'John Dugard's account of apartheid in South Africa, Namibia and Palestine serves to remind us of the depths to which humankind may sink in its determination to secure the supposed superiority of one racial group over another.'

– Archbishop Emeritus Desmond Tutu

'John Dugard's vivid historical and comparative study of injustice in three societies not only shows how law has been – and is being – used as an instrument of racial injustice, but reminds us powerfully of the need to confront racial oppression wherever it occurs.'

– Edwin Cameron, Justice of the Constitutional Court

'A number of books have explored the question of apartheid and Israel but never by so competent and knowledgeable a jurist who has first-hand experience of living under a system of apartheid. Dugard writes with academic rigor, a lawyer's precision and the experiences of a sensitive human being who has personal involvement in opposition to apartheid not only in his own country but in Palestine and South West Africa/Namibia. His book, written more as a memoir than an academic study, successfully weaves a highly readable narrative that brings to bear his vast experiences and contributes to a deeper understanding of urgent issues of Justice in our time.'

– Raja Shehadeh, prominent Palestinian human rights lawyer and author

'John Dugard's captivating account of the struggle against apartheid and his lucid analysis of the role of law in both oppressing people and in fighting for human dignity and freedom is as powerful in its sound moral message as it is a great read. Spanning from Namibia and South Africa to Israel and Palestine, Dugard's work and now fascinating book provides insights essential for every person interested in human rights and especially for cause lawyers.'

– Michael Sfard, leading Israeli human rights lawyer

Confronting Apartheid

A personal history of South Africa, Namibia and Palestine

John Dugard

First published by Jacana Media (Pty) Ltd in 2018

10 Orange Street
Sunnyside
Auckland Park 2092
South Africa
+2711 628 3200
www.jacana.co.za

ISBN 978-1-4314-2735-2

Design and layout by Shawn Paikin and Maggie Davey
Editing by Russell Martin
Proofreading by Lara Jacob
Index by Josh Bryson
Set in Ehrhardt MT 10.3/14pt
Job no. 003339

See a complete list of Jacana titles at www.jacana.co.za

Printed by **novus** *print* solutions, a Novus Holdings company

For Ietje, Jackie and Justin – with love

Contents

Preface

This book was conceived at the Bellagio Center of the Rockefeller Foundation on Lake Como, Italy, where I enjoyed a writing residency in 2013. The idyllic setting and intellectual companionship of my fellow residents provided an environment that enabled me to conceptualize the present study. In the same year and the year thereafter, I was invited to be a fellow in residence at the Stellenbosch Institute for Advanced Study (STIAS), which, like Bellagio, provided an opportunity for reflection and an intellectual exchange of ideas in beautiful surroundings. Here I commenced writing what was to become *Confronting Apartheid.* I am indebted to both the Rockefeller Foundation and STIAS for the enriching experience their residency afforded and the opportunity it gave me to develop my ideas.

In 2016 I was invited to deliver the annual Edward Said Memorial Lecture in Adelaide by the Australian Friends of Palestine Association (AFOPA), which compelled me to further develop my thoughts on the disparity in the treatment of South Africa and Israel by the international community for applying substantially similar policies.

Friends and family have read and commented on the manuscript of this book. Their criticisms have undoubtedly improved the portrayal of the events I describe as well as the language employed. I have benefited tremendously from these suggestions and criticisms. I am particularly grateful to those who drew my attention to sensitive issues that I had treated insensitively. I am grateful to Jane Dugard for correcting my recollection of several important events. I also wish to thank the following persons who read and commented on my manuscript: Edwin Cameron, James Crawford, Jackie Dugard, Max du Plessis, David Dyzenhaus, Norman Finkelstein, Denis Herbstein, Amelia Keene, Michael Sfard, Martin

Willner and Liesbeth Zegveld. Amelia Keene's thorough edit of the manuscript and constructive suggestions for the final shape of the book were particularly helpful.

My children, Jackie and Justin, are referred to all too briefly in this memoir. They participated in many of the events described in my life in Johannesburg and, together with Jane, provided a haven in a difficult society. I thank them for this. I also wish to thank them, Jackie's partner Itumeleng and Justin's partner Ingrid, and my grandson Dillon, my sister Sally and my stepmother Lilian, for their love and support in the years following my departure from South Africa. My thanks are due, too, to my stepchildren Alexander and Nastascha and their families for securing the happiness of my new life in the Netherlands.

My wife Ietje has shared in the events of the past twenty years. She encouraged me to continue my work as UN special rapporteur on the human rights situation in the Occupied Palestinian Territory when I was faced with competing professional demands, and accompanied me on many of my visits to Palestine. The knowledge that she shares my concern for justice in Palestine has given me strength in the face of setbacks for this cause. Ietje has guided the conceptualization, content and structure of the present study. Her criticisms of the manuscript have been honest and constructive – and resulted in much rewriting. Without her love and encouragement there would have been no book.

This book is a history of the injustices of apartheid in South Africa, Namibia and Palestine. It is also a personal memoir of the way in which these injustices touched my own life. It makes no claim to be an autobiography providing a comprehensive account of my life, my family and friends, and what might be described as my personal life. Many – most – friends do not feature in this history, not because their place in my life was unimportant but because this is a memoir of political and public events and not an account of my private life. This failure does not detract from my indebtedness to them for their friendship.

I am fortunate in having had Russell Martin to edit my manuscript. His advice on both substance and form has been wise, correct and insightful. His skilful hand has undoubtedly improved the final text. I appreciate too the encouraging and tactful manner in which he has done this.

Finally, thank you to Bridget Impey and her team of Nadia Goetham, Lara Jacob, Shawn Paikin, Tarryn Talbot, Neilwe Mashigo, Sibongile Machika and Lutendo Mabata at Jacana Media for making the publication of *Confronting Apartheid* possible and for the efficient and pleasant manner in which this has been done.

– John Dugard

1

Introduction

I was eleven when apartheid entered my life. I remember it well. On 26 May 1948 (twelve days after the declaration of the state of Israel) the National Party won the South African general election on the platform of apartheid. The next morning, at school assembly, the headmaster of Umtata School announced with tears choking his throat that General Smuts had lost the election. We now had a new government. I had grown up in a South Africa dominated by General Smuts, who had led the war effort on behalf of South Africa during World War II and triumphed. Now he was gone. It was difficult to contemplate a South Africa without him.

Although I was too young to understand what was to come, most of my subsequent life was dominated by apartheid – and not only in South Africa. For many people, apartheid is associated with South Africa. From 1948 to 1990 this system of racial discrimination, humiliation and political repression was used by the ruling National Party government to subjugate and oppress the black majority of South Africa and also the mandate territory of neighbouring South West Africa, which South Africa administered until the territory gained independence as Namibia.

Today, apartheid as it was applied in southern Africa is largely forgotten outside South Africa. This was brought home to me by a recent experience in The Hague where my wife Ietje and I live. We were just about to take our leave after a dinner with friends when the hostess, Noor, a young woman of Turkish descent, asked, 'John, before you leave, I want to know what it was like living in South Africa during apartheid.' The question sounded simple enough and obvious, but I realized that I had never been asked it before in my twenty years in the Netherlands or for that matter anywhere else. The night was late and I did not give a satisfactory answer. It required much more attention and a more nuanced reply.

Afterwards, Ietje commented how strange it was that I had never been asked that question before. Were people not interested? Or were they embarrassed, not wishing to probe one's moral response to apartheid? Were Germans who had lived under Nazi rule questioned about their daily lives? This memoir attempts to provide a more satisfactory answer to Noor's question.

While apartheid is generally associated with South Africa, today it is widely accepted that the term may be used to describe political systems in other countries that practise racial discrimination and political repression. Indeed, apartheid has been defined in a number of international conventions as a universal crime involving 'an institutionalized regime of systematic oppression and domination by one racial group over any other racial group',[1] with no mention made of geographical location. Thus, while apartheid in South Africa no longer arouses such heated emotions as in the past, the question whether the occupation of Palestine constitutes apartheid is, on the other hand, very much alive. Proponents and opponents of this claim clash in the media, political forums, the classroom and on the street. Although there appear to be similarities between apartheid as applied in southern Africa and Israel's occupation of Palestine, every effort is made by Israel's champions and sympathizers in the West to refute this. Some refuse to consider the evidence and simply dismiss such suggestions as a sign of anti-Semitism, an effective way of stifling debate. A more sophisticated argument employed to challenge the allegation of apartheid in occupied Palestine focuses on Israel itself. Here it is argued that Israel cannot be viewed as an apartheid state because, unlike apartheid South Africa, it extends the franchise to its Palestinian minority, allows Palestinians to become members of the Knesset, appoints Palestinians to high office and does not have a legal system that institutionalizes racial discrimination. From this it follows that there is no question of apartheid being applied in occupied Palestine.[2] This refutation of the apartheid analogy fails, however, to address the main charge against Israel, that its policies and practices in *occupied* Palestine – East Jerusalem, the West Bank and Gaza (and not Israel itself) – may be compared to those of apartheid South Africa.

Indeed, besides the system of apartheid, the mandate territory of South West Africa (Namibia) and the Palestinian territory occupied by Israel have much in common. South West Africa and Palestine were both mandate territories under the League of Nations designated as a 'sacred trust of civilization'. Unlike other mandate territories, both survived the demise of the League of Nations and presented a problem to the international community of how to dispose of them while ensuring that the right of self-determination was respected. South West

Africa achieved independence and membership of the United Nations in 1990 as Namibia, after a long struggle to free itself from its racist mandatory power, South Africa. The greater part of Palestine achieved independent statehood and membership of the United Nations in 1948–9 as Israel. The remaining part, 22 per cent of Palestine, was occupied by Israel in 1967. This occupation remains in force and, although this territory has achieved recognition as a state by the General Assembly of the United Nations and many states, it has yet to be admitted to membership of the United Nations in fulfilment of the 'sacred trust of civilization'.

South Africa and Israel have similar histories and narratives. The dominant people in apartheid South Africa – the Afrikaners – and the dominant people in Israel and occupied Palestine – the Jews – have both claimed to be people chosen by God to fulfil his destiny. Both have argued that they had historical title to the land. Both founded states inspired by genocidal traumas: the Anglo-Boer War (1899–1902) and its memories of British concentration camps in which thousands of Boer women and children died; and the Holocaust in which six million Jews perished. Both struggled to free themselves from British rule, but at the same time were influenced by the English language, culture and respect for the rule of law. Both commenced their independent statehood with the sympathy of the international community and high expectations of democratic behaviour. Both disappointed that community when they adopted discriminatory and repressive measures to subjugate their indigenous populations – what is often referred to nowadays as apartheid, though this usage in respect of Israel has its critics.

A criticism frequently levelled at those who seek to consider the question whether Israel's policies and practices resemble those of apartheid South Africa is that they have insufficient knowledge of either apartheid South Africa or occupied Palestine to allow them to pass judgement on this matter. The present memoir cannot easily be faulted on this ground. I am a South African who lived and worked – as an academic, director of a human rights centre and a practising lawyer – in South Africa during the life of apartheid. As an international lawyer I was involved in the dispute over the legal status of South West Africa and the treatment of its peoples. Later, I chaired international fact-finding missions concerned with the violation of human rights in occupied Palestine and served as United Nations special rapporteur on human rights in Palestine. The present memoir is not an academic study but an account of apartheid, or a system akin to it, by one who was deeply involved in opposition to apartheid in both South Africa and South West Africa and was fully exposed to Israel's practices as occupying power of Palestine in regular visits to the region. It is the memoir of one familiar with the facts on the ground.

What is more, the memoir is not that of a victim, either of apartheid or of the occupation. I write as a white, English-speaking South African, as a lawyer concerned about human rights and the inequalities of apartheid, and as a liberal who believes that the pen and the voice are mightier than the AK-47. Inevitably my portrayal of events and life in South Africa is coloured by colour – the colour of my skin. It is written from the perspective of privilege, for all whites were privileged. So, too, is my coverage of events in Palestine. As a United Nations official I received privileged treatment. Possibly this privilege provides a distance that allows me to offer a clearer picture of the situations of which I was both a part and an observer.

While I am a lawyer, this book is not a legal treatise, but it does view the policies and practices of South Africa, South West Africa and Palestine through the spectacles of the law. The conflict between the international community and these societies was and is characterized by claims of violations of international law and disputes over questions of law. These conflicts cannot be fully understood without an understanding of the legal perspective. Namibia achieved independence in compliance with international law. South Africa's democracy is premised on notions of international law. The conflict between Israel and Palestine can only be satisfactorily resolved in accordance with the rules of international law.

Now that apartheid as a legal system has been abolished in Namibia and South Africa, it remains my hope that the assessment of the situation in occupied Palestine, which forms the final part of this memoir, will provide greater understanding and assist in some small way in finding a peaceful solution to a problem that has dominated history since the end of World War II. If the present memoir has any purpose apart from telling the story of my experiences with apartheid, it is this.

2

Early days, 1936–1965

Unlike many lawyers, I was not born into a family of lawyers. Both my parents were teachers who arrived in South Africa in 1926–7 from England to teach at the Methodist mission school of Healdtown in the Eastern Cape. My father, Jack, was a science teacher, of Huguenot extraction, whose ancestors had fled France for England after the St Bartholomew's Day massacre. My mother, Rita, was a teacher of English literature who had spent her childhood in Kent.

While Healdtown was situated near the villages of Fort Beaufort and Alice, the Presbyterian mission school of Lovedale was situated in Alice itself. Healdtown and Lovedale were regarded as the Eton and Harrow of black mission schools in South Africa before they were destroyed as educational institutions by the National Party government in the 1960s. Many prominent South African black leaders studied at these two schools. Nelson Mandela was a pupil at Healdtown High School when my father was principal of the Training School. In his autobiography *Long Walk to Freedom*, Mandela wrote of Healdtown:

> It was, at the time, the largest African school below the equator, with more than a thousand students, both male and female. Its graceful ivy-covered colonial buildings and tree-shaded courtyards gave it the feeling of a privileged academic oasis, which is precisely what it was … Healdtown was a mission school of the Methodist Church, and provided a Christian and liberal arts education based on an English model.[3]

Nelson Mandela was not the only prominent alumnus of Healdtown. Robert Sobukwe, leader of the Pan Africanist Congress, was also a student there; as was Govan Mbeki (father of President Thabo Mbeki) and Raymond Mhlaba, both of whom would stand trial with Mandela at the Rivonia trial in 1964 and be sentenced to life imprisonment.

I was born in the village of Fort Beaufort and spent my early childhood at Healdtown, with my older sister, Sally. When I was four, my father became a school inspector and we moved from one village in the Transkei to another for the following twelve years: Butterworth, Engcobo and Umtata. At the time, and until the early 1990s, these villages and the neighbouring villages of Cofimvaba, Idutywa and Qunu were unknown to most South Africans. But then, when it emerged that they were the home villages of leaders of the African National Congress, such as Mandela, Hani, Mbeki and Sisulu, they became part of the South African consciousness. Walter Sisulu, lifetime friend, activist and fellow prisoner of Nelson Mandela, was born in Engcobo.

The six years spent in Engcobo were my formative years. Engcobo, in the heart of the Transkeian Native Territories, as they were officially known, is situated near another mission school, Clarkebury, where Nelson Mandela first went. Engcobo was a mix of colonial presence and trading outpost. Its small white community numbering several hundred consisted mainly of officials charged with the task of ministering to the needs of the black community and comprised the magistrate, missionaries, medical doctors, the local lawyer and traders. There was a small school for white children only: black children attended nearby schools, such as the school at All Saints Mission. Engcobo, among rolling hills and surrounded by gentle streams, was idyllic. I grew up like any colonial child, accepting the superiority of the white community but somehow aware that it carried with it responsibilities. This was the time of World War II. I grew up in the knowledge that there was a war somewhere 'up north', to which many of the village's young men had gone and where some had been taken prisoner at a place called Tobruk in North Africa. One of my earliest memories was the village barbeque – *braaivleis* – held to celebrate the end of the war and the return of prisoners of war.

In 1946 my father was transferred to the capital of the Transkeian Territories, Umtata, as the chief school inspector of black, white and coloured schools in the Transkei. My mother taught English at the prestigious Anglican mission school for black boys – St John's College. She claimed that the boys there were more receptive to Shakespeare than any other pupils she had taught. I attended the local school for white children.

Life in the villages of the Transkei at this time differed from that of other parts of South Africa. Relations between black and white were not intimate.

Paternalism prevailed. But there was no great distance between blacks and whites. There was a mutual dependency between white traders and their black customers. Similarly, the white officials and missionaries worked closely with their black colleagues in a relationship governed by mutual respect. Strict racial separation of the kind known in most of South Africa was not practised. My parents invited black colleagues to our home and it was not unusual for me to find them having tea with black colleagues. Inevitably this early childhood experience had an influence on me.

It was the practice for white children from Umtata, and indeed the Transkei, to go to boarding school in East London, King William's Town or Queenstown, where the boys' schools of Selborne, Dale and Queen's were situated. These schools were government schools but considered themselves replicas of English public schools, on which they modelled their culture and traditions. I chose Queen's College in Queenstown, where I spent four happy years. Although the school was exclusively for white boys, I cannot recall any evidence of racism on the part of the teachers. On the contrary, this was the time of the Defiance Campaign, the nationwide protest by blacks against passes, and the constitutional crisis, caused by the National Party's devious measures aimed at removing coloured voters from the common voters' roll.[4] Many teachers were open supporters of the Torch Commando, a protest movement comprising ex-servicemen, led by 'Sailor' Malan, who had distinguished himself as a pilot in the Battle of Britain, against the government's determination to change the constitution by unconstitutional means. They made their opposition to the government clear and at school I understood that it was 'right' to oppose the National Party government. I fear that many of my school friends, like most white South Africans, later became supporters of apartheid. But certainly not all. David Evans served five years in prison for participation in the activities of the African Resistance Movement in the 1960s, and Allister Sparks became editor of the *Rand Daily Mail* and one of South Africa's foremost journalists opposed to apartheid.[5]

I had grown up to believe that English was the dominant language of South Africa and that only a token knowledge of Afrikaans was required. But as the National Party became more powerful it became clear that, although both English and Afrikaans were official languages, Afrikaans was more 'official' than English. Certainly it soon was apparent that one would not succeed in many walks of life unless one was bilingual. For these reasons I accepted my father's decision that I study for one year at the University of Stellenbosch, South Africa's oldest and most revered Afrikaans-language university, rather than at the English-language University of Cape Town (UCT), which had been my own choice. After one year I would be free to move to UCT.

I stayed at Stellenbosch for five years and completed both a BA (in law) and an LLB degree there. Stellenbosch, with its oak-lined streets and colonial architecture, beneath a backdrop of majestic mountains and close to valleys of vineyards, is undoubtedly the most beautiful university town in South Africa. For most of my time there I was a resident of Stellenbosch's most illustrious residence – Wilgenhof - which had produced more leaders of Afrikanerdom than any other South African institution. In my time Wilgenhof claimed as old boys the governor general (E.G. Jansen), the prime minister (J.G. Strijdom), the chief justice (H.A. Fagan) and two of South Africa's best-known (and notorious) cabinet ministers, Eben Dönges and Eric Louw. Later I was to ask myself why I chose to remain and study in what was to me a foreign language at an all-white, conservative, pro-government university and why I did not move to an English-language university with a racially mixed student body (for at that time blacks were admitted in small numbers to the universities of Cape Town and the Witwatersrand), liberal teachers and students, and much greater freedom of expression and behaviour. I did not give this question much thought while I was at Stellenbosch. I suppose the answer is that I was happy there: I had good friends, enjoyed the academic scene, played rugby, cricket and hockey, and found some stimulation in being an 'outsider' from a different cultural background with different political views.

I still find it difficult to understand why I chose to study law. Probably it was because I realized even then that I needed a qualification for a profession that might allow me to earn a living. Legal education at Stellenbosch was not stimulating, with rote learning, little encouragement to question legal rules, and no consideration of legal policy. I learnt the rudiments of Roman law and Roman-Dutch law, South Africa's common law. Every effort was made to minimize the traces of English law despite the fact that South Africa's common law was in legal practice a blend of Roman-Dutch law and English law. International law appeared in the title of one of the courses, but was completely ignored in favour of an eighteen-month exposition and analysis of the constitutional crisis over the removal of the coloured voters from the common voters' roll, which introduced me to the real world of law and political intrigue. And then there was Professor J.C. de Wet, who taught me criminal law and the law of contract. Most lawyers of that time showed great deference to judges and were slow to criticize them. But 'JC' was different. He ridiculed judges and questioned their intelligence. If 'JC' was to be believed, most judges were wrong most of the time. From 'JC' I learnt that the law, lawyers, legal institutions, judges and politicians were to be critically questioned and openly criticized. In time, this lesson was to prove invaluable.

Political debate was part of the Stellenbosch culture. However, it was conducted almost entirely in terms of parliamentary politics, which meant white politics and the confrontation between apartheid's National Party and the opposition party – the United Party, premised on the legacy of J.C. Smuts. No black person ever spoke at Stellenbosch in my time. Moreover, there was an obsession with the threat of communism, reminiscent of McCarthyism in the United States. For instance, the National Party Youth Front at Stellenbosch claimed that communism was taking hold of Stellenbosch and provided as evidence for this the fact that more than half the inter-varsity rugby songs were in English. My introduction to radical politics was largely through *New Age*, the mouthpiece of the Communist Party (banned in 1950), then operating under the flag of the Congress of Democrats. But increasingly, real politics, in the form of the confrontation between the African National Congress and white intransigence, entered my world. The arrest of radical leaders from the Congress Alliance in 1956 on charges of treason, which was to lead to the notorious Treason Trial of 1956–61, featured prominently in my political education of the time.

Law and politics were kept separate. Policy and morality were not part of our legal education. No attempt was made to assess the morality of the new discriminatory and repressive laws of apartheid or to measure them against the United Nations Universal Declaration of Human Rights of 1948 or its South African equivalent, the Freedom Charter, adopted by the Congress movement at Kliptown, near Johannesburg, in 1955.[6] I do not recall these instruments ever being mentioned in my legal education at Stellenbosch. The constitutional crisis over the removal of coloured voters from the voters' roll, which had been enshrined in the political compact of 1910 creating the Union of South Africa,[7] was carefully considered but only in strictly technical legal terms. The question whether the entrenched clauses of the 1910 constitution allowed coloured voters with protected voting rights to be removed from the common voters' roll, and placed on a separate roll for coloureds only, by enlarging the Senate to secure the necessary two-thirds majority in a joint parliamentary sitting, was debated in terms of precedent and constitutional rules and not morality or the standards of some nebulous higher law.

In 1951 my parents moved to Cape Town when my father was appointed chief inspector of the Western Cape. At that time all education fell under the authority of the provinces, which meant that my father was responsible for inspecting white, coloured and black schools. However, in 1953 the Bantu Education Act[8] was passed. This law removed the education of black children from the control of the provinces and placed it in the hands of a department of the central government, the Bantu Education Department. The purpose was to allow the central government to impose a national education system upon black children that would be in line with the policy of apartheid. In particular it would make it clear to black children that they could not aspire to offices, jobs and positions reserved exclusively for whites and that their role was to serve their own community. The law was aimed primarily at the mission schools which saw it as their task to provide black children with the same education as white children – a goal interpreted by the National Party as being to produce 'black Englishmen'. As a result of the Bantu Education Act, most churches felt compelled to hand over their schools to the central government.

This presented my father with an unenviable choice. Should he remain involved in black education or not? He was given the choice of remaining in Cape Town as chief inspector of coloured education or becoming regional director of Bantu education for the Cape Province under the new dispensation. In what he was to describe in his memoirs, *Fragments of My Fleece*, 'as the most important decision I had to make in my career',[9] he decided that his background in missionary work and black education made him better qualified for the latter post. I suspect that his heart was more in black education, to which he had devoted his life. Certainly he felt that he could ameliorate the harshness of Bantu education. But his colleagues were divided. Some resigned rather than work under the new system. Others decided to stay on and do what they could to salvage black education from within. Old friendships were destroyed by these decisions. My father remained regional director of Bantu education, based in King William's Town, before being promoted to serve for a short spell at headquarters in Pretoria. There he found his position as a liberal English-speaking person who was not a member of the secret Afrikaans society, the Broederbond, intolerable. He was then transferred to the post of regional director of Bantu education in Natal, where he stayed until he retired in 1965.

I had mixed feelings about my father's decision to work in Bantu education. I was to become an outsider, criticising the system from without. But I could see that one with a senior position within the system could achieve much by interpreting law and policy benevolently and by making it clear to black teachers that he disapproved of the system. When I grew older I frequently met black political leaders and educationists who spoke highly of my father. None criticized him for remaining in the system. On the contrary, many told me that he had made the right decision and that generations of black children had benefited from his presence. My father was a liberal who hated apartheid. This I knew from many conversations. I believe that he made the right decision, but it took me years to accept this.

In December 1958 I graduated from Stellenbosch. In those days no pupillage was required for admission to the Bar and I was duly admitted as an advocate of the Supreme Court of South Africa in April 1959. For three months, at the beginning of 1959, I worked as a clerk in the King Williams's Town magistrate's court. As I resigned to travel abroad shortly after I was employed, I was given menial desk jobs. I did, however, have an opportunity to see the law in practice, which consisted mainly of blacks being tried for criminal offences. Punishment took the form of imprisonment and whipping for adults, while 'light cuts' (strokes administered with a cane) were a favourite punishment meted out to black juvenile offenders. One day the magistrate told me that I should witness light cuts being administered. I am not sure why he felt this to be part of my education but it certainly was educative. Having been at a school where light cuts with a cane were part of school discipline and tradition, I believed that 'light cuts' administered as punishment for juvenile offenders could not be very different. I was wrong. I saw a hefty black police officer beat the naked buttocks of a young boy stretched out on a bench. The boy cried and screamed; and blood oozed from his buttocks. This was my introduction to the administration of justice in South Africa. I had not been prepared for it in my legal studies at Stellenbosch.

In April 1959 I embarked upon an overseas adventure. These were the days before the gap year. In any event I had no plans for the future. My idea was to travel to Europe and become a writer. I envisioned a bohemian life in London or Paris while I wrote the great South African novel. In fact it did not work out that way. I travelled widely in Europe at a time when hitch-hiking was safe and youth hostels were welcoming. The nearest I came to a literary adventure was a conversation with Ernest Hemingway. One night in Pamplona during the feast of San Fermin, John Spottiswoode,[10] an American friend, and I refused to give way in a narrow street to a group of American students who were accompanied by a white-haired, white bearded, red-faced man and were loudly told to 'fuck off' by the man, who seemed to have had more to drink than we had. We responded loudly with 'and fuck you too' and thought no more about it. The next day, after I had run with the bulls through the streets of Pamplona, I saw the red-faced, white-haired man again at the bull fight. My neighbour pointed at him and said, 'That is Ernest Hemingway.'

While in London I shared a flat in Swiss Cottage with two South Africans, Denis Herbstein and Dudley Kessel. Denis and I were both employed as supply teachers, which meant being allocated at short notice to schools in need of teachers in greater London. I taught virtually everything from mathematics to needlework in schools where discipline was unknown.

I enrolled as a research student at the University of London and attended lectures in jurisprudence at King's College, where I was introduced to the writings of Gustav Radbruch. Radbruch had been dismissed from his professorial post at the University of Heidelberg by the Nazis, and after the war argued that Hitler's laws had failed to qualify as 'law' at all because they violated the fundamental principles upon which legal norms are based. Law was not simply a cluster of legal rules and principles to be applied to a given factual situation, as I had been taught at Stellenbosch. Radbruch taught that there were higher norms by which the validity of laws was to be measured. I had not previously related the philosophy of law to the problems confronting South Africa and now, for the first time, I began to ponder whether the laws of apartheid qualified as law in terms of Radbruch's thesis.

In March 1960 my world was shaken. A peaceful demonstration against the pass laws of South Africa at Sharpeville, organized by the Pan Africanist Congress, was brutally suppressed by the South African police and sixty-nine persons were killed. London burst into demonstration. I marched in one such demonstration from Hyde Park Corner to Trafalgar Square, where I heard Father Trevor Huddleston, who had left South Africa with a reputation as a troublesome priest, condemn apartheid and the pass laws. Before Sharpeville I had no plans to return to South Africa. I was happy in London. Teaching was not satisfactory but the great South African novel was still to be written. There was no hurry to return home. Sharpeville changed everything. I felt I had to go home. At a time when many were leaving the country, I decided to return.

South Africa for me was Cape Town. There was no other city in South Africa in which I wished to live. When I returned to South Africa in September 1960 I was employed as a judge's registrar in the Cape Provincial Division of the Supreme Court, a task which involved reading court records and sitting in court with a judge. For most of the time I acted as registrar to Acting Judge D.P. ('Lang David') de Villiers, one of the leading senior counsel ('silks') in South Africa. Two years later he was to lead South Africa's legal team in The Hague in the dispute with Ethiopia and Liberia over South Africa's administration of South West Africa. I also acted as registrar for a short period to Judge President Theo van Wyk, who was later appointed by South Africa as judge ad hoc in the International Court of Justice in the dispute over South West Africa.

I soon realized that I would have difficulty in making a career as an advocate at the Cape Bar as I had intended. South Africa, like England, had and still has a divided legal profession under which attorneys (solicitors) brief advocates (barristers) for opinions and court appearances. The success of an advocate at this time depended more on who one knew as an attorney than what one knew about the law. I knew few attorneys as I had not studied in Cape Town and Afrikaans attorneys tended to brief advocates who were politically acceptable. Consequently when Solly Leeman, who had been the star in my law class at Stellenbosch, approached me about taking his job as a law lecturer at the University of Natal in Durban to allow him to take up a teaching post at the University of Cape Town, I agreed with alacrity. I did not apply for the job and I did not produce evidence that I had the requisite legal qualifications. Solly's word was sufficient for my appointment as temporary lecturer in law at the University of Natal. Until then I had never seen myself as a university lecturer; it was not a career option I had considered. It was a post I took because my preferred career choice, the Bar, seemed closed and I had nothing else to do.

The Law School of the Durban campus of the University of Natal was situated in City Buildings adjacent to the parking ground of the Durban market. It was hot and noisy. The professor in charge was Exton Burchell, who was professor at the university's Pietermaritzburg campus. The student body at the Durban campus was racially mixed and was evenly constituted of whites, blacks and Indians. It should not have been. Blacks had been excluded from the 'open universities' of Cape Town and the Witwatersrand by the cynically named Extension of University Education Act of 1959,[11] which provided that henceforth universities would be racially segregated, with new universities to be created for black students. The University of Natal had never been 'open' to all races and was an all-white university. But it had a separate building for non-white, mainly Indian, students, called Marion Building, which was situated next door to City Buildings. I never quite understood how it was that in the early 1960s City Buildings was racially integrated. Legend had it that the independent and unpredictable vice-chancellor of the university, Ernie Malherbe, had deliberately misinterpreted the Extension of University Education Act to allow Natal to admit black students, mainly from the only black university then in existence – Fort Hare – on the ground that this was permissible in the years of transition to university segregation. So it was that I was faced with a politically aware and politically active racially mixed student body. One of my students was later to achieve fame: Navi Pillay (née Naidoo) became a judge of the International Criminal Court and UN high commissioner for human rights.

I lectured in the advanced course in Roman law, a subject which I had studied at Stellenbosch but never taken seriously. Now I found myself rapidly preparing lectures on this subject so that I could be one step ahead of my students. The Law School in Durban was in disarray as nearly all its lecturers were newly appointed and, like me, had little experience. Students soon sensed the insecurity of their new teachers and bombarded them with difficult questions designed to test their competence. In defence I resorted to Latin. I would open each lecture with a Latin text and call upon students known to be troublemakers to translate. This silenced them and created the impression that I was a serious scholar. When students presented a petition of complaint about their new teachers to Exton Burchell in Pietermaritzburg, I was not mentioned.

A.S. (Tony) Mathews was the lecturer in advanced Roman law in Pietermaritzburg. We became firm friends, particularly as it soon became apparent that we shared a common political outlook. Several years later we were to join forces as the main academic critics of the government's security laws.

The early 1960s was a time of political turmoil. The Communist Party had been proscribed in 1950 but it was not until 1960 that the African National Congress and the Pan Africanist Congress were banned. Thereafter radical political opposition was mobilized mainly by the Congress of Democrats, which had replaced the Communist Party, the South African Indian Congress and the Liberal Party, which had been established by the author of *Cry, the Beloved Country*, Alan Paton, and was hostile to the Marxist ideology of the Congress parties. I was not a 'joiner'. I refused to commit myself to any political party. However, I attended meetings of the Progressive Party, which had recently been formed as breakaway from the United Party, as well as the Liberal Party and the Congress of Democrats and socialized with their members. My Liberal Party friends included David Evans, an old school friend, and John Laredo, an old university friend, both of whom would be imprisoned for five years in 1964 for their activities in the militant wing of the Liberal Party, the African Resistance Movement. Congress of Democrats friends included Ronnie Kasrils and his girlfriend and later wife, Eleanor Anderson.[12] In 1963, at her request, I lent my Volkswagen Beetle to Eleanor. My car was returned the next day and I read in the newspaper that a pylon had been sabotaged near Durban. Only later did I connect the loan of my car to this act of sabotage and only in 2010 did Eleanor confirm that she had indeed used my car for the purposes of sabotage.

After I had convinced law students that I was to be taken seriously academically, and once it became known that I was politically involved, if not active in any party, it seemed to follow naturally that I would be asked to address student protest meetings. I accordingly addressed large student rallies on both the 'Sabotage Act',[13] which defined sabotage widely to include protest action, and the 90-day detention law,[14] which allowed incommunicado detention for ninety days for the purpose of interrogation. Already it was clear that there was a need for academics to take the lead in opposing the repressive measures of apartheid. It was equally clear that none of my fellow law lecturers was prepared to do so. So it was that a Romanist came to lead student protests against the excesses of the security laws.

I was a temporary lecturer at the University of Natal. The insecurity of my position led me to consider other options, including becoming a member of the

Durban Bar. Reluctantly, the university allowed me to combine teaching with legal practice and I took up chambers. The Durban Bar comprised a small, cohesive group of advocates whose members were ever ready to help and socialize with each other. I became firm friends of many advocates, several of whom, such as John Milne, John Didcott, Andrew Wilson and David Friedman, were later to constitute a small coterie of judges prepared to challenge the injustices of the apartheid legislative arsenal.

I was not a great success at the Bar. Perhaps it was because I was known to be a lecturer at the university, perhaps it was because, as a non-Natalian, I was largely unknown to Durban attorneys. Whatever the reason, it took some eighteen months before I received my first paid brief. In the meantime I was kept busy doing *pro deo* work. *Pro deo* counsel were appointed by the Bar Council, and paid a token sum by the state, for defending persons charged with capital crimes. In less than three years at the Durban Bar I defended some seventy persons, all black, charged with the common law crimes of murder, rape, housebreaking and robbery, all of which were capital crimes. It was wrong that inexperienced advocates like me should have been permitted to defend such persons unaided by more senior counsel. But the more senior counsel were busy with lucrative legal practices and it was left to the inexperienced juniors at the Bar to defend indigent blacks arraigned on capital charges. A friend at the Durban Bar had the misfortune to be appointed to defend persons who were sentenced to death, and executed, in his first four *pro deo* cases. I was marginally more fortunate in that my first client, after giving me a coherent account of how he had stabbed his uncle to death in self-defence and agreeing to plead not guilty, warmly invited the judge to go fishing with him when the charge was put to him on the day of his trial. He was found to be guilty but insane and detained indefinitely at the pleasure of the state president. I was furious, as I was convinced that had he not been persuaded by old hands in the prison to change his plea to one of insanity, he would have been acquitted.

I did not have to wait long for my first client to be sentenced to death: a rural black man who had killed a neighbour for naming his dog after him. Thereafter eight of my clients were sentenced to death. Five were executed despite petitions to the state president. Four were killed when they staged a jail break while awaiting execution in Pretoria. These four were members of a gang who broke into premises and were pursued by the police in a car chase through central Durban, in the course of which one member of the gang produced a gun (the existence of which had been concealed from other members of the gang) and shot one of the police pursuers dead. I argued that the gang members who had been unaware of the gun could not be held responsible for the death of the policeman, but the court held that they had a common purpose to commit a crime and must be held responsible for the consequences. I took the matter on appeal – on my own – to the Appeal Court in Bloemfontein but lost. The court handed down its decision in *State* v. *Malinga*,[15] which was to become a leading precedent on common purpose in criminal activity.

Prior to my experience as an advocate, I had opposed the death penalty on moral grounds. But this was largely an intellectual opposition to the penalty. There is nothing like seeing a person sentenced to death to concentrate the mind on the death penalty as a form of punishment. One moment your client is a person who must be defended. He remains a person throughout the trial. One gets to know and, in many cases, like that person. Then suddenly, at the end of the trial, he is told in a low and serious voice by a man whom one knows – the judge – that his life is to be cut short, very short. It was all so formal and clinical. But the reality of the death sentence was clear. I hated the death sentence; it gave me sleepless nights. I came to oppose it not only on moral grounds but because of the effect it had on the integrity of the legal process. How, I asked, could the legal process be rational and objective if it was to end in such an act of brutality?

My time at the Durban Bar introduced me to judges. I learnt that judges were human. Four judges of the Natal Supreme Court had been prisoners of war during World War II. They understood from their own personal experience what four years in confinement meant. A convicted person must have committed a very serious crime to receive a prison sentence in excess of four years from one of them. They also disliked the death sentence and did their best to avoid it. At the other end of the judicial spectrum were the hanging judges who were careless or carefree when it came to imposing the death sentence.

Although there were many political cases before the courts – that is, prosecutions of persons for contravention of the country's race and security laws – I was only once briefed to appear as counsel in such a case. The matter concerned Jacqueline Arenstein, wife of a prominent radical lawyer, Roley Arenstein, who had left the Communist Party on ideological grounds. She was charged with violating an order imposed on her under the Suppression of Communism Act, prohibiting her from attending meetings, by participating in a demonstration against the restrictions imposed on her husband.[16] As expected, she was duly convicted and her appeal failed. I would have liked to be briefed in such matters but realized that I was too inexperienced. Strangely, this lack of experience did not disqualify me from defending persons charged with non-political capital crimes.

In 1962 I met Jane Irwin, who was completing her master's degree in zoology at the University of Natal in Pietermaritzburg, and we became engaged to get married. Jane had recently been awarded a scholarship to study at Cambridge. I had wanted to study at Cambridge ever since I visited the university in 1960. I successfully applied for a British Council scholarship to enable me to join Jane. We were married in July 1963 and set sail for Cambridge in August of that year.

In my application for the British Council scholarship I had proposed that I study international law as this was a field in which few South African lawyers, I included, were qualified. I argued that I could make a useful contribution to South African academic and public life on my return with such a qualification.

At this time Cambridge was unquestionably the leading university in international law, having four of the world's top public international lawyers – Professor R.Y. Jennings, Derek Bowett, Clive Parry and Elihu (Eli) Lauterpacht. I spent two years at Cambridge, one year in the graduate LLB degree and one year writing a thesis on the Organisation of African Unity and its support for liberation movements for a Diploma in International Law under the supervision of Lauterpacht.

Jane was a student at Newnham College while I was a member of Sidney Sussex College. It was pure chance that I became a student at Sidney Sussex and it was only after I had been placed there that I learnt that several of my Dugard ancestors had been members of the college at about the same time as Oliver Cromwell. As a married couple, we did not live in college. I loved Cambridge with its medieval colleges and the Cam quietly flowing through the town. Images of the Backs in spring and autumn still haunt my mind and I came closer to heaven in King's College Chapel at evensong than at any other time. I made friends. Bob Hepple, who had just escaped from South Africa where he had been arrested with the leaders of the African National Congress at Rivonia, became a firm friend.[17] Another friend, from the international law group, was Hussein Hassouna from Egypt, with whom I was later to serve on the International Law Commission.

In South Africa I had studied law; in Cambridge I *read* international law. New fields of law and new ideas presented themselves. I learnt of the role played by law in the ordering of international society. International human rights law was still in its infancy but I became obsessed with the Universal Declaration of Human Rights and the European Convention on Human Rights and the notion that there were international norms by which national legal systems might be judged. South West Africa was a topical subject as the International Court of Justice had just handed down its decision, finding that it had jurisdiction to consider the dispute with South Africa over the status and administration of South West Africa. Increasingly I saw international law as a normative structure by which law in southern Africa might be examined and judged. Whereas initially I had chosen to study international law with little conviction that I might really use it in South

Africa (as I had promised the British Council), I now became convinced that it provided an answer to questions about the usefulness of law in apartheid society.

Prior to my stay in Cambridge I had no intention of pursuing an academic career. My intention was to return to practise at the Durban Bar. Everything changed at Cambridge. I now had a mission in life: to teach and write in South Africa about international law and to oppose apartheid by appealing to a higher international legal order. I did not expect to change South Africa in this way but at least I felt that I had a calling to pursue. The main problem was that this could only be done by teaching international law at a South African university, and only the University of the Witwatersrand ('Wits') took international law seriously, but there was already a teacher in that post. Then, as my stay at Cambridge came to end, I learnt that the post at Wits was vacant. I applied and was offered the position. Jane was delighted because she had no wish to return to Durban.

Jane and I returned to South Africa via Egypt, where we spent a delightful week with Hussein Hassouna, whose father was then secretary-general of the Arab League. We attended a political rally addressed by President Nasser and saw the sun set on the pyramids. We wished to spend a couple of days in Kenya en route home but were unable to obtain visas in Cairo for this purpose. So we decided to take our chance and apply for visas when we arrived in Nairobi – against the advice of our travel agent. When we arrived in Nairobi, I saw two immigration officers at the desk, one white, one black. Assuming that power lay with the white official, I approached him for visas to remain in Nairobi for two days in order to catch our flight to Johannesburg. He refused point-blank and said we would be deported to Cairo on the next flight. Reluctantly, when his back was turned, I approached the African immigration officer. 'Welcome to Kenya,' he said with a big smile. 'How long do you want to stay in Kenya?' Africa had changed. Kenya, Zambia and Malawi had all become independent during our time in Cambridge. Power was no longer with the whites. I had been taught a salutary lesson in the most delightful manner.

Jane and I arrived in Johannesburg in July 1965, in time for the start of the second term in the Law Faculty of the University of the Witwatersrand. In my early years at Wits I was intent on establishing myself as an academic lawyer who would be taken seriously by his peers. I concentrated on teaching and on building a respectable body of legal publications, mainly in the field of international law. My writings on international law were primarily concerned with the dispute over South West Africa, which was then before the International Court of Justice. I begin with this chapter of my life.

PART ONE

South West Africa/ Namibia

3

A brief history of South West Africa/Namibia, 1884–1960

Namibia, previously known as South West Africa, was colonized by Germany in 1884.[1] Following the outbreak of World War I, the South African army defeated German forces in South West Africa and occupied the territory. At the end of the war, South West Africa, together with Germany's other colonies in Africa and the Pacific Ocean and Turkey's possessions in the Middle East, was placed under a system of international tutelage or trusteeship, known as the mandates system.

The mandates system was established by article 22 of the Covenant of the League of Nations, which provided that to colonies and territories of Germany and Turkey which were 'inhabited by peoples not yet able to stand by themselves under the strenuous conditions of the modern world, there should be applied the principle that the well-being and development of such peoples form a sacred trust of civilization'. Advanced nations were entrusted with the task of administering these territories, to be known as mandates, in order to give effect to the 'sacred trust of civilization'. They were, however, to be accountable to the Council of the League of Nations for their administration. A distinction was drawn between the developed former possessions of the Turkish Empire – Palestine and Transjordan, Iraq, Syria and Lebanon – and the less developed colonies of Germany in Africa and the Pacific Ocean. The former were designated as Class A mandates whose existence as independent nations might be provisionally recognized subject to the rendering of administrative assistance by the mandatory state to which they had been entrusted, until they were able to stand on their own. The less developed German colonies in Africa and the Pacific Ocean were designated as Class B and Class C mandates and were subjected to greater administrative control by the mandatory powers.

In 1920 South West Africa, a Class C mandate, was placed under the tutelage of South Africa, which was authorized to administer it as an integral part of South Africa but was obliged to 'promote to the utmost the material and moral well-being and social progress of the inhabitants of the territory'. It was also required to prohibit the slave trade and forced labour and to ensure freedom of religion in the territory. The mandate made South Africa accountable to the Council of the League of Nations and required it to submit annual reports to the satisfaction of the council. In addition, South Africa agreed in article 7 of the mandate that 'if any dispute whatever should arise between the Mandatory and another Member of the League of Nations relating to the interpretation or the application of the provisions of the Mandate, such dispute, if it cannot be settled by negotiation, shall be submitted to the Permanent Court of International Justice'.

South Africa administered South West Africa as part of the Union of South Africa during the period of the League of Nations, treating the indigenous inhabitants of the territory in the same paternalistic and discriminatory manner that blacks were treated in South Africa itself. South Africa dutifully submitted reports to the Council of the League of Nations and there was no serious confrontation with the League. The League of Nations was essentially Eurocentric in its outlook, colonial powers played a major role in its affairs, and South Africa was a popular member.

In 1945, at the end of World War II, the Charter of the United Nations (UN) was signed. It created a new international trusteeship system to replace the mandates system of the League of Nations and to apply to territories detached from enemy states as a result of the war and to 'territories now held under mandate'.[2] Article 80 of the UN Charter, in a clear reference to the mandate agreements of the League of Nations, provided that the Charter was not to be construed as in any manner altering the rights of peoples under existing international instruments.

In April 1946 the League of Nations was dissolved. However, on 18 April, it was unanimously resolved by the League that, although the functions of the League relating to the mandates would come to an end on its dissolution, chapters XII and XIII of the UN Charter establishing the new trusteeship system embodied principles corresponding to those contained in article 22 of the Covenant of the League of Nations, which had established the mandates system. Both the League of Nations and the United Nations therefore anticipated that mandated territories would be placed under trusteeship but imposed no clear obligation on mandatory states to do this.

From the outset South Africa made it clear that it had no intention of placing South West Africa under trusteeship. When the UN Charter was being drafted, South Africa served notice of its intention to incorporate the territory into South Africa and in 1946 it formally requested the General Assembly of the UN for permission to do so. The General Assembly rejected the request and instead recommended that the territory be placed under trusteeship. South Africa, under the United Party government of General Smuts, refused to do so but it undertook to administer the territory 'in the spirit of the Mandate' and to submit reports on its administration of the territory to the United Nations. In 1949, after the National Party came to power in South Africa on the platform of apartheid, which it proceeded to apply to South West Africa, it announced that it would discontinue the submission of reports to the UN. The scene was now set for a forty-year political and legal confrontation between South Africa and the UN over South West Africa.

In 1950 the General Assembly requested the International Court of Justice to give an advisory opinion on the status of South West Africa. In its opinion,[3] the court rejected South Africa's claim that the mandate had lapsed on the demise of the League of Nations, held that the mandate continued in force, and ruled that although South Africa was not obliged to place the territory under trusteeship, it was obliged to account for its administration of the territory by submitting reports to the UN. The opinion of 1950 was endorsed by two further opinions[4] dealing with the manner in which the UN might exercise its supervisory role. All three advisory opinions were approved by the General Assembly but rejected by South Africa.

Advisory opinions are not legally binding. When it became clear that South Africa would not accept the opinions of the court, two former members of the League of Nations, Ethiopia and Liberia, instituted proceedings against South Africa in 1960.

4

Academic and legal counsel

The dispute over the status of South West Africa had been simmering for as long as I could remember. Events such as the rejection by the United Nations (UN) of South Africa's request for incorporation of the territory, the three adverse advisory opinions of the International Court of Justice, and the UN's hearing of petitions by the Reverend Michael Scott ensured that the matter remained on the South African political agenda. But it was not a serious issue. For all intents and purposes South West Africa was a fifth province of South Africa and the UN could not do anything about it. After all, advisory opinions were by definition only advisory and not binding. In the late 1950s the UN strategy changed. Frustrated by South Africa's intransigence, the UN now sought to obtain a legally binding judgment from the International Court of Justice in a dispute between states. Ethiopia and Liberia as the only former African member states of the League of Nations – apart from South Africa – agreed to bring the case before the court.

The applicant states, Ethiopia and Liberia, claimed not only that South Africa was obliged to place South West Africa under the supervision of the UN but also that apartheid as practised in South West Africa violated the mandate for South West Africa, which required South Africa 'to promote to the utmost' the welfare of the local inhabitants. Although ostensibly a challenge only to South Africa's administration of South West Africa, in fact it was a challenge to the survival of apartheid in South Africa itself. This was clear from the fact that the applicants sought a ruling that apartheid violated *universal* norms of international law and that the ultimate goal of the proceedings was to secure a binding judgment against South Africa. Whereas advisory opinions might be ignored, a judgment of the court in a dispute between states was legally binding and might be enforced by the Security Council in terms of the UN Charter. Literature began to appear that predicted a decision adverse to South Africa, sanctions imposed by the Security Council, and the end of apartheid in southern Africa.[5] South West Africa had become South Africa's Achilles heel.

In my early years at Wits University, the South West Africa dispute was my main preoccupation as I sought to employ the knowledge acquired at Cambridge to explain the issues to a confused South African public and to challenge the legal arguments raised by the government. The Wits Law School provided an excellent environment for such an exercise, as its academic leaders, Dean Bobby Hahlo and Professor Ellison Kahn, edited the premier South African legal periodicals, and relied heavily on contributions from Wits staff for these publications.

When I started my career at Wits, the proceedings before the International Court of Justice were at the stage of the hearing on the merits. In 1962 the court had dismissed South Africa's objections to the court hearing the case and found by a majority of eight votes to seven that it had jurisdiction to hear the dispute. I had written an article in the *South African Law Journal*[6] commenting favourably on this decision. This, together with comments to the press, established me as someone who knew something about the matter and who, unlike other international law commentators in South Africa, was not favourably inclined to the government's position. So it was that in July 1966 I was invited to the offices of *The Star* to listen to the radio broadcast of the decision of the International Court of Justice and comment on a decision that was widely expected to herald doom for the apartheid state.

I knew the issues. I knew that the applicants had argued that the mandate for South West Africa had survived the demise of the League of Nations, that South Africa was obliged to place the territory under the supervision of the UN as successor to the League, and that apartheid violated the terms of the mandate. Like most international lawyers, I expected the court to rule on these matters after it had rejected South Africa's preliminary objections in 1962 and found that it had jurisdiction and was therefore competent to pronounce on the substance of the claims. This was what I had been led to believe at Cambridge. But as I listened to the court's judgment, I felt bewildered and betrayed. The court announced that before it could pronounce on the merits of the case, the substance of the claims, it was necessary to consider a preliminary point – the question whether the applicant states had the necessary legal interest in the case, in particular whether their own nationals had been affected by South Africa's administration of South West Africa. This was confusing because the 1962 judgment had already decided that the applicants had the necessary legal interest in their concern for the welfare of the inhabitants of the territory. Not so, said the court; there was a difference between preliminary objections involving jurisdiction, which had indeed been decided by the court in 1962, and preliminary objections involving the admissibility of the claims. One such issue involving the admissibility of the claims concerned the question whether the applicant states had shown that they had a legal interest in the claims on the ground that they were directly affected by the treatment of their own nationals. This the applicant states had failed to do, said the court. There was no evidence of maltreatment of nationals of the applicant states; only of maltreatment of the indigenous population of South West Africa. Consequently the applicant states were not entitled to any decision on the merits of the case.

The court reached this decision on a point of law not argued by South Africa in the 1965 because it believed that the question of the required legal interest had already been decided in favour of the applicants in 1962. This controversial and much criticized decision was reached by eight votes to seven, with Sir Percy Spender of Australia, the president of the court, exercising both a casting and deliberative vote to enable the court to reach its decision. In effect the court had overturned its decision of 1962 and the minority of 1962 had become the majority of 1966, largely as a result of the death, illness and recusal[7] of judges known to be opposed to South Africa.

The South African government rejoiced at the outcome. Its lawyers were elevated to the status of national heroes, despite the fact that they had not raised the point taken by the court on its own initiative. My comment to *The Star* was meaningless as I had yet to understand the enormity of the court's decision. The liberation movements of both South West Africa and South Africa were dismayed. They had placed great hope in the court and they had lost.

All I could do was to express my opinion on the International Court's decision in print. I wrote a highly critical assessment in which I stressed that the court had in effect overturned its decision of 1962 by reverting to a preliminary issue that had already been decided. I was strongly critical of the judicial reasoning of the majority and praised dissenting judges, such as Jessup of the United States and Tanaka of Japan, who had challenged the views of the majority and addressed the merits of the case.

I had written the review of the 1966 judgment of the court under great time pressure as I was determined that the first critical comment on the decision should appear in a South African legal journal to indicate that many South Africans were appalled by the decision. I submitted it to the editors of the *South African Law Journal*, Professors Hahlo and Kahn. The next morning they summoned me to Hahlo's office. Hahlo stated: 'John, your article is good, but we cannot publish it. Imagine that your brother was charged with murder and acquitted on a technicality. Would you write an article criticizing the court for acquitting him? I am sure you would not. So I want you to rewrite the article praising the court.' Ellison Kahn looked at Hahlo in amazement. 'Bobby,' he said, 'you can reject the article but you cannot ask John to rewrite it saying something that he does not believe in!' To which Hahlo responded: 'I do not see why not.'

I replied that I could not, and would not, change my views and that I would submit the article to a foreign law journal, possibly with an explanation as to why I had not published it in a South African journal. The next day, Hahlo and Kahn again summoned me to Hahlo's office. 'We have decided that we will publish,' announced Hahlo.

Publishing critical articles in the *South African Law Journal* was difficult. The editors operated in a hostile political environment in which the government might, in retaliation to a critical piece, refuse to purchase legal publications from the publishers of the journal, Juta and Co. Hahlo and Kahn were both politically cautious and disinclined to criticize the government. But they were men of integrity and understood that ultimately they were accountable to their own consciences, whatever the consequences. On this occasion, as on others, I admired them for their decision.

My article was duly published. Other comments on the decision published in foreign legal journals, particularly one by Rosalyn Higgins, later herself to become president of the International Court of Justice, adopted the same line. I was pleased that the first article criticizing the court had appeared in a South African journal. Hitherto there had been little questioning of foreign policy or international law issues from within South Africa. I was determined that this would change. The government's monopoly of international law discourse within South Africa was at an end.

Understandably, the international community was angry with the International Court. It was accused of being racist, Eurocentric and colonialist. My own view is that these accusations were incorrect and that the majority of the court were simply out of touch with the evolution of international law from a legal order that protected state interests to a legal order that sought to advance human rights. The judges constituting the majority were advanced in years and belonged to an earlier era of international law.

The UN was determined to do something to repair the harm done by the court. A few months after the decision the General Assembly adopted Resolution 2145(XXI), which made the finding that the International Court had failed to make – that South Africa, by applying apartheid to the territory of South West

Africa, had violated and disavowed the mandate. Consequently the General Assembly revoked the mandate and declared that South Africa no longer had any right to occupy or administer South West Africa. It was present illegally in the territory. In 1968 the General Assembly declared that South West Africa 'shall henceforth be known as "Namibia"'.[8]

Resolution 2145(XXI) was not accepted by many Western states, particularly the United Kingdom and France. I set out to establish that the resolution was sound in law by examining the competence of the League of Nations to revoke a mandate and the succession of the General Assembly to this power. The result was a highly technical and historical piece. I chose not to submit it to the *South African Law Journal*, firstly, because this article was more controversial than the critical piece on the 1966 decision and it seemed only fair to protect both the journal and its publisher from a hostile response by government; and secondly, because I wanted it to reach a wider audience of international lawyers. Consequently, it was submitted to the premier international law journal, the *American Journal of International Law*. To my delight it was accepted.[9]

The South African government did not like my article because it challenged its central legal argument that Resolution 2145(XXI) was illegal and exceeded the powers of the General Assembly. Messages of disapproval from the government were conveyed to me and my article was subjected to a detailed, but ineffective, criticism by Professor Whitey van der Westhuizen, my former professor at Stellenbosch, at a meeting of the South African University Teachers of Law. More serious was the approach made by Donald Sole, a former South Africa ambassador, to Stanley Jackson, a deputy vice-chancellor at Wits, not to appoint me as a professor because of my disloyal publication. Fortunately it did not have the required effect on the selection committee.

The UN was not the only body that was disappointed by the 1966 decision of the International Court. Members of the South West Africa People's Organization (SWAPO) listened in amazement to the decision in their camps in Angola on the border of South West Africa. They had naively believed that they would be able to enter South West Africa triumphantly as victors after the court had ruled against South Africa. Confused and impatient, they crossed the border bearing arms only to be met by the South African security forces. Many were killed, others were captured. The South African government seized upon this opportunity to bring not only those captured to trial, but also the SWAPO political leadership in South West Africa. Windhoek was judged to be too unsafe, and too far from the media, for such a trial. It was staged in Pretoria's Old Synagogue, the scene of the Rivonia trial. This was to be SWAPO's 'Rivonia trial'.

There were many laws under which the accused might be brought to trial.

The common law crime of treason, which had been held to be applicable to South West Africa,[10] was an obvious one. But the government decided instead to enact the Terrorism Act, No. 83 of 1967, for this purpose. This was an extraordinary statute, even by the legislative standards of the apartheid regime. It created the new capital offence of terrorism, which was defined as meaning the commission of any act, with intent to endanger the maintenance of law and order, which was likely to have a number of results, such as creating hostility between the races or embarrassing the administration of the affairs of state. Consequently it included not only violent acts against the state but also legitimate protest action. The burden of proof was placed on the accused. In addition, the Act provided that anyone held under the Act might be detained incommunicado and indefinitely for the purpose of interrogation. Finally it made the Act retrospective to acts committed after 1962. The Terrorism Act applied to both South Africa and South West Africa and was later savagely implemented in South Africa itself. As a result, the original purpose of the Act – to provide for the arrest and trial of SWAPO leaders – was often forgotten.

The South African Bar, and particularly the Johannesburg Bar, had many fearless advocates who had not hesitated to defend leaders of the African National Congress (ANC) charged with serious political crimes. However, the attorney chosen to defend the SWAPO leaders, Joel Carlson,[11] had difficulty in finding senior counsel in this case. After some searching, he was able to brief Nami Phillips QC, a senior counsel at the Johannesburg Bar with a general commercial practice, who had hitherto not appeared in major political trials. Carlson also briefed as junior counsel three advocates with considerable experience in political trials, George Bizos,[12] Ernie Wentzel and Denis Kuny.

In discussions with Carlson and junior counsel I suggested that the Terrorism Act under which the SWAPO leaders were to be tried might be challenged on the ground that it had been enacted subsequent to Resolution 2145(XXI) and therefore was null and void in so far as it purported to apply to South West Africa. They liked the argument but feared that Nami Phillips would not agree. A meeting to discuss this matter with Nami was held one night at the Wits Law Library. He was highly sceptical about the validity of the argument and raised many objections, particularly that a South African court could not consider a resolution of the General Assembly. At the end of the meeting he enquired several times whether, even if it would not succeed, it was a tenable argument. I replied that it was. The meeting broke up with no decision. The next day Phillips told us that he was prepared to argue that the Terrorism Act was invalid on the basis that it was a tenable argument and that professionally he was obliged to raise all issues that might assist the accused, particularly when the death sentence was a real possibility. It was the right decision, though in the political climate of the day it was also courageous.

The heat of the political climate was soon evidenced by the publication of a report in an Afrikaans-language Sunday newspaper that the defence team was being funded by the proscribed Defence and Aid Fund, a fund established to provide money for the defence of persons charged with political offences. As it was unlawful for lawyers to receive funding from this body, Joel Carlson was compelled to reveal the source of funding: Lord Campbell of Eskan, a philanthropist whose family had made its fortune in the sugar plantations of the West Indies. (In fact, it later became known that Lord Campbell was indeed a front for the Defence and Aid Fund.)[13]

So it was that the *State* v. *Tuhadeleni and Others*,[14] the trial of thirty-seven members of SWAPO, including the movement's internal leadership, commenced in the Old Synagogue in Pretoria before Judge Joe Ludorf, with a preliminary exception to the indictment based on my argument that the Terrorism Act was invalid. I was not able to present the argument myself as I was not a member of the Johannesburg Bar, and Bar rules precluded me from appearing with members of the Bar. So Phillips carefully set out the arguments I had advanced in my article in the *American Journal*. The effect of this was to transform the trial from that of a group of 'terrorists', as the government wished to portray it, to a political trial involving the self-determination of the people of South West Africa and the confrontation between South Africa and the UN over the territory. A heavy police presence underlined the determination of the government to present the accused as terrorists who posed a threat to security, but the technical arguments of counsel, the attendance of foreign envoys and observers, and the knowledge that it was of concern to the UN gave it a decidedly international character.

Although the prosecutors in the case did not present a convincing rebuttal to the arguments raised by Phillips, it came as no surprise when Judge Ludorf, a staunch supporter of the apartheid regime, ruled against the motion and the trial proceeded. Although it was now a criminal trial, it retained its international character as the jurisdictional objection had succeeded in keeping it before the international media. Also, it was clear that there would be an appeal against the judge's ruling on the validity of the Terrorism Act should there be a conviction.

I attended the trial irregularly and came to know several of the SWAPO trialists well. They had all been brutally tortured in prison and were convinced that they would be sentenced to death. However, the international law argument and the widespread international publicity it engendered gave them new hope.

Although the first accused was Eliaser Tuhadeleni, Herman Toivo ya Toivo was the real leader. He was an impressive man and later made a moving statement from the dock after his conviction in which he accused South Africa of having failed to promote the 'sacred trust' conferred on it by the mandate. He recalled that he had joined the South African army during World War II to fight Nazism while Judge Ludorf had belonged to a pro-Nazi underground organization. I came to know Jason Mutumbulua and Johnny ya Otto particularly well. They were both teachers active in mobilizing political support for SWAPO in Katutura, the township of Windhoek. Both spoke excellent English and were responsible for conveying the views of the group to their lawyers. Joel Carlson was a controversial lawyer and many were critical of his legal acumen. But he restored the spirits of the thirty-seven after their long period of solitary confinement and torture by providing them with all the material comforts that the prison authorities allowed and making contact with their families.

In due course the trial ended and the accused were convicted of terroristic activities. Under the Terrorism Act such activities were punishable by death. Although the death penalty had not been imposed on the ANC leadership in the Rivonia trial of 1964, there was a real fear that the death penalty might be imposed in this case. This was the first major trial under the Terrorism Act and the government wished to send out a clear message that terrorism, as it sought to call subversive political activities, would be dealt with severely. In addition, Ludorf was known to be a hanging judge, unlike the more fair-minded judge in the Rivonia trial.

Joel Carlson was convinced that only international intervention could save the SWAPO thirty-seven. He discussed visiting the UN for this purpose with me. I suspect he discussed it with George, Ernie and Denis too. Whether he discussed it with Nami, I do not know. In any event, the next thing we knew was that Carlson was in New York lobbying the UN to intervene. It did. The Security Council adopted a resolution condemning the trial and demanding that sentence of death not be imposed.[15] This resolution served another purpose. It raised the issue of South West Africa before the Security Council for the first time in its history. I am convinced that Carlson's visit to the UN saved the accused. Carlson told the story that Prime Minister John Vorster summoned Ludorf to Cape Town to tell him not to impose the death sentence and that Ludorf, reluctantly, had accepted this advice. Judge Ludorf imposed life imprisonment on several of the accused and periods of imprisonment on others. Later, he told my Wits colleague, Barend van Niekerk, that he regretted not having imposed sentence of death on many of the accused.

State v. *Tuhadeleni and Others* was taken on appeal to the Appellate Division of the Supreme Court, sitting in full plenary session with eleven judges for the first time since the Senate case of 1957. I assisted Nami Phillips in the preparation of the appeal and journeyed to Bloemfontein with the legal team. We received a good hearing but, predictably, we did not succeed. South Africa's judges were not sympathetic to arguments premised on international law, and the spectre of terrorism made them close ranks in support of the government. The unanimous decision handed down by the court failed to deal convincingly with the arguments that Phillips had presented.

Now South West Africa was firmly before the Security Council. *State* v. *Tuhadeleni and Others* had succeeded where other efforts to persuade the Security Council to consider the question of South West Africa had failed. In 1970 the Security Council, for the first time in its history, requested the International Court of Justice to give an advisory opinion on the legal consequences for states of the continued presence of South Africa in South West Africa/Namibia.

In my article on the decision of the International Court I had thoroughly examined the competing schools of treaty interpretation. I had shown that the majority of 1966 (and the minority of 1962) belonged to the positivist, literal school of interpretation, which had resulted in a conservative, narrow interpretation of the instruments before the court, while the minority of 1966 (the majority of 1962) had adopted an expansive method of interpretation which allowed the judges to interpret instruments to give effect to their ultimate object. As the composition of the court had undergone changes since 1966, the South African government anticipated that the more liberal school would be in the majority. I was informally approached by Professor Marinus Wiechers of the University of South Africa, who had been briefed to advise the South African legal team, to establish whether I might informally advise the team on the likely method of legal reasoning to be employed by the court. Marinus was a colleague and a friend. I promised to give him an answer a few days later when I was scheduled to be in Pretoria. I agonized over the matter as the 'cab-rank' rule prescribed that an advocate should accept any brief, however unpopular the cause and however unacceptable the subject of the brief might be to the advocate. Although I was not a member of the Johannesburg Bar, I was an advocate and I felt constrained to honour my obligations. I discussed the matter with my friend Rex Welsh QC, one of the most successful and respected members of the Johannesburg Bar. 'Don't be silly,' he said, 'you cannot possibly advise a government you dislike on a case you hope it will lose!' So I decided to refuse. Marinus did not, however, keep the appointment. Some time later he told me, with some embarrassment, that the government had vetoed the suggestion that my advice be sought.

None of the states that presented oral argument before the International Court in the advisory proceedings asked me for advice. My article in the *American Journal* did, however, feature in the arguments of states[16] and was cited by Judge de Castro of Spain in his separate opinion.[17]

In 1971 the International Court of Justice handed down its advisory opinion on *Legal Consequences of States for the Continued Presence of South Africa in Namibia (South West Africa) notwithstanding Security Council Resolution 276 (1970)*.[18] The court held that the mandate had survived the League of Nations, that South Africa had succeeded to the obligations contained in the mandate, that South Africa had violated the mandate by applying apartheid in the territory, and that the General Assembly had lawfully terminated the mandate. Although my argument on the revocation of the mandate had been summarily rejected by the South African courts, it was accepted by the International Court.

In 1969 Jane and I spent six months in the United States. While we were there, Bill McClung of the University of California Press persuaded me to prepare a collection of edited documents and writings on the Namibian question. This task kept me busy for several years and in 1973 *The South West Africa/Namibia Dispute: Documents and Scholarly Writings on the Controversy between South Africa and the United Nations* was published.

The 1971 advisory opinion became the lodestar for the UN and set the parameters for its strategies on Namibia. In the years that followed, the UN did not compromise. It studiously followed the principal rulings of the court in its negotiations and actions.

As was to be expected, the opinion was subjected to severe criticism from the South African government. Prime Minister Vorster claimed that the court had been packed for the proceedings to secure a decision unfavourable to South Africa and that it had adopted an untenable method of reasoning, a view supported by most politicians and many South African legal scholars. In defence of the opinion I examined the composition of the court to refute the argument it had been specially constituted and sought to explain that the court had employed a method of legal reasoning in 1971 that accorded with its previous jurisprudence. It was the 1966 decision and not the 1971 opinion that was out of step with the court's jurisprudence.[19] For the next twenty years I urged the government to accept the opinion, to recognize SWAPO as the authentic representative of the people of Namibia, to repeal discriminatory and repressive laws, and to end the occupation of Namibia. Namibia was one of the world's last colonial problems, and in an age of decolonization South Africa could expect no sympathy for its policies of apartheid in the territory.[20]

In January 1976 I was invited to attend a major conference in Dakar, Senegal, on human rights in Namibia, hosted by the Senegalese government under President Léopold Senghor and sponsored by the UN commissioner for Namibia, Nobel laureate Sean McBride. The conference was attended by some three hundred people, including the leadership of SWAPO. Two white

South Africans were invited: Professor Barend van Niekerk and I. Barend van Niekerk, a controversial Afrikaner, about whom I will have more to say later, was primarily invited because he was a friend of President Senghor, having written a thesis in Paris on the influence of *négritude* on Senghor's poetry. The conference demanded that the Security Council call upon the South African government to permit the UN to supervise free and fair elections in Namibia, failing which mandatory sanctions should be imposed on South Africa. There was strong support for the legitimacy of the armed struggle.

Throughout the 1970s and 1980s the UN sought to secure the independence of Namibia. In 1978 it established the UN Transition Assistance Group – UNTAG – with the task of implementing Namibian independence through free and fair elections under UN supervision. Five Western members of the Security Council that took the lead in the search for a settlement agreed on a set of Constitutional Principles in 1982 to give effect to Resolution 435 and to form the framework for a future constitution of Namibia.

The twenty-year period between the 1971 opinion and independence in 1990 was characterized by diplomacy and conflict. While the UN attempted to broker peace and independence for Namibia, South African forces waged a bitter border war against SWAPO forces. SWAPO, which had been recognized as the authentic representative of the Namibian people by the General Assembly in 1973, was able to operate from bases in southern Angola after that country became independent in 1975. The presence of Cuban forces sent to assist the government of Angola complicated the situation as they assisted both the Angolan government in the civil war and SWAPO units. Fierce battles were fought between South African forces and SWAPO in southern Angola and along the northern border of Namibia. South African counter-insurgency forces waged a war against SWAPO both within Namibia itself and in southern Angola in the course of which many Namibians were killed and tortured. This had different consequences for me.

Under the law of South West Africa, captured members of SWAPO's military wing were terrorists who might be tried before the courts on charges of terrorism and, if convicted, sentenced to death and executed. Under international law it was, however, arguable, particularly since the adoption of the 1977 Protocols to the Geneva Conventions, that members of liberation movements were entitled to be treated as prisoners of war. As South Africa refused to sign the 1977 Geneva Protocols, it was impossible to argue in a South West African court that captured members of SWAPO were entitled to prisoner-of-war status. But it was arguable that such persons might claim that they reasonably believed they were entitled to be treated as prisoners of war if captured and that this should be taken into account in mitigation of sentence. I had advanced this view in several publications and was asked to present it as an expert witness in *State* v. *Sagarius and Others.*[21] The argument succeeded. The accused were convicted of terrorism but not sentenced to death. The court accepted as mitigating factors that the international community regarded South Africa as being in illegal occupation of Namibia and that captured members of SWAPO should be treated as prisoners of war. This decision was followed in other cases and no member of SWAPO was ever sentenced to death by a South West African court for military activities (or terrorism, as South Africa preferred to see it). This was the second time that an international law argument had saved Namibians from the gallows. It was clear that the internationalization of the case deterred judges from imposing sentence of death. The likely harm to the national interest caused by adverse publicity surrounding the death penalty in such cases was seen to outweigh the interest of harsh punishment.

In order to execute its war in Angola and South West Africa, the South African government intensified its conscription of young white men for two years' compulsory military service. This compelled young white South Africans to make a moral decision as to whether they could in all conscience take up arms in support of their country's illegal occupation of Namibia. This led to the formation of the End Conscription Campaign in 1983 to oppose conscription, support conscientious objectors and advocate an end to conscription. The organization was very active in mobilizing support for those who refused call-up until it was banned under emergency regulations in 1988. Many young men, numbering thousands, quietly left the country rather than serve. Some claimed religious convictions for refusing to serve. Others refused call-up on account of the illegality of the occupation and the policy of apartheid. I gave evidence before court martials on behalf of two leading conscientious objectors – Charles Yeats[22] and Ivan Toms[23] – on the illegality of South Africa's occupation of Namibia and the consequent illegality of the war in Namibia and Angola. Strangely, the presiding officers seemed genuinely surprised to learn that South Africa's occupation of Namibia was regarded as unlawful by the international community and initially showed some interest in the argument. But soon they realized the implications of upholding such an argument, and bewilderment turned to hostility. Inevitably the defence failed, and both Yeats and Toms were sentenced to substantial terms of imprisonment. However, the argument did succeed in drawing attention to the illegality of the occupation of Namibia – a taboo subject in South Africa.

I remained involved in the Namibian cause throughout the 1970s and 1980s, advising SWAPO on questions of international law, attending conferences and working with the office of the UN commissioner for Namibia. In 1989 I acted as an international monitor in the UN-supervised elections. On 21 March 1990 Namibia finally became independent.

PART TWO

South Africa

5

A brief history of apartheid in South Africa

The history of apartheid dates back to 1652 when the Cape of Good Hope was settled by the Dutch East India Company to provide a refreshment station to facilitate trade with the East Indies.[1] Racial segregation and white domination, the hallmarks of apartheid, were evidenced by the Dutch settlement's subjugation of the indigenous people in the region and the introduction of slaves from the Dutch East Indies and elsewhere. The British colonial occupation, which began on a permanent basis in 1806, saw the end of slavery but the continuation of segregation and white domination. In the interior of the country, the Boer republics of the Orange Free State and the South African Republic (Transvaal) were likewise premised on racial inequality. After the defeat of the republics in the Anglo-Boer War of 1899–1902, the four British colonies joined to form the Union of South Africa in 1910. The compact that emerged from this Union was founded on white domination. Only whites enjoyed the franchise in the Transvaal and Orange Free State while in the Cape Province (and technically in Natal) non-whites were allowed to retain the old qualified franchise, which was entrenched in the constitution by a clause requiring amendment by a two-thirds majority vote in both Houses of Parliament sitting together. In 1936 African voters (but not coloured voters) in the Cape were removed by the required procedure from the common voters' roll and given separate parliamentary representation.

South Africa played an important role in World War II under the leadership of Prime Minister Jan Smuts. After the war Smuts was welcomed in the peace-making councils of the new world order and enjoined with the task of drafting the Preamble of the Charter of the United Nations, committing the world body to the promotion of human rights. But his vision was confined largely to the international stage. At home he simply followed the traditional paternalistic and discriminatory policies towards blacks.

Smuts's United Party seemed assured of victory in the election of 1948. But it was not to be. The National Party, under Dr D.F. Malan, supported largely by Afrikaner voters, secured a narrow victory on the platform of apartheid. Segregation had always been part of South African life. Interracial marriage was rare; public facilities were in practice mainly segregated; most skilled jobs were reserved for whites; African men were required to carry documents – 'passes' – authorizing their movement from one place to another; and only qualified coloured voters in the Cape Province enjoyed the franchise in addition to all whites. Segregation was a way of life for South Africa before 1948. Now it was to become an ideology with the distinctive name of apartheid. South Africa was to embark on a policy of institutionalized and systematic racial discrimination and domination in which there would be no respect for human rights.

The National Party government soon set about translating the policy of apartheid into law. One of the hallmarks of apartheid was to be its legislative transparency. Other states might quietly and secretly practise segregation, but this was not to be the case with South Africa. The law was to be used as an instrument to enforce separation and no attempt would be made to conceal its discriminatory intent.

A number of laws were immediately passed to ensure racial 'purity'. The first was the Prohibition of Mixed Marriages Act[2] of 1949, which forbade marriages between 'Europeans and non-Europeans'. This was followed by a law making sexual relations between 'Europeans and non-Europeans' a punishable offence.[3] To prevent crossing from one racial group to another, the apartheid regime then enacted the Population Registration Act,[4] which could be described as the cornerstone of the whole system of apartheid. This statute provided for the compilation of a register of the entire South African population, reflecting the classification of each individual as a white person, a coloured person (this included not only persons of mixed descent, known as coloureds in South Africa, but also Malays, Indians and Chinese) or a Bantu (the term used by the apartheid regime to describe black Africans). Disputes over race classification were to be settled by reference to a person's physical appearance, social acceptance and descent. Race classification boards were charged with making the determination of race classification in disputed cases. This led to great suffering as families were torn apart by being classified as belonging to different racial groups, with all the ensuing consequences for their personal, social, economic and political lives.

Once racial identity was clear, it was necessary to spell out the consequences. In practice, separate social and public facilities had been reserved for different races from time immemorial. But in 1953 the Reservation of Separate Amenities Act[5] made it clear that there was no obligation on persons in charge of public amenities and places to provide substantially equal facilities for all racial groups. The separate but unequal policy was now enshrined in law. This law covered parks, restaurants, toilets, cinemas, theatres and beaches. Large signs indicating that particular facilities were exclusively for 'whites only' became a common feature of South African life.

Residential segregation had always been practised in an uncontrolled manner, with some neighbourhoods partially integrated and many coloured and Indian residential areas situated in the centre of the city close to white neighbourhoods. In 1950 the Group Areas Act[6] was passed to provide for the creation of separate 'group areas' in towns and cities for whites, Africans and coloureds. Persons of another race in areas zoned for exclusive white occupation were prohibited from acquiring property in such areas and committed a crime if they remained in occupation in premises in such areas. In theory such areas were supposed to be equal but in fact they were not. The Act was administered in a grossly discriminatory manner in favour of whites, a discrimination that was condoned by the Appeal Court.[7] The population removal under the Group Areas Act that achieved the greatest notoriety was the removal of sixty thousand coloureds from District Six in the heart of Cape Town, which they had occupied since the nineteenth century, to a bleak area with no amenities and far from places of employment kilometres away from Cape Town.

The Group Areas Act was used mainly to remove coloureds and Indians from their established homes in the 'white' cities and towns. Other legislation was employed to move Africans from their ancestral homes in the countryside to the African reserves, constituting some 13 per cent of South African territory. Under these laws hundreds of thousands of Africans were moved from so-called black spots near white farms and resettled on land in the areas reserved for African occupation that were to become Bantustans.

Education was next. Although schools were largely separated along racial lines before 1948, black scholars were subject to the same provincial educational regime as whites. However, in 1953 the Bantu Education Act[8] removed the education of black children from the control of the provinces and the churches and brought it under a central government department determined to ensure that black children would be educated in accordance with their status in South Africa. Ironically this law was passed at the same time that the United States

Supreme Court rejected school segregation on the ground that 'separate educational facilities are inherently unequal'.[9] At this time the University of Cape Town and the University of the Witwatersrand in Johannesburg were open to all races though the numbers of non-whites who enrolled were small. Nelson Mandela, for instance, studied law at the University of the Witwatersrand. In 1959 these universities were closed to all non-white students by the cynically named Extension of University Education Act.[10] Separate universities, later referred to disparagingly as 'bush colleges', were established for each non-white racial group.

The reservation of skilled jobs for whites was a product of law and convention before 1948. The National Party extended the existing laws to cover a wide range of jobs in the mining, building and clothing industries and in a host of occupations.[11] African trade unions were not permitted under the law providing for collective bargaining and industrial conciliation. Africans were prohibited from striking and the security laws were invoked to restrict the activities of African leaders in the workplace.

In the 1950s the government embarked on the disenfranchisement of the sole remaining non-white voters.[12] As it lacked the necessary two-thirds majority in both Houses of Parliament to remove the coloured voters from the common voters' roll in the Cape Province as required by the constitution and the courts,[13] the government resorted to the devious strategy of packing the Appeal Court with well-disposed judges and increasing the size of the Senate by adding new members nominated by the government itself. In this way the coloured voters were disenfranchised and the supremacy of the all-white Parliament affirmed.[14]

Discriminatory restrictions on the freedom of movement of blacks dated back to the early nineteenth century. Blacks were largely confined to their own reserves except when they were released to serve the agricultural and industrial interests of the white community. When they entered white towns and cities, they were required to carry 'passes', or documents that provided evidence of authorization to be in such an area. Movement to the cities was, however, difficult to control as there were no job opportunities in the African reserves and the white economy desperately needed black labour. But the National Party was determined to curb the flow of blacks into the cities. Existing pass laws were consolidated and tightened in 1952 by the cynically named Bantu (Abolition of Passes and Co-ordination of Documents) Act,[15] which also extended the pass laws to black women. It now became an offence for a black person to reside for longer than 72 hours in an urban area without permission. Failure to produce such permission in the form of a pass was a punishable offence. The pass laws were vigorously enforced by Bantu commissioner's courts, which provided a sausage-machine-like form of justice for blacks, who in almost every case were tried without legal representation and sentenced to a short term of imprisonment of several weeks or months followed by an order to leave the urban area. In 1974, for instance, there were 386,400 prosecutions under the pass laws, representing 28 per cent of all 'criminal' cases sent to trial in South Africa: that is, a thousand trials every day of the year. Further restrictions on movement were to be found in curfew laws in the cities and in a law allowing a Bantu Affairs commissioner to deem a black person 'idle and undesirable' and to order his removal from an urban area.

Discriminatory laws of this kind provoked protests and demonstrations, mainly led by the African National Congress (ANC), which had been established in 1912. This prompted the enactment of repressive laws to suppress extra-parliamentary political action. The Suppression of Communism Act of 1950[16] was the most draconian security law of the first decade of apartheid. This statute outlawed the Communist Party, and prohibited and punished the advocacy of communism. Communism was defined in such a way that it encompassed ideologies, beliefs and actions completely unrelated to that ideology. Communism included any doctrine which aimed at 'bringing about any political, industrial, social or economic change … by the promotion of disturbance or disorder by unlawful acts or omissions'. This law and the Criminal Law Amendment Act of 1953[17] made civil disobedience protest action unlawful. This was illustrated by the prosecution of ANC leaders during the Defiance Campaign of 1952 for advocating and organizing a civil disobedience campaign against discriminatory laws in general and the pass laws in particular.

The Suppression of Communism Act made the advocacy of communism a punishable offence. However, in practice the government preferred to silence its opponents by administrative means in so-called banning orders, which permitted the minister of justice to impose restrictions on the freedoms of assembly, gathering, speech and movement of persons who he believed were engaged in activities furthering the objects of communism. Publications might also be prohibited under this Act. So too might organizations: in 1962 the Congress of Democrats was banned, and in 1966 the South African Defence and Aid Fund, an organization devoted to the defence of persons charged with political offences, was prohibited in this way.

The ANC worked closely with other radical anti-apartheid movements and was the dominant member of the Congress Alliance, comprising the ANC, the South African Indian Congress, the (white) Congress of Democrats and the South African Coloured People's Organization. In 1955 the Congress Alliance adopted the Freedom Charter at a large gathering held at Kliptown, near Johannesburg, which committed the alliance to a democratic South Africa, outlawed racial discrimination and respected human rights. At the same time the Charter demanded nationalization of the mines and banks. The government responded by arresting 156 persons – 105 Africans, 23 whites, 21 Indians and 7 coloureds – and charging them with treason, on the allegation that they had sought to overthrow the state by violent means and establish a communist system of government. The trial dragged on for five years before all were acquitted in March 1961. The apartheid regime was greatly embarrassed by the acquittal by white judges whom it had viewed as sympathetic to its cause. It had succeeded, however, in tying down the leadership of the Congress Alliance, including Albert Luthuli, then president of the ANC, Oliver Tambo and Nelson Mandela, for several years while they attended court hearings.

Despite these repressive measures, protests continued. In March 1960, a protest against passes in Sharpeville, organized by the Pan Africanist Congress (PAC), which broke away from the ANC in 1959 and which was led by Robert Sobukwe, resulted in the killing of sixty-nine innocent African protesters. The country erupted in protest. In Cape Town a crowd of thirty thousand marched peacefully on the central police station. International condemnation was swift to follow. In response, the government declared a state of emergency which continued for 156 days, during which 11,503 persons were held in custody without trial.

A further response of the government was to enact the Unlawful Organizations Act,[18] which proscribed both the ANC and PAC in the interest of public safety. Initially this ban was to last for one year only, but in 1963 it was made permanent. The restrictions imposed on members of the ANC and PAC in terms of this ban followed the Suppression of Communism Act. Consequently it became a crime to further the activities of the ANC or PAC. Prosecutions were frequent, particularly in the Eastern Cape, a stronghold of the ANC. In the mid-1960s at least two thousand persons were prosecuted under the Unlawful Organizations Act for nothing more than belonging to the ANC or PAC or furthering their activities. Sentences ranged between five and seven years' imprisonment.

In October 1960 a referendum was held among whites on whether South Africa should cease to recognize the British Queen as the nominal, constitutional head of state and instead become a republic. After a majority of 52 per cent had voted in favour, South Africa became a republic on 31 May 1961. Shortly afterwards it decided to leave the Commonwealth of Nations.

The ANC had pursued a policy of non-violence from its inception. Sharpeville and the banning of the ANC brought about a change in thinking. Mandela, Sisulu and other members of the younger generation of leaders decided that there was no alternative to violence. In 1961 Umkhonto we Sizwe (Spear of the Nation), commonly known as MK, was created and began a campaign of sabotage of government buildings and installations. At the same time young men and women began leaving South Africa for military training in the Soviet Union and other African states.

The government response was to enact the 'Sabotage Act'[19] in 1962, which created the offence of sabotage, punishable by death, and the 90-day detention law in 1963,[20] followed by the 180-day detention law in 1965,[21] which authorized detention, in solitary confinement, without trial for 90 and 180 days respectively, for the purpose of interrogation.

The ANC and the Communist Party leaders set up a secret rendezvous at Lilliesleaf farm in Rivonia, north of Johannesburg, to plan the activities of MK. In July 1963 the security police swooped on the farm and arrested the leaders of the High Command, including Walter Sisulu and Govan Mbeki. Mandela himself was already in prison, serving a five-year sentence for inciting protests against the decision to become a republic and leaving the country unlawfully. However, he was charged with sabotage, together with those arrested at Lilliesleaf, in what became known as the Rivonia trial.[22] In June 1964 eight of the accused were convicted of sabotage and sentenced to life imprisonment.

The Rivonia trial was followed by a spate of other trials in which persons were charged with sabotage or furthering the aims of unlawful organizations. Most of them belonged to the ANC and PAC. The best known was Bram Fischer QC, a leader of the Communist Party, who had defended the accused in the Rivonia trial. He was released on bail, but later went into hiding before being rearrested, tried for sabotage, and sentenced to life imprisonment in 1966. Another sabotage movement of this time was the African Resistance Movement, a splinter of the anti-communist Liberal Party, which despite that party's commitment to non-violence, engaged in acts of sabotage. One of its members, John Harris, was convicted of murder for placing a bomb in the Johannesburg railway station concourse which killed an elderly woman. Harris was executed for this crime.

When the National Party came to power in 1948, it promised, and practised, more racial separation and more discrimination. Its policy was to strengthen the powers of the tribal chiefs and authorities in the reserves set aside for African occupation, but there was no suggestion of granting any form of self-government or independence to these territories. Essentially apartheid was a policy of white domination, or *baasskap* (boss-ship), premised on racial separation. Towards the end of the 1950s, it became clear that such a policy was completely unacceptable to the international community with its demands for self-determination and respect for human rights. Consequently the National Party government was compelled to produce a more sophisticated version of apartheid that might satisfy the demands of the international community but at the same time maintain white supremacy. Apartheid was now portrayed as 'separate development', which, according to the National Party regime, was in accordance with the principle of self-determination proclaimed in the Charter of the United Nations. This new policy envisaged the creation of 'self-governing Bantu units'[23] for each of the different tribal groups in South Africa. When this policy was introduced, there was no certainty that self-government would lead to independence, though the prime minister, Dr H.F. Verwoerd, did hint at this possibility. In order to show the world that it was sincere in its new policy of separate development (and in order to impress the International Court of Justice in the proceedings over apartheid in South West Africa then before the court), the government conferred self-government on Transkei, the territory set aside for the Xhosa people, in 1963. The success of South Africa in the proceedings before the International Court of Justice in 1966, which removed the urgency to appease international opinion, and the assassination of Dr Verwoerd, the architect of separate development, in the same year, slowed the pace of the implementation of this policy in the mid-1960s.

It was this racist and repressive country to which my wife Jane and I returned from Cambridge in 1965.

6

Speaking out

Before our return to South Africa, I had visited Johannesburg on several occasions. I did not like the city. I had never been to the University of the Witwatersrand ('Wits'). It was a strange new world. But, to our surprise, it was very welcoming. Both the Faculty of Law, where I taught, and the Medical School, where Jane was a research scientist, were friendly and sociable. Jane and I soon found that we were leading a very busy social life. Johannesburg was not an attractive city – except in spring when the jacaranda trees were in full bloom – but it was a place characterized by vibrancy and energy. We came to like it. We started our Johannesburg life in a flat in Berea, wedged between Yeoville and the fashionable suburb of Houghton, and then moved to a house in the leafy suburb of Craighall Park. In 1970 Jackie was born, followed by Justin in 1972. We were the happy family of four J's.

At Wits I initially taught international law, company law and criminal procedure: international law because that was my passion and reason for coming to Wits, company law because all lecturers were then expected to teach a course to commercial law students, and criminal procedure because I believed that it should be taught as a 'rights' course which emphasized the rights of accused persons and the need for procedural fairness.

Jane and I were not apolitical. We knew full well that we would be involved in the political life of the country and were determined not to become typical white South Africans who kept aloof from the injustices of the society in which they lived. On the other hand, we intended that our actions would remain within the law. We did not wish to suffer the fate of friends who now found themselves in prison for their political actions and whom I visited regularly there: David Evans, John Laredo and Marius Schoon, school and university friends who were serving prison sentences for sabotage committed in furtherance of the African Resistance Movement and the Congress of Democrats. Instead, my contribution to a better South Africa would be to use my newly acquired qualifications as an international lawyer to write and speak on South Africa's violations of international law and human rights. This, I believed, would be more useful, perhaps more effective, than futile illegal action. And this would be done within the law, even if it meant operating on the fringes of the law.

Acting within the limits of the law was more easily said than done, as the permissible bounds of free speech were ill defined. Moreover, lawful speech might easily be interpreted as unlawful by informers, spies and the security police, with serious consequences. I was to learn the uncertain limits of the law on free speech in my criticism of the courts and in my interpretation of the security laws.

Judges had long been immune from serious criticism for their part in condoning political repression and race discrimination, but this immunity began to erode when the Appellate Division of the Supreme Court handed down several decisions involving the rights of detainees under the security laws that displayed an unwillingness to interpret the laws in favour of individual liberty. This provoked an article in the *South African Law Journal*[24] examining these decisions by Tony Mathews, my former colleague from Natal, and Ronald Albino, professor of psychology at the University of Natal. They concluded that the Appeal Court had failed to uphold the rule of law and the traditions of the common law requiring ambiguous statutes to be interpreted in favour of individual liberty, and had shown a callous disregard for the well-being of detainees. In essence, they accused the court of having acted in bad faith in order to advance the interests of the executive.

It had taken courage for my colleagues Bobby Hahlo and Ellison Kahn, the editors of the *South African Law Journal*, to publish this article, as traditionally law review articles did not engage in such strong criticism of the courts. While the interpretation placed on a statute and the relevance of a particular precedent might be politely questioned in highly restrained language, the questioning of the moral integrity of the courts was hitherto unknown. Not surprisingly, the article had consequences. Chief Justice L.C. Steyn condemned it, the legal profession divided on both the tenor and the contents of the article, and the government retaliated against the publisher, Juta and Co., by handing a major publishing contract to a rival, uncritical publisher, Butterworths.

The Mathews and Albino article had a profound effect on me. I had believed that my opposition to the apartheid regime was best limited to challenging its legal position on South West Africa and international law, as I was the only qualified critic on these subjects and my voice was likely to be most effective there. But this article made me realize that there was a wider responsibility. Legal academics could, and should, it seemed, criticize not only the law and practice of apartheid but also the institutions charged with implementing apartheid. My colleague Jean Davids and I started to write critical commentaries on judicial decisions involving the security laws for the *South African Law Journal*. Although Hahlo and Kahn were troubled by confrontational comments of this kind inspired by the Mathews and Albino article, after cautious editing they did publish everything we wrote.

In 1967 the Human Rights Society of Wits University, which was closely associated with the Liberal Party, organized a series of lectures on liberal values, and I was asked to deliver the lecture on the law.[25] This lecture – 'Liberal Heritage of the Law' – took place at a time when the Law Society of the Transvaal, the official body representing attorneys, had come in for considerable criticism for its failure to protest against the banning of one of its members under the Suppression of Communism Act. This was Ruth Hayman, an attorney who had fearlessly represented persons charged with political offences. George Cook, the president of the Law Society, had made a statement on behalf of the society justifying its neutrality, arguing that it was the duty of the Law Society not to involve itself in politics. If it had questions or complaints, he declared, the Law Society should make representations to the government privately and not in public. Public protest would achieve nothing.

The meeting was held on the Wits campus with Rex Welsh QC in the chair. Rex, probably South Africa's most highly regarded corporate lawyer, was a member of the governing board of the Wits Law Faculty and I knew him slightly, but after this address we were to become firm friends. I chose as my principal theme the failure of the Law Society to uphold liberal values, particularly the rule of law, and responded in a highly confrontational manner to George Cook's statement. The speech, to a large audience, was well reported in the press and initiated a debate about the role of the legal profession in an unjust society. Several retired and sitting judges publicly criticized me, but I received considerable support from respected members of the legal profession.

Thereafter, I was much in demand with the press, particularly the *Rand Daily Mail*, the newspaper most critical of the government, under the editorship of Laurence Gandar. (I deliberately use the term 'press' and not 'media' because radio was monopolized by the government-controlled South African Broadcasting Company and television was not permitted in South Africa until 1976.) My popularity with the press was easy to explain. There was a culture of silence on criticism of judges and the administration of justice. In part, this was out of fear that robust criticism was illegal; in part, this was considered the safest course to pursue in an authoritarian state with wide administrative powers to silence critics. Practising lawyers refrained from public criticism, hiding behind professional rules which constrained them from commenting on cases in which they were involved, rules that they conveniently extended to cover comments on the general administration of justice. Academic lawyers, too, had imposed self-constraints upon themselves and, with the exception of Tony Mathews, refrained from commenting critically on the laws of apartheid to the press. Non-lawyers either did not have the expertise to comment on the law or were viewed by the media as lacking the authority to be cited by name. Now the press had a senior lecturer (professor after 1968) who was prepared to comment critically on matters affecting the administration of justice.

So I found myself commenting not only on matters of international law, particularly questions concerning the foreign policy decisions of government on South West Africa, Rhodesia and the United Nations, but also on police actions and judicial decisions in respect of political repression and racial discrimination. White South Africans were fearful of the law and believed that it imposed more restrictions on freedom of speech than it really did. The security laws had a chilling effect on freedom of speech. I knew the law, I knew what might be said and what was prohibited. I was careful to stay within the limits of the law – except in one case to be mentioned later. I was, however, seen as skating on thin ice by most white South Africans, many of whom admired my public criticisms of the government but lacked the courage to speak out themselves. Jane was frequently asked, 'Isn't John afraid that he will get into trouble?'

In 1968 I was appointed as a professor of law. By this time the Wits Faculty of Law had undergone important changes. Jean Davids and I had changed the image of the Law Faculty from an institution that was neutral and uncritical of government to one in the forefront of legal activism. At that time we were joined by Barend van Niekerk.

I had known Barend at Stellenbosch where he had distinguished himself by his vigorous support for the National Party Youth Front (Nasionale Jeugbond). But he had changed as result of his further education in France. He was now an outspoken critic of the government and was unable to get an appointment in an Afrikaans-language university despite his excellent academic qualifications. He revelled in pursuing particular causes. The abolition of the death penalty was his main concern when he joined Wits and he soon found himself on the wrong side of the law when he published an article on the death penalty in which he showed convincingly that statistics proved that the death penalty was implemented in a racially discriminatory manner. Of course, everyone knew that a black person was more likely to be sentenced to death than a white person, but the publication of such an assertion, backed by statistics, in the *South African Law Journal*,[26] was too much for some judges, particularly the judge president of the Transvaal Provincial Division, Piet Cillie. Barend was prosecuted for contempt of court but acquitted on a technicality, after a thorough dressing down by the trial judge.[27] This case demonstrated that judges were now determined to use contempt of court as a weapon to protect themselves against hostile academic critics – particularly Mathews, Van Niekerk and myself.

In 1969 I was awarded a travel fellowship to visit the United States by the United States–South Africa Leadership Exchange Program (USSALEP). My visit was divided into two parts. The first consisted of a spell teaching a course on comparative civil liberties at the Woodrow Wilson School of Public and International Affairs at Princeton, to which I had been invited by Professor Richard Falk, who had acted as an observer at the SWAPO trial. It was an exciting time at Princeton as the campus was divided on two issues – the war in Vietnam and the admission of women students for the first time in the university's history. The second part of my stay comprised a three months' journey through the United States to universities of my choice, which enabled Jane and me to see the East Coast, Midwest, West Coast and South. All university campuses we visited were alive with dissent over the Vietnam War, and there was an idealism and vitality among students that I was not to encounter on subsequent visits to the United States. I spent one day at the notorious Chicago Conspiracy Trial of eight accused who had orchestrated the demonstrations at the Democratic Party Convention in Chicago in 1968, and marvelled at the contemptuous manner in which the accused treated the presiding judge, Julius Hoffman. Hoffman's comments and rulings routinely elicited the response from the accused of 'Fuck you, Your Honor'. Why 'Your Honor' was added to this abuse I could not understand. I compared this with the respect shown by both accused and counsel to judges in political trials in South Africa.

The American experience of race relations and opposition to the Vietnam War were highly relevant to the anti-apartheid struggle. This explains why American law and institutions had a profound influence on South African human rights lawyers during the apartheid years. The decisions of the Warren Court on racial equality and procedural rights, such as *Brown* v. *Board of Education of Topeka*,[28] which held that the separate but equal doctrine was unconstitutional, were an inspiration, and the work of public interest law groups such as the Legal Defense and Educational Fund of the National Association for the Advancement of Colored People (NAACP) provided examples of how lawyers might advance human rights through the courts.

This visit to the United States was the first of many during the apartheid years. In part, this was because I later became the recipient of American funding for the Centre for Applied Legal Studies (of which more later). In part, this was because I was welcome in American universities, but not welcome in their British and European counterparts, which had imposed a boycott on South African universities extending to all white academics, irrespective of their views. Invitations to European and British academic conferences were seldom forthcoming. Certainly, I never received one. American universities, on the other hand, distinguished between academics who opposed apartheid and those who did not. The former were much in demand as visitors and at conferences.

In 1971 I was required to deliver my inaugural lecture as professor at Wits. Initially I thought that I would speak about international law, but, on reflection, I decided that international law was too esoteric for an audience of South African lawyers. Consequently, I chose to speak on the subject of 'The Judicial Process, Positivism and Civil Liberty'.[29] The principal thesis of my lecture was that South African judges had interpreted the law of apartheid in favour of the government and that they had been misled into doing this by adopting the philosophy of legal positivism. This philosophy encouraged a sharp division between law and morality and saw law as the command of the sovereign power – the all-white Parliament – which was not to be challenged by judges in applying the law. Relying on the American school of legal realism, which maintained that the judicial decision, largely inarticulate, was the product of a judge's background, education and life, I argued that white South African judges had been influenced by their inarticulate premise in favour of white superiority in the interpretation of race and security laws. Positivism had provided judges with a philosophical justification for refusing to consider the immorality of apartheid's laws and to accept such laws without question. I urged judges to confront and neutralize their inarticulate premise in favour of white racial superiority and to interpret the law in accordance with the liberal values of the South Africa common law based on the philosophy of natural law.

A full-page report of my lecture was published in the *Rand Daily Mail*.[30] This was followed by extensive press coverage and editorial comment. The *Sunday Times* discussed my lecture approvingly in an editorial and concluded: 'The professor has blown a breath of fresh air into an atmosphere which had been rather overpoweringly laden with incense.'[31] Of course, not all approved and several judges publicly criticized my views, arguing that it was the duty of judges to interpret the will of Parliament and not to criticize the law even if they profoundly disagreed with it.

Shortly afterwards I attended a conference of the Association of South

African Teachers of Law at Buffelspoort near Hartbeespoort Dam. Recently retired Chief Justice L.C. Steyn was the keynote speaker at the dinner, and it was expected that, as the occasion was essentially a farewell to him, he would make a few warm comments about academic lawyers and graciously accept the accolades that had been bestowed on him by his hosts. Instead he launched into an attack on an unnamed academic who had suggested that judges were guided by their inarticulate premises into making decisions that favoured the executive in matters of security. He said that judges had considered laying charges of contempt of court against the unnamed academic but that the academic in question had been very smart in suggesting that judges had not deliberately ruled in favour of the executive but had only negligently and subconsciously done so. This meant that a charge of contempt of court would not succeed as there was no claim that judges had intended to favour the executive. Needless to say, this address divided the association, which comprised law academics from both English-language and Afrikaans-language universities. Many Afrikaans academics felt that political loyalty compelled them to side with L.C. Steyn, but several quietly told the unnamed academic that they agreed with his views and that Steyn had been wrong to use this occasion to castigate critics of the judiciary.

Academics were now under threat from the judiciary for contempt of court. I had the bizarre experience of a visit from the head of criminal investigation (CID) and the head of security police from Grahamstown arising out of a criticism I had made of a decision of Judge President Cloete of the Eastern Cape Division of the Supreme Court, suggesting executive bias. In a decision in which the court had been asked to set aside Ciskei independence in 1981 because the people of Ciskei had not been consulted, Cloete stated that the legislation granting independence had been passed by a sovereign Parliament and no court of law was competent to pronounce on its validity. I simply commented that the judgment was 'a rather brutal statement of parliamentary sovereignty and one which showed the extent to which the courts were willing to accept the notion of parliamentary sovereignty'.[32] The two officers explained that they had been instructed by the judge president to travel from Grahamstown to Johannesburg to interview me and ascertain whether I was correctly reported and, if so, whether I was prepared to apologize for my comment. I replied that I had been correctly reported and that I was not prepared to apologize. The security police officer then left and the head of the CID quietly apologized to me for the inconvenience caused. He said that in his opinion I had said nothing unlawful and that judges were oversensitive and arrogant. 'You will be the same when you are appointed a judge,' he added. I thanked him and assured him that I had no intention of becoming a judge. No prosecution followed and the matter was dropped.

In 1983 Judge Solomon was reported as having said in passing sentence on two white men convicted of killing a black woman in East London: 'I take into account this woman was black. If the boot were on the other foot, if two black men did this to a white woman … I would have had to deal with them more severely.' I commented that all Supreme Court judges were white, which meant that they 'should be particularly careful when making these kinds of comments which tend to violate the confidence of the man in the street that all people are equal in the eyes of the law'.[33] Judge Solomon laid a complaint. I was visited by a police officer and again made a statement saying that I stood by what I had said. Again there was no prosecution.

Barend van Niekerk was not so fortunate. Now a professor in Durban, Barend addressed a meeting in the Durban City Hall protesting against the detention-without-trial laws. He castigated lawyers and judges for their failure to condemn the Terrorism Act of 1967, which allowed indefinite detention without trial, and called on judges to 'kill' the Act by refusing to accept the testimony of any detainee held under this law. He was prosecuted for contempt of court and defeating the ends of justice by urging judges to reject the testimony of all such witnesses without proof that they had been subjected to duress. He was convicted by the Supreme Court and the conviction was upheld on appeal in a judgment designed to silence academic critics.[34]

The contempt of court weapon was not the only means for silencing academics who became too critical. The Internal Security Act, as the Suppression of Communism Act had been renamed in 1976, prohibited and punished the quotation of anything said or written by a person who was banned from attending gatherings on the ground that he had, in the opinion of the minister of justice, engaged in activities which endangered the security of the state; or by an ex-resident of South Africa who in the opinion of the minister of justice engaged in activities abroad calculated to achieve any of the objects of communism. This meant that academics writing in South Africa had to be very careful not to quote such a person, however scholarly the statement or publication might be. In 1978 I fell foul of this law in two cases.

While at Princeton in 1969 I had been persuaded by the Princeton University Press to write a book on the law of apartheid, which I worked on for many years. In 1978 the press published *Human Rights and the South African Legal Order*, in which I examined the history of discriminatory and repressive legislation in South Africa, and the response of the judiciary to it. South African law and jurisprudence were compared and contrasted with international standards and foreign jurisprudence, particularly the decisions of the United States Supreme Court. I returned to the theme of my 1971 inaugural lecture, that legal positivism and respect for the notion of parliamentary sovereignty had been harmful to South Africa. It was a thorough, scholarly study running to nearly five hundred pages. I was very careful not to quote any banned person or publication.

Without consulting me, obviously, the Princeton University Press selected two distinguished readers to review my manuscript. One was Albie Sachs, author of *Justice in South Africa*, then teaching at the University of Southampton. But Albie, who was to become a member of the Constitutional Court of South Africa, was banned under the Internal Security Act, which meant that he might not be quoted in South Africa. Without informing me, the press included a warm statement from Albie recommending my book on the dust cover of the hardback and on the cover of the paperback. Princeton had no distributor in South Africa and relied on Oxford University Press for local distribution. The local manager of Oxford University Press, Neville Gracie, without consulting me, referred the book to the Department of Justice for approval because of the statement by Sachs on the cover. This was a spineless act. I am convinced that the Sachs statement was in substance so harmless that it would have gone unnoticed had it not been drawn to the attention of the Justice Department. As it was, the book was predictably prohibited and declared to be undesirable in the same Government Notice as Philip Roth's *Professor of Desire*.[35] In order to secure its release, it was necessary to remove the dust cover and to delete the offensive statement on the paperback. Ultimately, the book was distributed, but Oxford University Press, which did not wish to undermine its educational sales which depended on government support, saw to it that it was not properly marketed. Publishing houses of this time, with some notable exceptions like Juta, were responsible for serious internal censorship of this kind. The book remains the most comprehensive account of the law of apartheid and clearly influenced some judges. But sadly it did not receive the attention it deserved, thanks to its timid distribution.

My second brush with the Internal Security Act in 1978 was more serious. In September 1978 the Senate of Wits University organized a special lecture series to consider important national issues. The first was titled 'Politics and Education', and I was invited to speak on a panel with Professor Wynand Mouton, rector of the University of the Orange Free State and Dr Nthato Motlana, chairman of the Soweto Committee of Ten. On the day of the meeting, several hours before the meeting was due to begin, Dr Motlana was banned under the Internal Security Act from attending any political gathering and any gathering held on the premises of the University of the Witwatersrand until the end of the month. The banning order was clearly intended to prevent him from speaking at the meeting. I was outraged. I was also in considerable pain as a result of trouble with my back. Anger and pain tend to cloud reason.

Shortly before the meeting Jane and I met with Dr Motlana just outside the campus of the university, which he was prohibited from entering in terms of his banning order, and he gave me a copy of his banning order. I hastily read it and was immediately struck by the fact that it was more limited than banning orders I had previously seen, in that it only prohibited him from attending gatherings and did not prohibit him from publishing anything. I asked Nthato for a copy of his speech, which to me did not appear to be an inflammatory statement. I told him that in my view his banning order did not prohibit me from reading out his speech and asked for permission to do so. He agreed.

The packed hall – of three hundred and fifty, black and white – that night included a number of senior lawyers, including the cautious Ellison Kahn as chairman. I hastily told Kahn that in my view there was no legal objection to my reading Dr Motlana's speech if he had no objection. He raised none. I told the audience that I had read Dr Motlana's banning order and that it did not expressly prohibit the publication of his speech. I read the banning order out aloud. None of the lawyers in the meeting questioned my decision. Jane told me afterwards that she had raised her hand to object to my interpretation of the banning order as the prohibition on being quoted was in the Internal Security Act itself and not the banning order. I either did not see Jane's raised hand or, more probably, deliberately chose not to see it. I then read the speech, which, predictably, contained a reasoned but strong attack on the education of black children in the wake of the Soweto uprising of 1976.

After the meeting, when Jane and I were driving home, Jane said: 'I am pleased that you read Motlana's speech but it was clearly illegal.' 'What do you know about the law?' I responded. 'You are a biologist.' Calmly Jane said, 'The prohibition on publication of a banned person's speech is surely in the Act itself and does not have to be repeated in the banning order.' Jane was right. 'You are absolutely correct,' I said. 'I even wrote about it in my book on *Human Rights and the South African Legal Order*.' It was clear that I had in error violated the Internal Security Act. When I returned home, I phoned the reporters from the English-language newspapers, the *Rand Daily Mail* and *The Star*, to warn them not to publish. However, I did not know that a reporter from the Afrikaans-language newspaper *Die Beeld* had been at the meeting. The next day Motlana's speech was published in *Die Beeld*.[36] *Die Beeld* and I were charged under the Internal Security Act.

It was clear from the surrounding circumstances that I had mistakenly read Motlana's speech. Ellison Kahn confirmed this; so did my statement before I read Motlana's speech and my request to the newspapers not to publish. I was informed by the chairman of Wits Council, Dr Nico Stutterheim, that the minister of justice, Jimmy Kruger, had told him that the charge would be dropped if I apologized. Supported by the vice-chancellor of the University, Dr D.J. du Plessis, I refused. This would have made me perpetually beholden to the minister of justice and precluded me from ever again criticising him. And so it was that I appeared before a Johannesburg magistrate, defended by the best counsel in South Africa – my friends Sydney Kentridge SC and George Bizos, instructed by Raymond Tucker. Kentridge informed the court about the error I had made, how my wife had corrected me and that I had accordingly stopped the press from publishing the speech. 'Mr Kentridge,' said the magistrate, 'is the accused's wife a lawyer?' 'No,' said Kentridge very solemnly, 'she is a biologist.' The court broke into laughter. I was convicted, fingerprinted as a criminal, cautioned and discharged. Public ridicule was my sentence. Had I not acted in error, and had this not been supported by the evidence, the sentence would have been more severe, as I might have been charged with disobeying a law in protest against the Internal Security Act, which would have exposed me to a prison sentence of three years – and whipping.[37]

7

Civil society and opposition to apartheid

The concept of civil society, in the sense of the aggregate of non-governmental organizations reflecting the will of the people, was unknown in South Africa during the apartheid era. The term 'non-governmental organization' – NGO – was likewise largely unknown. But there were many organizations of a decidedly non-governmental nature engaged in lawful opposition to apartheid that advocated human rights and racial equality. Political parties are generally excluded from the notion of civil society, but the Progressive Party between 1960 and 1974, with only one member of Parliament, Helen Suzman, could better be viewed as an NGO rather than as a political party. Other organizations opposed to apartheid that today would be seen as belonging to civil society were the English-language universities, the National Union of South African Students (NUSAS), the churches, represented in particular by the South African Council of Churches, the Christian Institute and the University Christian Movement, the Women's Defence of the Constitution League, better known as the Black Sash, and the South African Institute of Race Relations. After 1978 and the creation of the Centre for Applied Legal Studies, the Legal Resources Centre, the Black Lawyers Association, Lawyers for Human Rights and the National Association of Democratic Lawyers – of which more later – there were a number of public interest law groups opposed to apartheid that might also be broadly described as NGOs.

These organizations all operated within the law – or, perhaps more accurately, on the fringes of the law. For all were condemned as 'non-South African' by the apartheid regime, many were subjected to legal investigation, and some were proscribed by government decree. With the main opposition party in the all-white Parliament, the United Party, a collaborator with the National Party in the suppression of human rights, and the African National Congress (ANC), Pan Africanist Congress (PAC), South African Communist Party (SACP) and other radical political organizations proscribed by law, the burden of opposition to the apartheid regime within South Africa fell upon these NGOs. South Africans of all races who wished to oppose apartheid within the law in a concerted, collective manner did so through one or more of these organizations. Jane and I therefore found our political home in them.

Although my principal professional and academic interest was international law, my work on apartheid and the legal order that it had spawned had made me an expert in a branch of law in which few lawyers practised and from which most lawyers kept a fearful distance – the law of apartheid. This meant that my advice was sought by organizations that opposed apartheid and their leaders.

Progressive Party

Political opposition to apartheid was conducted underground through banned organizations, such as the ANC, PAC or SACP, or lawfully through the non-Marxist Liberal Party, which supported a universal franchise until its closure in 1968, or the Progressive Party, which favoured a qualified franchise. The official parliamentary opposition, the United Party, differed so little from the ruling National Party in its attitudes towards racial discrimination and human rights that it failed to provide an avenue for serious opposition to apartheid. When I arrived in Johannesburg in 1965, the Liberal Party had been largely destroyed by banning orders and the arrest or flight of members of the African Resistance Movement, which had attracted some of the brightest members of the Liberal Party.

The Progressive Party, established in 1959 when eleven members of the United Party broke away, presented an opportunity for meaningful political opposition to those determined to bring an end to apartheid within the law and through parliamentary means. And before 1968 it was open to all races, though in practice the party was predominantly white. Helen Suzman, the sole Progressive Party MP, represented Houghton, the constituency in which we resided. Jane and I became members of the Progressive Party but we soon found working for the party to be frustrating. It was too much concerned with rallying support in the white community and too little with the real issues facing South Africa. However, it was in theory a non-racial political party of whose platform of racial equality and respect for human rights we largely approved. That was before 1968.

In 1968 the National Party introduced the Prohibition of Political Interference Bill, which made it an offence for a person belonging to one of the four racial groups – white, coloured, Bantu and Asian – to belong to a political party of which a member of another racial group was a member; to assist in the election campaign of a person belonging to another racial group; or to address a meeting of a political party of which the majority of members belonged to another racial group. The Liberal Party made it clear that it would disband if the Bill became law. The Progressive Party was, however, divided. Some believed that the party should make a stand and engage in civil disobedience or even consider disbanding, while others believed that the Party should continue as a white party within a white Parliament, fighting for racial justice. Jane and I felt that some serious protest should be made, and that the Progressive Party should not meekly submit to the apartheid regime.

It was in this mood that we attended the meeting of the Houghton constituency to consider this issue. It was badly attended, reflecting the lack of concern shown by most members of the party for the legislation and the principle of racial equality it raised. Only eight persons were present. The chair asked for suggestions, and I made a passionate plea for strong action from the party in the form of disobedience or disbanding of the party. Jane supported me and I persuaded three other members of the meeting to support my motion. This meant that the most important Progressive Party constituency in the country had decided to engage in disobedience or disband. Clearly this decision could not stand. The party machinery went into action. Our meeting was declared to have been held without a quorum and a new meeting was called at which a large majority voted against my proposal.

After the Bill became law,[38] Jane and I ceased to involve ourselves in the affairs of the Progressive Party. My membership lapsed, though I continued to give Helen Suzman all the support I could. And I canvassed for the party in the 1974 election, which saw the party win five seats, and send Colin Eglin, Zach de Beer, Van Zyl Slabbert and Alex Boraine to Parliament with Helen. I shared in the excitement of a larger parliamentary voice. But in the following year the party joined with the liberal wing of the United Party to form the Progressive Reform Party and I became even more disillusioned and distant from the Progressives. (Later this party joined other political groups to become the Progressive Federal Party, then the Democratic Party and finally the Democratic Alliance.)

For me, the main attraction of the Progressive Party was Helen Suzman, with whom I worked closely. Helen[39] was undoubtedly South Africa's most prominent liberal parliamentarian. From 1961 to 1974 she was the sole member of the Progressive Party in Parliament and the only MP with the conviction and courage to oppose apartheid. Vilified in the all-white, mainly male, reactionary Parliament, she became the voice of the voiceless and disenfranchised, speaking out fearlessly against racial discrimination and political repression. Her activities were not confined to Parliament: she visited political prisoners on Robben Island, banned and banished persons, families who had been forcibly relocated to barren areas from their homes, and she spoke bravely and forcefully at protest meetings called by civil society. In Parliament she had the unenviable task of defending human rights and liberal values and opposing countless apartheid laws with little, if any, support from the United Party. Although she was not a lawyer, she made it her business to lecture Parliament on the rule of law and how this was violated by discrimination and repression in South African law and practice.

Without colleagues in Parliament, Helen was obliged to speak on virtually every Bill presented to Parliament. Although she was assisted by dedicated and competent research assistants, she needed outside help, particularly on legal matters. I became an informal legal adviser to Helen, helping her to prepare speeches on the legal aspects of parliamentary Bills. I became a regular visitor to the Suzman home at 49 Melville Road, Johannesburg, where we would consider the most persuasive and effective way to address a hostile audience in Parliament on legal matters. I greatly admired the fact that she never lost her sense of outrage at the government in general, and certain members of government in particular, over their laws and actions. She did not mince her words in her condemnation of apartheid or its protagonists. At the same time she never lost her sense of humour. From Helen I learnt that there could be no compromise on human rights, but that it was essential to be correct on the law and accurate with the facts. What irritated her political opponents most was the thoroughness of her preparation of speeches and the fact that she could not be faulted on the law or the facts. I later put these lessons to good effect in my work as UN special rapporteur on human rights in the Occupied Palestinian Territory (OPT). The Israelis and Americans complained bitterly about my reports on the violations of human rights in the OPT, declaring that they were biased and inaccurate. However, when challenged to provide evidence of any inaccuracy, I received no reply. I had done my homework in the best tradition of Helen Suzman.

Black Sash

The Black Sash was a women's group formed in 1955 as the Women's Defence of the Constitution League to protest against the removal of coloured voters in the Cape from the common voters' roll. Its members wore black sashes to mourn the passing of the constitution of 1910, and it thus became known as the Black Sash. Later it extended its protests to cover all aspects of apartheid, particularly the pass laws and the detention-without-trial laws. It established advice offices to advise blacks on the pass laws in order to help them manage their lives in an unjust system. The pass laws, which determined the right of blacks to be present in urban areas, constituted an intricate and complicated legal order that few lawyers understood. Moreover, as fees were not forthcoming from those affected, it was of little concern to lawyers. Raymond Tucker, honorary legal adviser to the Black Sash, was *the* expert on the subject, but over time women advice officers developed an expertise in advising the victims of these laws. I was occasionally consulted and developed some knowledge of the laws. I worked closely with the organization and advised its founder, Jean Sinclair, and her successor (and daughter), Sheena Duncan, on both the pass laws and the limits of protest against the security laws. Like Raymond, I became an 'honorary woman' for the purposes of the Black Sash. Jane was an active and full member.

Women wearing black sashes standing in silent protest outside Parliament and government offices troubled the regime, and the organization came to be hated and reviled. It became a sign of courage and independence for women to join the Black Sash. Husbands were often embarrassed by their wives becoming members, as this discredited them in the eyes of government. Many women resisted pressure from their husbands, but many succumbed. Black Sash fêtes and social occasions were an opportunity for liberals, mainly white, to meet and to feel confident and comfortable in the knowledge that they were not alone in their opposition to apartheid. Undoubtedly the Black Sash was the most significant white protest group in South Africa.

The Churches

There was no established Christian church in apartheid South Africa though the Dutch Reformed Church, to which the majority of whites belonged and which in the main supported the government, was politically the most powerful. Other Christian churches that had large followings among all racial groups were the Anglican, Roman Catholic, Methodist and Presbyterian churches. Although the white suburban congregations of these churches were generally restrained in their opposition to apartheid, many white church leaders were outspoken in their condemnation of apartheid on moral and theological grounds. Black church leaders and congregations showed less restraint. Active church opposition to apartheid was mobilized largely through the South African Council of Churches, the Christian Institute and the University Christian Movement. The two foremost church leaders in the opposition to apartheid were undoubtedly Desmond Tutu and Beyers Naudé.

I first met Desmond Tutu[40] when he was Bishop of Lesotho and came to know him well after 1978 when he was appointed general secretary of the South African Council of Churches in Johannesburg, which had close ties with the Institute of Race Relations. In 1978, as director of the Centre for Applied Legal Studies (CALS), I made sure that he became a member of the centre's board of trustees, in which capacity he gave sound advice on the direction of CALS and on the issues it should address. In 1984 he was awarded the Nobel Peace Prize for his leadership in the opposition to apartheid and the following year he was appointed Bishop of Johannesburg. 'John,' he said to me shortly after his appointment, 'I want you to be my chancellor.' At that time I did not understand what this meant and he explained to me that the chancellor was the legal adviser to the bishop and a senior officer in the diocese. I told him that although I was an Anglican, I was not in good standing as a communicant. 'God will understand,' he replied. So it was that I became chancellor of the diocese of Johannesburg until 1986 when Desmond became the 'Arch' – the archbishop of the Anglican Church of Southern Africa, based in Cape Town.

As chancellor I participated in the major services and events in St Mary's Cathedral, dressed in full regalia and following in the footsteps of the bishop in procession. I also attended regular meetings of the diocese to discuss its ecclesiastical affairs. At the same time I was kept busy advising the bishop on the law. There were many legal problems that confronted the diocese, some political and some mundane church matters, but what kept me most busy was the bishop and the law governing economic sanctions. The security laws made it a serious crime to advocate economic sanctions against South Africa. Desmond Tutu was a firm supporter of sanctions and did little to conceal his views both at home and abroad. Whenever I read in the newspaper that Bishop Tutu had called for sanctions in Europe or the United States, I feared that prosecution would follow. On one occasion I recall going to meet him at Jan Smuts Airport (as Johannesburg's airport was then known) on his return home from such a visit abroad to explain how he had been reported and to enquire what he had actually said. He giggled and made no attempt to deny that he had advocated sanctions. No prosecution was brought.

In 1982, before Desmond became bishop, his passport was removed by the government. I suggested that we challenge the withdrawal despite the fact that there was clear judicial authority to support the power of the executive to withdraw a citizen's passport. I reasoned that litigation would serve to publicize the case, but, more important, there was a possibility that a victory for the government in the courts would satisfy the government politically, which would then in all probability return the passport. We brought an application to set aside the withdrawal, in which I argued that international human rights law viewed a passport as a basic human right. As predicted, we lost the application.[41] But, as predicted, the government soon returned Desmond's passport. This was a classic example of the importance of the losing case.

Tutu was a controversial figure, both nationally and within his own congregation. White congregants were particularly critical of him, which was very unfair as he was highly sensitive to white opinion within the Anglican Church. I found it frustrating, for instance, that he defended the refusal of the leading Anglican boys' school in Johannesburg, St John's College, to admit black students at a time when Catholic schools were doing so. 'We must go slowly,' he would say. 'We cannot afford to alienate white opinion.' I spent many hours defending him to fellow Anglicans who believed that Tutu was an ANC agent in disguise and would discard his clerical cloth for political office if the ANC came to power. I have been fully vindicated by Desmond Tutu's career subsequent to South Africa's political transformation. Not only did he not join government but he has consistently been a critic of the South African government – and many others. He is the conscience of South Africa: a brave, impish figure full of good humour and warmth.

South Africa's other great church minister was Beyers Naudé. He had studied at Stellenbosch and, like me, was in residence at Wilgenhof. As a Dutch Reformed Church minister and member of the Broederbond, the secret society that guided both Afrikanerdom and the government, Beyers commanded great respect in Afrikaans society. However, in 1963 he resigned from the Broederbond and left his position as *dominee* because the Dutch Reformed Church was not prepared to reject apartheid, which made him a leper in his own Afrikaans community. In the same year he founded the Christian Institute, an ecumenical organization committed to uniting Christians to oppose apartheid.

The Christian Institute was one of the organizations investigated by the Schlebusch Commission appointed in 1972 because they were deemed to be subversive by the government.[42] Beyers, and other members of the Christian Institute, refused to testify before the commission on the ground that as a matter of conscience they could not testify before a body that failed to observe the principles of natural justice in its proceedings. Beyers was convicted by a magistrate and sentenced to a fine of R50 and three months' imprisonment, which was conditionally suspended. Judges in the appeal courts were divided on whether this conviction should be upheld, but eventually the conviction was confirmed.[43] Clearly, Beyers commanded the respect of many judges.

In October 1977, in the wake of the Soweto uprising and the killing of Steve Biko, the Christian Institute was declared an unlawful organization under the Internal Security Act and Beyers was banned under the same Act for a period of five years. This banning order, imposed by the minister of justice, prohibited him from leaving the magisterial district of Johannesburg, from entering any African township, factory, educational institution or place where publications were prepared, from preparing anything for publication and from giving educational instruction. The order also prohibited him from attending any political gathering and 'any social gathering, that is to say, any gathering at which the persons present also have social intercourse with one another'. From this it followed that it became an offence to quote anything said or written by him. The courts had no power to set aside a banning order. His banning order was renewed but was then withdrawn in 1984.

I first met Beyers at the Institute of Race Relations, in which he took an active part. The director of the institute, Fred van Wyk, had previously worked at the Christian Institute, and he made sure that the Institute of Race Relations worked closely with the Christian Institute.

When Beyers was banned, he was forced to resign from all organizations in which he was involved as a result of the prohibition on attending gatherings. One of these was the Christian Fellowship Trust, which administered a programme that enabled South African clergy to study abroad and invited foreign church ministers to visit South Africa. Beyers asked me to take his place on the administrative committee of the trust, which comprised Beyers's wife Ilse and another dissident clergyman, Professor Albert Geyser. Albert himself had suffered for his views on the church's support for apartheid. He had been tried for heresy by the Nederduits Hervormde Kerk when he was a professor of theology at the University of Pretoria, and he was subsequently appointed professor of divinity at Wits. He had also been responsible for leaking documents to the press on the Broederbond, which he had obtained from Beyers.

The main task of this committee was to select South Africans whose visits abroad the trust was to fund. It was certainly not a subversive committee, which held meetings in Albert's home in Parktown over afternoon tea. But, as the purpose of Beyer's banning order was to isolate him from society, he was prohibited from participating in the work of the committee.

I met frequently with Beyers while he was banned when I visited Ilse at the Naudé home in Greenside in connection with the affairs of the trust. This provided me with the opportunity to discuss the state of the nation with him and to experience the restrictions under which he lived. In 1976 the Appeal Court had ruled that a social gathering prohibited by a banning order was constituted by any number of persons 'from two upwards'.[44] This made conversations with Beyers unlawful, but I was careful to visit only when Ilse was at home and could legitimately argue that I had not come to visit Beyers or spoken to him. Nevertheless, we were careful not to be seen talking and there was always the fear of a knock on the door from the security police.

Like Tutu, Beyers was a man of principle. His convictions gave him the strength to cope with his exclusion from Afrikanerdom and the restrictions of his banning order. He never showed hatred for those who had persecuted him. Although he lacked the exuberance of Tutu, he retained his optimism and sense of humour. On one occasion, when I told him how the security police had ordered sand to be delivered and dumped in my driveway and had advertised the sale of my house in *The Star*, he laughed and told me how the police had ordered a fully stocked liquor cabinet to be delivered to his house, cash on delivery. We agreed that the police had not lost their sense of humour in their determination to harass enemies of the state.

Wits University

It is difficult to explain how Wits managed to remain an independent centre of academic excellence in the world of apartheid. Of course, the university was not unaffected by the laws of apartheid. In 1959 the Extension of University Education Act had extended apartheid to universities.[45] The universities of Cape Town and Witwatersrand, which had once admitted students of all races in small numbers, were now prohibited from enrolling non-white students, that is, Africans, Indians and coloureds. Other universities, which in practice had not admitted non-white students, were likewise prohibited from admitting such students. New universities were established for Africans (in addition to the historically black University of Fort Hare, founded in 1916), coloureds and Indians. Black professors were not permitted to teach at white universities, but there was no ban on white teachers at the black universities.

Strangely, although the apartheid regime determined who might teach and who might be taught, it did not interfere with what might be taught. No doubt it was not necessary to legislate on this matter for the black universities, where the security police and university authorities kept a watchful eye on signs of dissent and independent thinking. Afrikaans-language universities were freer but were constrained by their overall support of the apartheid regime. University courses at the English-language universities addressed all the issues that a good university in Europe or North America would teach in a critical manner. Every university seemed to have an exponent of Marxism with a student following.

Wits University was intellectually vibrant. Critical thinking and dissent were actively encouraged. Students were not afraid to express their opposition to apartheid. Protests against apartheid laws and government actions were a regular feature of university life. Students would line the major thoroughfare of Jan Smuts Avenue, which bordered the campus, with placards denouncing the government and after a while the police would cross the road, enter the campus, assault students with whips, and perhaps make a few arrests. On other occasions the police would enter university buildings and use tear gas to break up meetings. Academic staff also protested regularly but more sedately.

For many years I served on the university's Academic Freedom Committee, which monitored government interference in the autonomy of universities and held protest meetings against university apartheid. Every year the university would commit itself institutionally to the restoration of full academic freedom, in particular the admission of black students. On these occasions the chancellor, vice-chancellor, deans, lecturers and students would gather solemnly in full academic regalia to reaffirm the values of the university. The Academic Freedom Committee organized regular lectures addressed by prominent South Africans or foreign guests, such as Senator Robert Kennedy. I have a vivid recollection of Bobby Kennedy acknowledging the acclaim of students as he stood on the roof of a moving car.

Despite its institutional opposition to apartheid, Wits was later subjected to the international academic boycott which severed ties between South African and foreign universities. This meant that South African scholars were unwelcome at universities abroad and were seldom invited to participate in international conferences. European universities were particularly strict in their support for the academic boycott of South Africa. It was unfair that Wits and the University of Cape Town (UCT) were tarred with the same brush as other South African universities that had never admitted black students and that were institutionally supportive of the government.

Wits and UCT, the two universities previously open to all races, co-operated closely in the advocacy of the restoration of full academic freedom. In 1968 the two joined in strong protest against the refusal of the government to allow UCT to appoint a distinguished African anthropologist, Archie Mafeje, with whom I had studied at Cambridge. The following year I delivered the Annual Day of Affirmation of Academic Freedom at UCT and spoke in favour of a broad approach to freedom that concerned itself with freedom beyond the university.

There could be no academic freedom, I argued, if society itself was not free.[46]

The students at the English-language universities and black universities belonged to National Union of South African Students (NUSAS), which co-ordinated and initiated many anti-apartheid projects and protests. I was appointed as legal adviser to NUSAS in 1969 and advised it mainly on the legality of meetings and publications. Students from the black universities, however, broke with NUSAS in 1968 to form the South African Students' Organization (SASO), which, under the charismatic leadership of Steve Biko, pursued a policy of black consciousness.

The government was concerned about the opposition of the universities to apartheid and from time to time threatened to reduce funding if they failed 'to put their houses in order'. As all universities in South Africa were largely dependent on government funding, this would have brought the universities to their knees. But in fact this never happened. The government continued to fund all universities, including those that were institutionally hostile to it. There were several reasons for this. Firstly, the government was fully aware that the English-language universities produced top graduates in the fields of engineering, mining, science, medicine and dentistry. South Africa could not survive without them. Secondly, the English-language universities were highly regarded abroad. Thirdly, I suspect that the government realized – correctly – that the majority of students and staff were apolitical and that it could afford to tolerate the dissent of a minority. But while white student dissent could be tolerated, black student dissent was another story. The security police made sure that dissent was not allowed at the black universities.

The government kept a watchful eye on Wits. The various intelligence agencies employed student spies to monitor both teachers and fellow students. Not infrequently these spies acted as agents provocateurs who led students into illegal activities, with serious consequences. It later appeared that the agents of the different intelligence agencies were not informed about each other and spent time reporting on the provocative actions of their fellow spies. Telephone tapping was also used to collect information and to intimidate. At one time Wits employed an expert to identify which staff members' phones were tapped. Not surprisingly my phone was tapped, together with a small group of academic colleagues. One of these, Eddie Webster, a sociologist, was indignant. 'Eddie,' I said when he phoned to complain and demand that we take action, 'imagine how you would have felt if the investigation had not shown you to be one of the chosen few for tapping!' That silenced him. Telephone tapping was a sign that you were worth monitoring.

The Wits Law Faculty also changed its image from that of an institution neutral to apartheid to one that was actively opposed to government policy. The curriculum was altered to allow this. A comparative human rights course was introduced, which went under the innocuous name of Aspects of Public Law. Students maintained that the four courses that I taught – Aspects of Public Law, Criminal Procedure, Jurisprudence, and International Law – were Human Rights Law I,II, III, and IV in disguise. New young lecturers followed this example. Wits introduced a legal aid clinic to assist indigents, mainly blacks, with their legal problems. Wits was now seen not only as the premier law faculty in South Africa but also as the most politically aware.

When I joined the Wits Law School, its staff was all white and, with the exception of Jean Davids, all male. The student body too was exclusively white as a result of the prohibition placed on the admission of black students. Over the years the Law School changed its character. There was an influx of women teaching staff and a succession of women professors held the office of dean. This protected me from criticism in the United States at a time when gender equality had replaced racial equality as the priority in US law school composition. I would be asked if there were any women faculty members at Wits and, when I replied that the dean and half the staff of the faculty were women, critics were too embarrassed to ask the more difficult question of how many blacks there were on our staff. In fact there were none until the late 1980s. The student body, too, underwent a change in composition. The number of women students increased radically and in the 1980s the government gave permission to Indian and coloured students to study at Wits. In the late 1980s the university went further and admitted black students with little regard for the law.

I spent thirty-three years at Wits, during which time I served as dean of the Faculty of Law and head of the Law School.

The South African Institute of Race Relations

It was not easy for whites to meet and work with blacks in apartheid's racially structured society. Wits was segregated until the 1980s, and political parties were racially segregated after 1968. Social integration was difficult and contrived. Apart from the churches and church groups, the institution that provided the best opportunity for racial integration in some sort of political context was the South African Institute of Racial Relations.

The institute in my time was a body committed to both research in the field of race relations and community service. Its headquarters were in Johannesburg but it had branches in all the main centres of South Africa. All branches were racially mixed, with members drawn largely from the universities, churches and welfare organizations. Politically, its members were liberal in the broad sense. Some had belonged to the Liberal Party, which had dissolved in 1968, others were more at home in the ANC but had been obliged to suppress their political activities in the light of the organization's proscription, and yet others were active on the left wing of the Progressive Party. Generally its members were moderate leftists with social consciences. Church leaders were well represented in all the branches, and this ensured that white liberals were kept informed about the moods and views of the black community. Branches promoted interracial events, engaged in community service and organized protest meetings against the invasion of human rights. The national executive, of which I became a member in April 1968, met regularly, and each year a conference was held in a different city to address problems affecting race relations in the country. The research department of the institute was highly respected and its annual publication, *A Survey of Race Relations in South Africa*, was used by politicians of all persuasions and the media. The institute included as members some of South Africa's best-known liberals, such as Helen Suzman, Desmond Tutu, Beyers Naudé, Ellen Hellmann, E.E. Mahabane, Mike Savage, David Welsh, Cassim Saloojee, Wilkie Kambule and Laurie Schlemmer. Its directors in my time – Quinton Whyte, Fred van Wyk and John Rees – were prominent liberal figures respected in all communities.

The institute provided a home for those who believed South Africa's future lay in non-racialism. It enabled persons from different racial groups to meet and discuss political issues of the day under the guise of information gathering and community service. It provided a political home for those denied the right to engage in normal political activity. But its activities did not escape the scrutiny of the security police. Several of its research workers were banned under the Internal Security Act and others were detained for interrogation. Jeanette Curtis, a research worker at the institute, was detained under the Terrorism Act and reports were received that she was being tortured. The institute asked for an appointment with the minister of justice, Jimmy Kruger, to obtain assurances that she and others detained would not be tortured. Our delegation met the minister and his top security advisers in the Union Buildings in Pretoria, where we were given the assurance that no one ever laid a hand on detainees. 'But what about mental torture?' I asked. 'It is accepted under international law today that solitary confinement, deprivation of sleep and prolonged interrogation constitute psychological torture.' The minister and his advisers seemed genuinely surprised to learn this and for a time fell silent. Clearly, police interrogation methods depended heavily on psychological torture of this kind.

In statements and speeches made at its conferences, the institute protested vigorously about racist and repressive legislation. Based on its research, it made representations to government about the impact of its laws and policies on black communities. In the 1960s and 1970s, before the institute ceased to be a community-based institution and instead became primarily a research institute, and before the advent of legal human rights groups in the 1980s, it was undoubtedly South Africa's principal NGO, in modern parlance, concerned with human rights and racial equality.

In 1972, as we have seen, the government established a commission of inquiry, known as the Schlebusch Commission (after its chairman, a senior member of Parliament), to investigate organizations guilty of what it regarded as subversive activities. The commission comprised ten members, six from the National Party and four from the United Party. Those investigated were the Institute of Race Relations, the Christian Institute, the University Christian Movement and NUSAS. In common these organizations were racially mixed and critical of government and sought to bring about social change by means of interracial co-operation. All four groups were heavily dependent on funding from abroad. Modelled on the United States House Committee on Un-American Activities of the McCarthy period, the purpose of the Schlebusch Commission was clearly to discredit the organizations in question. The commission was empowered to summon any person under threat of criminal sanction and to interrogate that person in order to further its investigations. Both the personal beliefs and conduct of such persons might be explored. The commission received evidence in secret largely from the security police. It met in secret and evidence was not published so that those summoned to appear before it had no idea of the evidence that had been obtained against them.

The commission published in 1973 an interim report on NUSAS, which led to the banning of eight of its leaders under the Suppression of Communism Act. This was followed by the banning of leaders of the black consciousness movement. A branch of the University Christian Movement, the Wilgespruit Fellowship Centre (where my son Justin had been christened in 1972), was also investigated and one of its staff members deported.

In the light of this arbitrary action, the other organizations summoned to appear before the commission considered – and were divided – on the question whether to co-operate by testifying before it. As we have seen, the Christian Institute refused to appear. The Institute of Race Relations, after bitter and divisive meetings of its council, decided to co-operate and provide the commission with the information it required on the ground that it had nothing to hide. Individual members and employees might, however, refuse to testify before it. Several members of the Institute of Race Relations were duly prosecuted when they failed to appear. In the end, the institute was cleared of wrongdoing, when the commission found that it was in favour of evolutionary and not revolutionary social change.

Shortly afterwards the government enacted the Affected Organizations Act,[47] which allowed it to prohibit foreign funding for organizations it declared to be 'affected'. Both NUSAS and the Christian Institute were declared to be affected, which severely curtailed their future activities.

I was not to escape the tentacles of the Schlebusch Commission. I was summoned to appear before it as honorary legal adviser to NUSAS in the course of its investigation of NUSAS. My interview was scheduled after the questioning of a group of radical clergy from the University Christian Movement, who had been discredited by revelations about their drug taking and sexual activities. Counsel for NUSAS, Ernie Wentzel, warned me that I should expect questioning about any sexual relationship I had ever had. In fact I was spared this indignity. Instead I found myself questioned by Advocate Fanie van der Merwe on behalf of the security police about my advice to NUSAS and other 'subversive' activities on the basis of a dossier containing intercepted letters and taped telephone conversations, which were presented to me without notice. After some time Van der Merwe asked, 'Of which organizations other than NUSAS are you a member?' To this question I replied that I had never been a member of NUSAS, and that on the contrary I had been a member of the Afrikaner Studentebond (ASB), the rival student organization representing the Afrikaans universities. This led Chairman Schlebusch to exclaim: 'My God, hoe het dit gebeur?' (My God, how did this happen?) I then explained to the commission that I had studied at Stellenbosch University (which fact surprisingly did not appear in my dossier) and that as a student there I had automatically become a member of the ASB. After this, the mood of the commission changed dramatically. The chairman stated that I confirmed his view as an *oud-Matie* (old Stellenbosch student) that the Stellenbosch law faculty produced better lawyers than the University of Pretoria, where Fanie van der Merwe had studied. There was light-hearted banter about which law faculty was better. Hostile questioning then ended. It seems that the commission considered me as one of 'them' and not a subversive.

The Schlebusch Commission failed to achieve its primary objective, the discrediting of liberal and radical critics of the apartheid regime. Whereas American radical intellectuals had been discredited, ostracized and dismissed from universities and other institutions once they were called to testify on their ties with communism before the House Committee on Un-American Activities, no such stigma was attached to persons and organizations summoned to appear before the Schlebusch Commission. On the contrary, we were warmly applauded by our friends and the institutions for which we worked. To have been summoned before the commission became a badge of honour. Clearly the apartheid regime had miscalculated the response of liberals and liberal institutions in South Africa to accusations of undermining the apartheid state.

To return to the Institute of Race Relations, in 1979 I was elected as president of the institute for a two-year term, succeeding the Rev. E.E. Mahabane, a prominent church leader, whom I had had the privilege of presenting for an honorary doctorate at Wits in 1976. He was the grandfather of Itumeleng, who would become my daughter's partner.

The president's role was largely honorific. I presided over meetings of the national executive and delivered two presidential lectures. The legacy of the president was mainly to be found in these lectures.

My 1979 lecture was titled 'Failure of a Fiction' and examined the policy of Bantustanization. In 1979 'independence' had already been granted to Transkei, Bophuthatswana and Venda. My lecture traced the evolution of the policy and examined the National Party's expectation that its independent Bantustans would be internationally recognized and the refusal of the international community to confer such recognition. I concluded that the policy had therefore failed in its main objective. I then went on to examine a sinister feature of the policy, namely the denationalization of black South Africans. According to government policy, all black South African citizens were to be deprived of their South African citizenship and granted the citizenship of the Bantustan with which they were most closely linked by language and culture. Even blacks living in the urban areas with no connection with a Bantustan were to be deprived of their citizenship in this way. I declared that this was both immoral and contrary to contemporary international law. 'When fictions and fantasies fail', I said, 'it is time to face the realities of the situation: that we black, white and brown people share a common destiny in South Africa; and that the policy of separate development is acceptable neither to the majority of people of South Africa, nor to the international community.'[48]

My second presidential lecture was titled 'A National Strategy for 1980'.[49] The title was a response to the demand for a 'total national strategy' made by the recently elected prime minister, P.W. Botha. This address criticized the restraints imposed by the apartheid regime on freedom of political expression and called on the government to introduce a number of modest reforms as an indication of its willingness to create a climate for change. These included the repeal of the Prohibition of Mixed Marriages Act; a moratorium on the implementation of the pass laws; the relaxation of the security laws; the granting of amnesty to political prisoners; and the enactment of a Bill of Rights to guide courts and administrative officials.

8

The Centre for Applied Legal Studies and public interest law

Apartheid was a discriminatory and repressive system rooted in the law. Acts of Parliament, subordinate legislation issued by state officials and judicial decisions created the apartheid legal order. Persons who violated race or security laws were prosecuted in ordinary courts. The police and government officials were accountable under the law. It was a uniquely legalistic order.

The legal nature of the system called for a legal response from the legal profession. But this was largely unforthcoming. The legal aid system was completely inadequate and did not provide for funding in most cases under the laws of apartheid. Legal practitioners generally refused to defend persons charged under the laws of apartheid, either because they were unsympathetic or because they were afraid of being labelled as 'political lawyers'. This they feared would frighten off other clients who supported the government or, still worse, might incur the wrath of the government itself. Consequently, it was left to a small group of lawyers opposed to apartheid and committed to the rule of law to handle cases of this kind. This group included some of South Africa's leading advocates, who were much in demand in commercial litigation, and a smaller group of attorneys. As attorneys dealt directly with clients, they were more vulnerable to ostracism and pressure not to handle such cases.

This small band of advocates and attorneys did a magnificent job, particularly in defending people charged with major crimes such as treason, terrorism or sabotage. There was funding, mainly from abroad, for legal defence in such cases, but these limited resources could not be stretched to provide for the defence of persons charged with less serious offences, such as offences under the Group

Areas Act and the pass laws, nor could they cover civil litigation to challenge the validity and scope of the country's race and security laws. In these circumstances there was a serious need for some institutional machinery to provide for a legal response to apartheid's legal order.

The apartheid government was determined not to expand legal assistance as it realized that this would be used to challenge the apartheid system. This was well illustrated by its response to an international conference on legal aid organized by the University of Natal in 1973. Although the conference concerned itself largely with criticism of the existing legal aid system and discussion of how this might be improved, drawing on the experiences of other countries, the minister of justice not only prohibited all government officials charged with the administration of justice from participating but also issued a directive to judges not to attend the conference. Consequently, it was clear that legal assistance would have to be provided by institutions other than the state.

In the early 1970s Wits established a legal aid clinic and started to include legal aid in the law curriculum. Inevitably this gave rise to suggestions that we should establish a public interest law firm to engage in creative litigation along the lines of the American Legal Defense Fund, which had handled the litigation that gave rise to the desegregation of American schools. Felicia Kentridge, Raymond Tucker, Geoff Budlender and I were the primary proponents of such a venture.

Following the Soweto uprising of 1976, American foundation officers began to show an interest in funding public interest law in South Africa. Bill Carmichael of the Ford Foundation was well disposed to such a project but wanted time to consider the matter more carefully. David Hood of the Carnegie Corporation of New York, a former law school dean, was both enthusiastic and impatient. In order to ensure that no time was wasted, he proposed the establishment of a legal research centre attached to the Wits Law School that would research issues appropriate for litigation and that such litigation should be undertaken in collaboration with another centre, a proper public interest law firm. The Carnegie Corporation made a grant to Wits for this research centre, which was mandated to assist in the establishment of a public interest law firm. This move resulted in a commitment from both the Ford Foundation and the Rockefeller Brothers Fund, represented by Bill Carmichael and Bill Moody respectively, to join the Carnegie Corporation in funding public interest law in South Africa.

Although it meant sacrificing my career as an international lawyer, I agreed to direct the research centre, to be given the innocuous name of the Centre for Applied Legal Studies (CALS) rather than the Centre for Human Rights, which would have invited a hostile response from the government. The search was now on for a director of the public interest law firm to be known as the Legal Resources

Centre (LRC). Our first choice was Arthur Chaskalson, a leading senior counsel at the Johannesburg Bar. To our surprise he agreed to give up a lucrative practice and to accept the directorship of the LRC.

CALS was funded entirely by American foundations because the nature of its work made it impossible to raise funds locally. Although these foundations made no attempt whatsoever to influence the work we were doing, their involvement gave CALS a distinctly American character. This had major advantages. CALS and the LRC were regularly visited by distinguished human rights lawyers, such as Jack Greenberg of the NAACP Legal Defense Fund, Louis Henkin of Columbia Law School and Aryeh Neier, former director of the American Civil Liberties Union, who, in sharing their own experiences of advancing human rights in the United States, helped to guide public interest law in South Africa. On the personal level, it resulted in many visits to the United States to report to the Carnegie Corporation, Ford Foundation and Rockefeller Brothers Fund on the work of CALS and to study the strategies and practices of public interest law bodies in the US.

CALS did not quite work out as originally planned. It did pursue research and produced first-rate publications in the fields of administrative justice, censorship, constitutional law, human rights, international law, labour law, and the repressive and discriminatory laws that made up the legal apparatus of apartheid. It did engage in public education in these fields through research, publications, the media and conferences. But it did not become a collaborative partner with the LRC in respect of litigation. The main problem was that the organized legal profession – represented by the Society of Advocates and the Law Society (the attorneys) – was prepared to waive professional rules of practice relating to access to clients, *pro bono* work, and advocates and attorneys working together in the same institution, in respect of the LRC but not CALS.

The LRC was headed by a respected senior advocate and could be expected to behave responsibly and adhere to professional rules in so far as this was possible. CALS, on the other hand, was directed by a law professor, who was not eligible to become a member of the Society of Advocates, with a history of criticizing the legal profession and judiciary for their failure to confront the government on apartheid. Moreover, CALS provided free legal advice and assistance in litigation not only to those affected by discriminatory race laws but also to black trade unions. This offended the organized legal profession as it saw black trade unions as a potentially lucrative source of income. CALS was therefore denied recognition by the legal profession, which placed obstacles in the way of its engagement in *pro bono* litigation. Advocates at CALS were barred from appearing in court as co-counsel with members of the Society of Advocates, and attorneys were prohibited from practising from university premises. This made it difficult for CALS and the LRC to collaborate in litigation.

The situation did improve: the LRC and CALS were able to collaborate on some matters, and the Law Society did relax its rules in respect of attorneys working for CALS provided they operated off campus in a separate legal firm – which became the highly successful attorneys firm of Cheadle, Thompson and Haysom. But the close collaboration between CALS and the LRC envisaged by the funding foundations never materialized.

The attitude of the organized legal profession demonstrated the extent to which professional bodies were unwilling to bend their rules in the interests of *pro bono* human rights work. It was clear that the profession was prepared to tolerate public interest law provided it did not threaten its monopoly over those able to afford to pay for legal assistance and did not result in the profession being seen to be actively engaged in opposition to apartheid. The message was clear. The organized legal profession, and most lawyers, felt comfortable about practising law under the apartheid legal order and would assist the apartheid regime in resisting attempts to undermine its legitimacy.

CALS was an exciting institution. An advantage of not being subject to professional rules was that it was at liberty to engage in more imaginative litigation and research. The challenge of confronting apartheid through the law in a professionally creative manner attracted idealistic young lawyers dissatisfied with practising law in the traditional manner. I encouraged individual freedom of action, which at times was exasperating to me as director, but it ensured that each member of staff was at liberty to give full vent to his or her own talents. Although they were engaged in serious and often dangerous work, they retained their sense of collegiality, humour and *joie de vivre.*

CALS focused on a broad range of human rights issues. Bantustans, discrimination, political repression, capital punishment, censorship and planning for a future democratic South Africa, all fell within its purview. The work of CALS in these fields is examined in the chapters that follow. Two subjects in which CALS made a major contribution, in which I was largely uninvolved, were labour law and the political conflicts of the 1980s.

CALS played a leading role in the evolution of South African labour law from an instrument of racial oppression to rule by consensus and negotiation. The creation of CALS coincided with the establishment of the Wiehahn Commission of Inquiry into labour relations in 1978. Following the publication of the report of this commission in 1979, the country's labour laws were changed dramatically to provide for the recognition of hitherto unrecognized black trade unions and the establishment of a special court to hear industrial disputes. There were, however, few qualified labour lawyers that enjoyed the confidence of black trade unions. CALS soon occupied the role of principal legal adviser to these unions. Under the leadership of Halton Cheadle, the assistant director of CALS, who was ably supported by Clive Thompson, Paul Benjamin, Modise Khoza, Martin Brassey and later Edwin Cameron, labour law was substantially developed to take account of the new dispensation. The wide jurisdiction of the industrial court was fully exploited to persuade it to apply international standards of equity and fairness while unions were advised on the procedures for collective bargaining. CALS lawyers were involved in many of the landmark labour cases of the 1980s, including those dealing with standards of occupational health and safety, procedural fairness in dismissal and retrenchment, and the right to strike. Education was also a matter of concern. Regular labour law conferences were held for labour lawyers and unionists, and a new journal was produced, the *Industrial Law Journal*.

CALS became a meeting place for those involved in the new labour movement. Regular visitors to the centre included Cyril Ramaphosa, general secretary of the National Union of Mineworkers (NUM), who led the constitutional negotiations for the ANC in the early 1990s and was elected as president of South Africa in 2018, and Alec Erwin, general secretary of the Federation of South African Trade Unions (FOSATU), who later became minister of trade and industry (1996–2004) and minister of public enterprises (2004–8). It is not an exaggeration to say that South Africa's labour laws were shaped by CALS.

Of course, CALS' success in the field of labour law did not make it popular with the leaders of commerce and industry. The Law Society resented the fact that its members were deprived of the opportunity to provide paid legal services to black unions, which had more confidence in the advice they received from CALS. It also made fundraising for CALS difficult in South Africa as the major corporations were reluctant to support an organization that strengthened unions. At a meeting to raise funds from one of the giants of South African industry, Barlow Rand, I was told that it would not provide any funding to any of our programmes because we supported black trade unions, of which Barlow Rand disapproved. This incident had its positive side. I was able to use it as a reason to abandon attempts at fundraising in South Africa. American funders were impressed that our work was so effective that local funders were hostile.

The 1980s were characterized by serious political conflicts. In 1983 the government decided to create a Tricameral Parliament: one house for white representatives, one for coloureds, and one for Indians. Black Africans were excluded as their political life was to be found in the Bantustans. This led to the formation of the United Democratic Front (UDF), comprising churches, civic organizations, student bodies and unions, which embarked upon a programme of rent boycotts, protests, demonstrations and stay-aways from work. There were confrontations with the security forces in many parts of the country and in 1985 the government declared a state of emergency, which continued in force until 1990. In KwaZulu-Natal the conflict took the ugly form of violence between the Inkatha Freedom Party of Mangosuthu Buthelezi and members of the UDF and its affiliated organizations. Lawyers were in desperate demand and CALS staff, led by Nicholas (Fink) Haysom, with the assistance of other staff, including Halton Cheadle and members of the labour law unit, responded by travelling to the centres of conflict to give legal advice. Fink, a former NUSAS leader, was active in many parts of the country as adviser and litigator, and was himself detained without trial for four months in 1981. (In 1994 Fink became legal counsel to President Mandela, after which he was involved in the Middle East and Africa in conflict resolution. In 2014 he was appointed as head of the United Nations Assistance Mission in Afghanistan (UNAMA) and in 2016 he was appointed as UN special envoy for Sudan and South Sudan.)

In addition to giving legal advice, documenting and speaking about the violence in the country, CALS staff were involved in some of the major judicial decisions of that period. One such case concerned the case of the torture of several hundred detainees held under the emergency laws at prisons in Port Elizabeth in 1985.[50] In most cases of this kind there was no reliable evidence of torture as the law precluded family visits and the state medical doctors who visited detainees and took complaints were unwilling to testify on these experiences. However, on this occasion Dr Wendy Orr, a state district surgeon responsible for the care of detainees at two Port Elizabeth prisons, attested to systematic assaults on over a hundred detainees in the course of police interrogations. Reports to her medical superiors were simply ignored. A team of CALS lawyers, led by Halton Cheadle, assembled affidavits for a court action in great secrecy before bringing the case to court. The Supreme Court accepted this evidence of torture and interdicted the police from further assaulting emergency detainees. Following this success, a court order was obtained to allow lawyers to visit police stations without warning to collect evidence of torture. Sadly, despite these successes, the torture of detainees continued. Torture was part of the police culture.

In 1979 a highly successful conference on human rights, largely funded by the Ford Foundation, was held at the University of Cape Town. At the end of this conference it was resolved to establish an association of human rights lawyers to promote respect for human rights. On the suggestion of Johann Kriegler, this body took the name of Lawyers for Human Rights (LHR). Initially LHR recruited members and set up regional branches, presided over by a national executive. Without funding it had no office of its own, so for several years CALS managed its affairs. Later, LHR was able to establish an office of its own in Pretoria with Brian Currin as its director. Over the years LHR evolved from an association of individual lawyers that worked on human rights issues to a public interest law firm with a professional staff.

Two other important law bodies were established in the early 1980s – the Black Lawyers Association (BLA),[51] which, though confined to black lawyers, worked closely with CALS and the LRC, and the National Association of Democratic Lawyers (NADEL), which was open to all races and reflected the philosophy of the banned Congress movement. CALS maintained close relations with the BLA through its first two directors, Godfrey Pitje and Justice Moloto (later to become a judge of the International Criminal Tribunal for the former Yugoslavia), and its litigation officer, Dolly Mokgatle (she later directed the parastatals Spoornet and Eskom), who had been a research officer at CALS for four years.

The establishment of CALS, LRC, LHR, BLA and NADEL ensured that law became an important instrument in the struggle against apartheid and that lawyers were able to use their legal skills to this end. These bodies provided lawyers with avenues to engage in collective action to promote human rights. The campaigns against the Group Areas Act and the pass laws, described in chapter 10, were actions of this kind.

CALS, which occupied a central and co-ordinating role among public interest law bodies, itself grew in size and importance. The 1978 staff of three professional lawyers, a research officer and secretary had grown to twenty when I retired in 1990 and was replaced by Dennis Davis, later to become judge president of the Competition Appeal Court. CALS still operates as a successful advocacy and public interest law institution under the auspices of Wits, albeit under an entirely new legal order. The *South African Journal on Human Rights*, which had a modest beginning in the early 1980s as an avenue for the publication of more serious criticism of the apartheid order than mainstream academic journals would allow, is now an established academic law journal read both in South Africa and abroad. My daughter Jackie, now an associate professor in the Wits Law School, is an editor of the journal and worked at CALS for six years before establishing another human rights NGO, the Socio-Economic Rights Institute of South Africa (SERI).

9

Bantustans

The policy of separate development, as the government preferred to call apartheid, was a massive exercise in social engineering. On the face of it, separate development was a programme of decolonization designed to grant self-determination and independence to South Africa's tribal homelands or Bantustans. But in reality it was a racist, Machiavellian scheme that planned to relegate blacks to rural reserves glorified with the trappings of statehood and to replace their South African citizenship or nationality with the fictitious citizenship of an independent Bantustan. Conceived by the intellectual giant of the National Party, Dr Hendrik Verwoerd,[52] as a response to international criticisms of apartheid as a form of *baasskap* or crude white domination, it envisaged the creation of ten independent states, to one of which every black South African would be attached by citizenship. Within the Bantustan with which every black South African was affiliated, however loosely, by tribe or ethnicity, he or she would be entitled to exercise civil and political rights. In 'white South Africa', outside the Bantustans, in which most blacks would continue to live and work, they would be foreign visitors with no civil or political rights. In pursuance of this fantasy, blacks were forcibly relocated from white farms and so-called black spots into the homelands. There they were virtually abandoned and left to make a living without the most basic amenities, schools or hospitals, far from shops or opportunities for employment. Deprivation of nationality or citizenship – 'denationalization' – and forced population removals were the hallmarks of the Bantustan policy.

The ten Bantustans were Transkei and Ciskei for the Xhosa, Bophuthatswana for the Tswana, Venda for the Venda, KwaZulu for the Zulu, Lebowa for the Pedi or North Sotho, Qwaqwa for the South Sotho, KaNgwane for the South African

Swazi, KwaNdebele for the Ndebele, and Gazankulu for the Shangaan. Between 1976 and 1981 four Bantustans took independence: Transkei, Bophuthatswana, Venda and Ciskei, which became known as the TBVC states. The other six Bantustans, described as self-governing homelands, refused to become independent. KwaZulu presented a particular problem to the government because it represented the most populous homeland and because its head, Chief Mangosuthu ('Gatsha') Buthelezi, the most prominent of the homeland leaders, refused to lead KwaZulu to independence. Attempts to woo self-governing homelands into accepting independence by favours to their leaders and the offer of increased land failed. Despite the failure of the four independent Bantustans to obtain recognition by other states, which was the initial goal of the policy, the government persisted in its efforts to persuade the self-governing homelands to accept independence until 1990.

Independence was not without material benefits. Of course, the Bantustan leaders were well cared for financially. But in addition the South African government sought to improve the infrastructure of the TBVC states by encouraging industry to locate factories in these territories and by building schools, hospitals and universities there. Also, Sol Kerzner, the casino king of southern Africa, established glitzy casinos, of which the best known was Sun City in Bophuthatswana, to cater for South Africans bent on gambling but prevented from doing so by law in Calvinist South Africa. Undoubtedly this revenue contributed to the financial well-being of the TBVC states. Casinos were so much a feature of the TBVC states that it was said that the hallmarks of independence were a flag, a university and a casino.

On 26 October 1976 Transkei became the first Bantustan to accept independence.[53] The South African government hoped and perhaps believed, naively, that it would be recognized by other states, particularly its Western friends. This, despite the fact that the General Assembly of the United Nations had already warned member states not to recognize Transkei or any other homeland that sought independence. Thus the trappings of statehood were emphasized and the more sinister side of independence – denationalization of citizens – was downplayed. Transkei established its own Ministry of Foreign Affairs, with officers trained in diplomacy by Pretoria and sent abroad in anticipation of Transkei's busy international relations programme; it issued Transkei passports; and it established border posts for all visitors to Transkei, including South Africans. Two days after independence, the General Assembly adopted a resolution by 130 votes to none (with the United States abstaining) that condemned the independence of Transkei as a measure designed to consolidate apartheid, and called on states not to recognize the homeland.[54]

This call was endorsed by the Security Council.[55] No state recognized Transkei. Bophuthatswana became independent in 1977, followed by Venda in 1979 and Ciskei in 1981. None of these states was recognized either.

As a 'Transkei boy', I approached Transkeian 'independence' with mixed feelings. On the one hand, I knew that independence was the fulfilment of the fantasy of self-development and was therefore to be opposed. On the other hand, the boy in me wanted Transkei to succeed in becoming truly independent. Our family had enjoyed Christmas holidays at Port St Johns on the Transkei coast for several years before 1976. John Barratt, director of the South African Institute of International Affairs, another Transkei old boy, had also spent his holidays in Port St Johns. Both of us knew the full implications of Transkeian independence but emotionally, perhaps nostalgically, we hoped that somehow Transkei would break loose from South Africa and assert full independence. Of course, there were signs of independence. There was the immigration officer who proudly stamped our passports as we entered Transkei. With a big smile, which told that he no longer felt subservient to white South Africa, he welcomed us to Transkei. This new display of confidence was apparent wherever we went. In December 1976 the beaches of Port St Johns, which had hitherto been reserved exclusively for whites, were flooded with black children who arrived from Umtata by bus. I was able to introduce my children to the president of Transkei, Kaiser Matanzima, when he visited the hotel one day. Capital Radio, the only independent broadcasting station in southern Africa, operated from Transkei in order to escape the restrictions on radio freedom imposed by South Africa. To add to all these signs of independence, by chance I met Digby Koyana, previously a law professor in South Africa and now minister of foreign affairs of Transkei, at the airport in Zurich and watched in amazement as he went through immigration on a Transkei passport.

These were all outward signs of independence but they concealed the reality of continued South African control. This reality was soon brought home to me.

Shortly after independence I was asked to advise in the defence of three young men from Umtata, capital of Transkei, who were charged with furthering the aims of communism by belonging to a reading group that read and discussed radical writings, including George Orwell's *Animal Farm*. The three were Dumisa Ntsebeza, his brother Lungisile and Matthew Goniwe. The 'crime' was alleged to have occurred before the independence of the Transkei, which meant that the alleged crime was directed at the South African state, but the prosecution took place after Transkei became independent. I argued that the new 'state' of Transkei did not succeed to the old state of South Africa in respect of crimes against the state for the simple reason that the state had changed. The presiding judge was George Munnik, the chief justice of Transkei. He dismissed the argument and undertook to provide reasons for his decision later. He then convicted the accused men and sentenced them to three years in prison. Munnik never provided reasons for his decision despite repeated requests. He shortly afterwards became a judge in South Africa, beyond the reach of Transkeian lawyers. The case illustrated very well that independence was a fiction and a farce. In fact, South Africa and it officials retained control over Transkei. A crime against the South African state was a crime against its dependant, Transkei.

I wrote regularly to Dumisa while he was in prison about his legal studies. After South Africa's transformation, he became a successful senior counsel and a controversial member of and spokesman for the Judicial Service Commission. Lungisile is an acclaimed academic. Matthew was murdered by the security police in 1985, with three other activists, together known as the Cradock Four. This notorious assassination was a turning point in the struggle for freedom in South Africa. On the day of the funeral of the Cradock Four, President P.W. Botha declared a state of emergency, which was to be the last repressive step of the apartheid regime.

White South Africans were bemused by the Bantustan policy and the TBVC states. They saw the policy largely as a harmless exercise in decentralization which satisfied the political aspirations of some blacks and allowed them – whites – to attend performances by foreign artists who refused to appear in South Africa itself because of its race policies. The notion that all blacks would lose their South African citizenship and be given the worthless citizenship of and political rights in some rural statelet was too far-fetched for most to understand. I tried desperately to explain the implications of the policy in speeches and writings, recalling the statement of Dr Connie Mulder made when he was minister of Bantu administration and development in 1978 that

> If our policy is taken to its full logical conclusion as far as the black people are concerned, there will be not one black man with South African citizenship … every black man in South Africa will eventually be accommodated in some independent new state in this honourable way and there will no longer be a moral obligation on this Parliament to accommodate these people politically.[56]

I campaigned vigorously against the independent Bantustans and attacked their claims to statehood from the perspective of international law. My presidential address to the Institute of Race Relations in 1977 was devoted to this subject. Relying on resolutions of the United Nations, I argued that Bantustans had been created in violation of international law and that as a consequence they failed to qualify as states.[57] This was a theme that I pursued in other publications and at a meeting on the legal issues relating to apartheid organized by the United Nations in the Peace Palace in The Hague in 1985, under the chairmanship of Assistant Secretary-General James Jonah.[58]

At CALS I advised communities opposed to territorial changes with the aim of consolidating homelands that were designed to further the ideology of separate development. I also acted as counsel in a number of court challenges to Bantustans.

In 1982 the apartheid regime sought to rid itself of Swazi South Africans by excising the territory in which they lived adjacent to Swaziland and ceding it to that kingdom. A commission of inquiry under former Chief Justice Rumpff was established to receive representations on this subject. I was nominated to be a member of the commission by the government of the self-governing homeland of KaNgwane under Chief Minister Enos Mabuza, but was vetoed by Pretoria. The South African government wished to portray this as a generous cession of land to a neighbouring state in full accordance with international law. I submitted a substantial memorandum to the commission in which I argued that under contemporary international law the principle of self-determination required that the will of the people of any territory to be ceded should first be obtained by referendum. This argument substantially undermined the government's position, as it was clear that Swazi South Africans were opposed to cession to Swaziland. The self-determination argument prevailed and the Rumpff Commission advised against such cession. The government was compelled to accept this recommendation.

Military coups were a feature of the independent Bantustans, with coups succeeding in Transkei and Ciskei. An attempt on the part of the military to overthrow President Mangope of Bophuthatswana in 1988 was, however, thwarted by the intervention of the South African army. *State* v. *Banda*[59] involved the trial of several army officers who were charged with treason arising out of this failed coup.

Treason is defined as a crime against the state. On behalf of the accused, I argued in the Supreme Court of Bophuthatswana in Mafikeng that the charge could not stand, as Bophuthatswana failed to qualify as a state under international law. In order to qualify as a state under international law an entity must show that it has a population, a defined territory, an effective government and a capacity to enter into foreign relations. Assisted by Reagan Jacobus of CALS, I argued that, as a completely unrecognized state, Bophuthatswana had not demonstrated a capacity to enter into foreign relations. Some recognition on the part of other states was necessary for an entity to constitute a state. Furthermore, Bophuthatswana was designed to further the policy of apartheid, which meant that it had been created in violation of a peremptory norm of international law. My argument lasted the whole day. It was not easy, however, as security was tense. There were armed soldiers all around the courtroom and an armed soldier watched carefully over the judge from within the court itself. I had never before experienced presenting an argument in such circumstances. In most security cases the presence of the security police was enough to intimidate counsel, but an armed guard in court took intimidation one step further. Not surprisingly, Chief Justice Friedman, after listening intently, dismissed my argument, proceeded with the trial and convicted 126 of the rebels of treason. The internationalization of the trial did, however, as in the case of the SWAPO leaders tried in Pretoria, ensure that no death sentences were imposed.

In the last years of apartheid the government was determined to create a fifth independent Bantustan – KwaNdebele – for the Ndebele people. However, KwaNdebele, a self-governing homeland situated in the centre of the old Transvaal province, lacked sufficient territory and population to give it both credibility and viability. Accordingly, the apartheid regime decided to remove the community of Moutse from a neighbouring self-governing homeland, Lebowa, and attach it to KwaNdebele.[60] This move flew in the face of the ideology of apartheid, according to which separate independent states were to be created for each of South Africa's ethnic groups. But now the government planned to include the Pedi or North Sotho community of Moutse living in Lebowa, created for the Pedi people, in the state of KwaNdebele for the Ndebele people. I had many meetings with the leaders of the Moutse community. Dolly Mokgatle of CALS and I took them to Cape Town to lobby their case in Parliament, but to no avail.

This left a legal challenge as the only possible remedy. To me it seemed that the only basis on which the government's plan might be challenged was that it failed to give effect to the ideology of apartheid, which was recognized in a number of domestic statutes providing for the creation of separate Bantustans. However, this meant arguing in favour of the ideology of apartheid in order to prevent the creation of a new Bantustan, a strategy which was condemned by those who believed that no credibility whatsoever should be given to apartheid or separate development. In short, it was a highly politically incorrect argument. Fellow human rights lawyers were not slow to criticize.

Assisted by my CALS colleague Edwin Cameron, later to become a judge of the Constitutional Court, I presented this argument before the Transvaal Provincial Division of the Supreme Court. It came as little surprise that the argument was rejected. We then took the matter to the Appeal Court in Bloemfontein. Busloads of people from Moutse arrived at the court, dressed in their tribal outfits, intent on showing that they were ethnically attached to the Pedi tribe for which Lebowa had been created. Many in the crowd were from Johannesburg and Pretoria and I suspect had never worn tribal dress in their lives before. The hearing before the Appeal Court went well. It was clear that the judges were amused to find me, a known opponent of apartheid, arguing in favour of the need to apply the policy of apartheid correctly with due regard to ethnic purity, and William de Villiers, an ardent supporter of apartheid who habitually argued cases on behalf of the government, arguing that apartheid allowed a Bantustan to be created for different ethnic groups without regard to ethnic affiliation. The appeal succeeded.[61] KwaNdebele did not become an independent Bantustan.

After the court's decision John Mathebe, nephew of Gibson Mathebe, Moutse's acting chief, declared: 'We are grateful to Professor Dugard. In our tradition when someone does something to help us we do not give them money or cattle, we give them a wife. We want to give the professor a wife.' In fact I received neither money nor an additional wife. But my family and I were the main guests at a big party held in Moutse to celebrate the victory.

The failure of the plan to create an independent Bantustan in KwaNdebele did not deter the apartheid regime from embarking on a similar exercise in respect of the self-governing homeland of Qwaqwa, situated in the Orange Free State for the South Sotho people. Now the regime proposed to include a large township adjacent to Bloemfontein, Botshabelo, into Qwaqwa, to give it credibility and viability in terms of territory and population. The population of Botshabelo was not, however, ethnically uniform, and comprised Tswanas and Xhosas in addition to South Sotho. The argument raised in the Moutse case was again made and with the same success.[62] When I presented the argument in this case in the Appeal Court in Bloemfontein in 1990, I recall looking at rows of officials from Pretoria responsible for constructing and maintaining the policy of separate self-governing homelands and independent Bantustans and wondering what was going through their minds as they confronted not only another failure to expand the empire of apartheid but also the imminent demise of the empire itself. Soon, like the officials of former colonial empires, they would be without empire and without jobs, as President De Klerk had already made his landmark speech proclaiming the end of apartheid.

In the 1980s I attended many seminars and conferences in which the chief ministers of the self-governing homelands participated and I came to know them well. At these meetings there was always tension between these leaders and the supporters of the banned ANC. At one such seminar in an idyllic setting at Cintsa on the coast near East London, Chief Buthelezi was challenged with the comment that the 'true leaders' of the people were on Robben Island or in exile. He exploded in anger and the seminar almost broke down. Later I was presiding over a similar seminar in the Settlers Monument during the Grahamstown Festival when a speaker confronted Buthelezi in a similar way. Fortunately, I knew what to expect. I was not disappointed. Buthelezi made no attempt to conceal his anger in another outburst.

Perhaps I was too friendly with these homeland leaders. In the 1980s Chief Minister Cedric Patudi of Lebowa asked me to advise his cabinet on the advantages of federalism in a future democratic South Africa. I agreed and invited him to Wits to talk about the matter. I expected that he would be accompanied by one or two of his ministers for a low-key visit. Instead, on the scheduled day, the full cabinet of some ten ministers arrived, each in a separate long black Mercedes limousine with chauffeur. Such a display could not be concealed. Wits students learnt of the presence of hated 'homelands stooges' on campus and started to mobilize to confront them. Fortunately I received advance warning and was able to terminate the meeting hurriedly and ask my guests to leave for their own safety.

Although the TBVC states were recognized as independent states under the law of South Africa, and although they maintained diplomatic relations with each other, they remained unrecognized by the international community. Indeed, foreign states continued to hold South Africa responsible for the actions of the TBVC governments. When F.W. de Klerk announced the end of apartheid on 2 February 1990, this inevitably meant the end of the TBVC states. Although the National Party government accepted this, it preferred to have the TBVC states reincorporated into South Africa by formal cession, which implied that they had previously existed as independent states. Understandably, the ANC rejected this and insisted that they be reincorporated by the simple device of repealing the statutes that had purported to confer independence upon them. I wrote in support of this procedure,[63] and this view prevailed. The 'independent' Bantustans were reincorporated into South Africa by the repeal of the independence-conferring statutes,[64] and nationality was restored to the eight million black South Africans who had been denationalized by the 'independence' of the TBVC states.[65]

10

Race discrimination

Institutionalized race discrimination was the hallmark of apartheid. The legal order constituting apartheid, which provided for unequal separation and discrimination in the allocation of basic human rights, has already been described in chapter 5. Law was buttressed by convention and by a perception that the requirements of the law reached further than they did. Race discrimination was prescribed by law and enforced by law. Statutes, regulations and judicial decisions commanded and authorized race discrimination in almost every sphere of life. Signs in public buildings, parks and beaches indicated clearly the racial group allowed to use each amenity. But the law could not and did not cover every possibility. Here social custom played its part. Most whites believed that the race laws prohibited more than they did in fact. For instance, there was no prohibition on blacks dining in white homes, but most whites believed that such intercourse was forbidden by law and refrained from doing so.

Despite the breadth of the laws prescribing separation, there remained many areas of human and social interaction that were not covered by law. The city centres of South Africa were racially mixed. There were separate counters for the races in the post office and other government offices, but not in shops in most cities. The law did not prohibit persons of different races from attending church services (although an attempt was made to do this) and from most forms of social interaction. Some organizations, such as the Institute of Race Relations and the Christian Institute, were open to all races. Foreign visitors often expressed surprise at the amount of racial mixing in shops and hotels[66] in the major cities, in professional life, in church life and in interracial bodies.

The police believed that the law went further than it did, as was illustrated by a strange personal experience. One cold winter night shortly before midnight, I received a call from a friend who had been at a racially mixed dinner and dance party in Johannesburg organized by a group of radical clergy. At 11:30pm the police had disrupted the party and arrested them on the charge of interracial dancing. They had been taken to John Vorster Square, the police headquarters, and I was asked to secure their release on bail. I drove down to John Vorster Square and asked the desk officer why my clients were being held. 'There were blacks and whites dancing together, and this is against the law,' he said with disgust. 'There is no such crime,' I said. 'Of course there is,' he replied and went off to consult his colleagues. Half hour later, after consulting a lawyer, he returned. 'You are right,' he said angrily, 'but we are charging them instead with breaking the curfew law, which prohibits blacks from being in white areas.' 'But, officer,' I replied, 'the curfew only comes into force at midnight and they were arrested at 11:30!' Very reluctantly, and angrily, he was obliged to release my clients, who later sued successfully for wrongful arrest.

In addition to the gaps in the law, there was the fact that some of the race laws were seldom enforced, and as a result persons of different races could mix with impunity. It was unlawful to serve blacks liquor, which in theory meant that the host of a dinner party committed a crime by serving drinks to black guests. But in practice there were no prosecutions for such socialization. The law prohibited whites from entering black townships, but this prohibition was seldom enforced. I visited friends in Soweto frequently and was never stopped by the police. On occasion I would pass a police vehicle but the police seemed uninterested in my presence in a black township. Of course, most whites strictly observed this law, and this meant that whites had no idea of the conditions in which their fellow black South Africans lived.

In the 1970s, as South Africa entered into diplomatic relations with neighbouring African states, special dispensation was granted to black diplomats. Some of the better hotels were designated as 'international hotels' which might be frequented by black diplomats. But hotels made no attempt to police their visitors, with the result that wealthy local blacks had no difficulty in visiting or even staying in hotels in theory reserved for whites. I recall meeting our friend Constance Ntshona, a successful black Soweto businesswoman, in a theatre reserved for whites. When I asked how she came to be there, she replied, 'Tonight I am the ambassador of Malawi.'

Apartheid South Africa was a complex society. Most whites met and came to know blacks as servants in the home or as subordinates in the workplace. Many whites had been brought up by black nannies. Although the relationship between black and white was close, it was inevitably largely a master–servant one. Those who wished to mix with other races on equal terms could do so without breaking the law, but they did have to make a conscious effort to do so. And, of course, most failed to do this.

Whites were largely spared the brutality and ugliness of apartheid. They tended to see apartheid as a benign ordering of society along racial lines. Of course, many had contact with the pass laws, which required white employers to register black employees. They found it inconvenient and frustrating if an employee suddenly disappeared as a result of being arrested under these laws. But whites had little knowledge of the impact that apartheid had on the lives of their fellow citizens. In particular they had little empathy for the humiliation suffered by blacks on a daily basis. Few visited the homes from which their live-in domestic servants came in the rural areas. And few had any idea of the squalid conditions in the black townships where most South Africans lived.

The apartheid legal order was an abuse of law. All features of this legal order were obscene. The Group Areas Act and the pass laws, with which I had most experience in my professional life, were among the worst.

Group Areas Act

The Group Areas Act[67] authorized the zoning of cities and towns into grossly unequal residential areas for different racial groups. Separate and unequal residential areas for Africans were already a feature of South African city life when the National Party came to power in 1948. Consequently the Group Areas Act was directed largely at coloured and Indian suburbs in the cities. Many coloureds and Indians were forced to leave their homes and to relocate to areas far from their places of employment in new suburbs with inferior accommodation.

In the late 1970s accommodation for coloureds and Indians, in their separate suburbs on the outskirts of Johannesburg, became scarce. At the same time whites began to leave apartments in the city centre, zoned for exclusive white occupation under the Group Areas Act, for the more comfortable white suburbs. Landlords, deprived of income, responded by leasing apartments to coloureds and Indians. The government's response was to initiate the prosecution and eviction of hundreds of coloureds, Indians and blacks for unlawful occupation.

A community organization, Actstop, was established to oppose these prosecutions and evictions. Working closely with CALS and Lawyers for Human Rights, it compiled a roster of lawyers willing to act free of charge to oppose prosecutions. The lawyers who volunteered their services to Actstop were free to raise any defence that they believed might halt the prosecutions. Jules Browde SC, president of Lawyers for Human Rights, raised the defence of necessity, arguing that those prosecuted had nowhere else to live, as the coloured and Indian areas were completely overcrowded. Although this argument received a sympathetic hearing, it was dismissed.

When it came to my turn to defend a coloured family charged with illegal occupation – that of Ivan Werner, his wife and young child – I pondered about the defence to raise. The night before I was due to appear in court it suddenly occurred to me that I might challenge the validity of the government proclamation zoning central Johannesburg for exclusive white occupation on the grounds of unreasonableness. While the validity of laws enacted by Parliament might not be questioned by courts, the validity of proclamations enacted in terms of such laws – known as subordinate or delegated legislation – might be challenged on grounds of unreasonableness. Moreover, there was authority for the proposition that subordinate legislation that discriminated unfairly on grounds of race was unreasonable unless clearly authorized by the enabling Act of Parliament. My only difficulty – a major difficulty – was that this argument had previously been raised in respect of the Group Areas Act and rejected by the Appeal Court in the notorious case of *Lockhat* v. *Minister of the Interior*[68] on the ground that the Act authorized racial discrimination. In this case the court held that the Group Areas Act was 'a colossal social experiment' involving the large-scale movement of people throughout the country. 'Parliament must have envisaged', said the court, that it would 'cause disruption and, within the foreseeable future, substantial inequalities.' The court added, in the manner of Pontius Pilate, that it was not for it to decide whether this would 'prove to be for the common weal'.[69]

Decisions of the Appeal Court are not absolutely binding and might be challenged – even if this was very seldom done and most lawyers believed that it was irresponsible to do this. On the other hand, even if my argument failed – as was most probable – it would secure a suspension of all prosecutions pending the decision of the Appeal Court, which would take at least two years. This was because no prosecutions could be brought while the law was being challenged. During this time prosecutions might be overtaken by political events relating to the government's determination to provide political rights to coloureds and Indians. Elated by these thoughts, I went to the magistrate's court the next day and informed the magistrate that I was challenging the validity of the proclamation zoning Johannesburg 'white' under which my clients were prosecuted. The magistrate was surprised but accepted that in law he had no alternative but to postpone hearing pending a decision of the Supreme Court, which alone could consider such challenges to the validity of a proclamation.

Determined to have the matter argued by an experienced senior counsel, I asked Ernie Wentzel, a prominent human rights lawyer, if he would lead me. Ernie agreed, but the Johannesburg Bar Council ruled that he might not appear with me as, although I had been admitted to the Bar, I was not a member of the Society of Advocates. I was appalled at this invocation of a trade union rule in a matter of public interest, involving human rights, in which lawyers would appear free of charge. The decision of the Johannesburg Bar Council left me no option but to argue the case myself, with the assistance of Jonathan Burchell, a senior lecturer at Wits and an expert in criminal law, and Shun Chetty, one of the leading anti-apartheid attorneys, who had also volunteered his services to Actstop.

It was no easy task to challenge the validity of a proclamation on the ground that it discriminated on the basis of race. In order to do this, it was necessary to obtain evidence of discrimination not only in housing but also in respect of health, education, family life and delinquency, which were a necessary consequence of the zoning of separate group areas. This meant examining documents, speaking to experts in these fields, and persuading witnesses to testify to the discriminatory consequences of separate group areas.

The hearing of the challenge to the proclamation took place in Johannesburg in the Witwatersrand Local Division of the Supreme Court. In essence we produced for the first time in South Africa what is known in the United States as a 'Brandeis brief' (named after Louis Brandeis, who later became a member of the US Supreme Court), that is, a dossier of sociological, medical and educational statistical evidence combined with legal argument which was designed to show *on the facts* that the proclamation in its implementation discriminated against coloureds, Indians and blacks, and produced harmful consequences.

Fifteen witnesses attested to the fact that the overcrowded conditions in the areas set aside for coloured occupation contributed to diseases like tuberculosis, to family break-ups and delinquency. The partial and unequal treatment that resulted from the application of the proclamation, I argued, contravened not only South African common law but also the international obligation to promote and respect human rights which South Africa had assumed in signing the Charter of the United Nations. The mention of South Africa's international obligations under the UN Charter produced an outburst from the prosecutor. 'Counsel is making a political speech,' he protested loudly. I explained to the court that there was English authority for the proposition that a state's international obligations should be taken into account in the consideration of the reasonableness of subordinate legislation. The judge was not convinced by this or other arguments and ruled that the proclamation zoning Johannesburg for white occupation was valid.

A year later I presented the same argument to the Appeal Court in a joint appeal, with Jules Browde arguing that the defence of necessity prevailed while I argued that the proclamation was invalid on grounds of unreasonableness. Neither argument succeeded and the appeals were dismissed.[70] The court did not, however, suggest that I had acted irresponsibly in questioning the correctness of its decision in *Lockhat* v. *Minister of the Interior.*

The political climate had changed dramatically in the two years' moratorium on prosecutions afforded by the *Werner* case. The government had meanwhile determined that it would co-opt the coloured and Indian communities into the central political order by according them representation in Parliament. Consequently it was no longer politically expedient to continue with prosecutions under the Group Areas Act. An attempt to do this was cut short by judicial decisions, in one of which I appeared as counsel, ruling that no one might be evicted under the Group Act without a full inquiry into the availability of alternative accommodation.[71] As such accommodation in the coloured and Indian areas was unavailable, it became pointless to proceed with the prosecutions in which the matter of alternative accommodation might be raised.

The government persisted in its attempts to enforce the Group Areas Act. In 1987 I was asked to assist the Palkowich family. Mr Palkowich was white and his partner was Indian. He purchased a house in Kempton Park, zoned for exclusive white occupation, as a white person. Then he successfully applied to be reclassified as Asian to allow him to marry his partner. He was prosecuted for living in a white group area. I challenged the validity of the proclamation zoning Kempton Park white on the ground that it violated the 1983 constitution's commitment in its preamble 'to uphold Christian values and civilized norms'.[72] The magistrate duly postponed the prosecution and referred the matter to the Supreme Court, as had been done in *Werner*'s case. The argument that I intended to raise would clearly embarrass the government at the time when it was set on rapprochement with Indians and coloureds, who were now represented in Parliament. Indeed, that was my intention. It therefore came as no surprise to me when the government withdrew the prosecution and granted a permit to Mr and Mrs Palkowich to live in their home in Kempton Park.

Although the Group Areas Act was only repealed in 1991,[73] it was effectively destroyed by the Actstop litigation campaign. The *Werner* case convincingly demonstrated that a losing case might be politically successful. For me this was important, as I had arguments with colleagues about undertaking cases that might have positive political and social results even if they were likely to fail in court. *Werner* clearly vindicated this position.

The Pass Laws

The pass laws were undoubtedly the most hated laws in the legal apparatus of apartheid. As we have seen, these laws[74] obliged every black African in the cities and towns of South Africa to carry a document showing that the bearer was entitled to be in the urban area in question. Failure to present a pass on demand from a police officer was a criminal offence, punishable by a fine (which few workseekers could afford) or several months in prison. The pass laws were vigorously enforced and more than half of South Africa's prison population consisted of pass law offenders. The pass laws ensured that no stigma was attached to a criminal conviction and brought the whole legal system into contempt. This law, more than any other, demonstrated that justice played no part in the legal process.

The pass laws were enforced by Bantu commissioner's courts presided over by civil servants with minimal legal training. No legal representation was provided; the law obliged the accused to prove his own innocence; and commissioners refused to enquire into the personal circumstances that had led the accused person to enter the city without a pass. The whole procedure usually lasted for only two to three minutes. This conveyor-belt system of law enforcement was completely dependent on the absence of legal representation.

Before 1984 I had some experience of the pass courts from occasional appearances on behalf of the family of our housekeeper, Selena Molefe. Few blacks escaped arrest under the pass laws and Selena's family, who lived in the country near Rustenburg, were no exception. Not surprisingly, I had a high success rate before these courts. When I arrived at the court, the prosecutor would be visibly annoyed, as time spent on legal defence in one case would throw his roster of prosecutions into disarray. Even if the 'trial' resulted in a conviction, it would inevitably take a couple of hours with some cross-examination of the police witness who made the arrest (if the police officer was present, which was highly unusual) and a plea in mitigation. Consequently, in most cases the prosecutor would simply withdraw the case after seeking an assurance from me that I would ensure that the accused person obtained a valid pass.

I would often take foreign visitors to sit in at the commissioner's court to see apartheid in operation. This too was unwelcome. The clerk of the court would approach me to ask what my business was. When I told him that courts were open to the public and I had come to observe, he would convey this quietly to the commissioner and prosecutor, who would seldom be able to conceal their annoyance. Visitors also meant that the procedure had to be slower and this again meant that the number of cases scheduled to be processed that day would be reduced.

From its inception the CALS concerned itself with the pass courts. Ramarumo Monama, now a High Court judge, monitored the procedures employed in the courts and in 1983 submitted his findings into the structure and functioning of the courts to a judicial commission of inquiry under Judge Hoexter. In the following year, on the recommendation of the commission, the administration of the pass laws was transferred from Bantu commissioner's courts to magistrate's courts. CALS, Lawyers for Human Rights and the Black Sash then set up a roster system, modelled on that established for prosecutions under the Group Areas Act, to provide free legal representation in the pass courts. This meant that each case lasted several hours instead of a few minutes, with lawyers raising questions about the correctness of procedures, cross-examining police witnesses and offering defences based on the personal circumstances of each accused. I well recall the surprise on the magistrate's face when I arose to inform the court that I appeared as lawyer for the accused. This was simply not part of the game, his face seemed to say. To aggravate matters, the campaign secured the attention of the press, which provided publicity to the injustices of the system. The pass law courts simply could not work if principles of due process of law were to be observed. It was an indictment of South African lawyers that this form of civil disobedience, or rather civil obedience to the law, had not been tried before.

In 1986 the pass laws were repealed.[75] Various political and economic factors contributed to this, but there can be no doubt that the manner in which lawyers had rendered the system unworkable was also a factor.

11

The security laws and political repression

The security laws, which provided for political control through repression, were an essential part of the apparatus of apartheid. As shown in chapter 5, they were initially justified as anti-communist measures designed to save South Africa from communism. By the early 1960s it had become clear that the security laws were being used to suppress black nationalism and radical political dissent aimed at creating a democratic South Africa. Communism was simply a ruse. Consequently the government had to find another politically acceptable reason for suppressing dissent. Terrorism was the obvious choice. In 1967 Parliament enacted the Terrorism Act,[76] which created the crime of terrorism. In terms of this Act,[77] a person committed the capital crime of terrorism if, 'with intent to endanger the maintenance of law and order', he or she committed *any act* that was likely to have any of a number of results in South Africa. These included bringing about social and economic change by forcible means or in co-operation with any foreign government or international body; encouraging hostility between whites and other inhabitants of South Africa; or embarrassing the administration of the affairs of state. In effect this meant that any effective political opponent of the government fell within the definition of terrorism.

Whereas under the Suppression of Communism Act anyone was a communist if the government said so, under the Terrorism Act anyone was a terrorist if the government chose to call him so. The result of labelling political opponents as terrorists was that the term lost its true meaning, and to be called a terrorist was simply a way of saying that the person strongly opposed apartheid. To use the term simply as a way of discrediting one's political opponents is to make it impossible to take meaningful action against real terrorist acts.

Prosecutions were undoubtedly brought under the Terrorism Act against persons who had committed serious crimes of violence, often involving loss of life, with the intent to create a state of terror. But the Act was also used to prosecute persons for crimes that could not remotely be termed terrorism. For instance, the dean of Johannesburg, Gonville ffrench-Beytagh, was convicted of terrorism on the grounds that he had paid money to support the dependants of political prisoners. This, the court found, was terrorism because it would be likely to boost the morale of persons engaged in attempts to overthrow the state by violence. Happily, the dean was acquitted on appeal.[78]

No person was prosecuted under the security laws without being detained for a lengthy period of time under the Terrorism Act,[79] which authorized indefinite detention without trial for the purposes of interrogation, or else one of its predecessors which likewise allowed detention for long periods of time.

These laws did not expressly authorize torture. But in practice they were used to subject detainees to both mental and physical torture. The security police interrogators, who were known for their brutality, were unaccountable to anyone. Since no family members or private doctors were allowed to visit detainees, there was no one to whom the detainee might complain or display his or her injuries. Visits by magistrates or state doctors were meaningless as they were all part of the same state machine.

There were alarming reports of torture. Over fifty detainees died in detention in the most suspicious circumstances. The police explanations for such deaths – slipping on soap in the shower, falling down stairs, leaping from windows in police headquarters and hanging – were both implausible and incredible. But they were accepted by magistrates and judges and the white public at large. For most whites, security was paramount. They were not prepared to question explanations of the deaths of persons who threatened their safety. The deaths in detention of the black consciousness leader Steve Biko in 1977[80] and of the white trade unionist doctor Neil Aggett in 1982[81] received widespread national and international attention. But although inquests into their deaths produced evidence of police callousness and the collaboration of state medical doctors, the police interrogators were protected by the legal cocoon of non-accountability provided by the Terrorism Act. Moreover, inquest magistrates lacked both the courage and the inclination to probe the opportunities for torture provided by the Terrorism Act. Their findings that no one was responsible for the deaths of Biko and Aggett and others like them were outrageous, but they were to be expected of civil servants accountable to their masters in Pretoria. And they satisfied a white public determined to close its eyes to atrocities committed to ensure their safety and continued white rule.

Another weapon in the arsenal of laws at the disposal of the security police was the banning order. The Internal Security Act empowered the minister of justice to impose severe restrictions on persons who he was 'satisfied' were engaged in activities that endangered the security of the state. Such an order, usually imposed for five years, confined a person to a particular magisterial district or house (in which case it was known as 'house arrest'), prohibited that person from attending gatherings of two or more persons and from being on the premises of factories, educational institutions or publishers, and banned such a person from attending political gatherings. It was a criminal offence to publish anything said or written by such a person. This civil death was not subject to judicial review: the minister's arbitrary decision was final. Political activists released from prison were invariably subjected to such an order.

The banning of persons under the Internal Security Act was not uncommon. During the apartheid years some two thousand persons received banning orders. Most orders were imposed on unknown blacks or whites perceived to be a threat to the security of the apartheid state, with the result that this form of executive punishment made little impact on white opinion. One had to know a banned person to comprehend the injustice of the system, and most whites did not know banned persons.

The restriction on social gatherings was a particularly harsh one. Banned persons were prosecuted for attending dinner parties and picnics and for playing bridge. Initially this restriction was interpreted as outlawing gatherings of a considerable number of persons or of more than two persons outside the family circle, but in 1976 the Appeal Court ruled that a social gathering was constituted by any number of persons 'from two upwards'.[82] Jane and I knew and socialized with several banned persons, but we were aware that a knock on the door might mean arrest.

The security police and government officials were vindictive, at times sadistic, in their enforcement of banning orders. One of the most notorious examples of such vindictiveness was the treatment of Robert Sobukwe,[83] the founder and leader of the Pan Africanist Congress. In 1960 Sobukwe was imprisoned on Robben Island for his role in the Pan Africanist Congress call on black South Africans to burn their passes, which had resulted in the Sharpeville massacre of 21 March 1960. When his prison sentence expired, special legislation was passed each year to hold him on Robben Island. In 1969 he was released but subjected to a banning order under the Suppression of Communism Act, which restricted him to the Kimberley magisterial district. Sobukwe, a distinguished academic, was in 1970 offered a teaching post by an American university. His application for a passport having been refused, he applied for an 'exit permit', allowing him to leave South Africa with no right of return, which was duly granted by the minister of the interior. He then requested the minister of justice for permission to leave the Kimberley magisterial district to enable him to embark on an aircraft for the United States. This request was refused. Sobukwe then applied to court for an order allowing him to leave South Africa on an exit permit.

Sobukwe's attorney, Raymond Tucker, briefed the doyen of the Johannesburg Bar, Isie Maisels QC, and Ernie Wentzel to make this application. I was asked, this time on brief, to advise on the common law right, and the right under international law, of a person to leave a country. The purpose of this advice was to guide the court in the interpretation of contradictory statutes on the law governing freedom of movement and the right to leave one's country. My opinion focused largely on the recognition of such a right under Roman-Dutch law by seventeenth-century jurists such as Grotius. The application failed and Sobukwe's confinement to Kimberley was renewed until his death in 1978. The Appellate Division's decision in this case[84] was but one of many disgraceful judicial decisions of the apartheid era in which courts exercised a policy choice in favour of executive action in their interpretation of repressive statutes. (Although I had been briefed as one of his lawyers, I never met Sobukwe as he was strictly confined to Kimberley. Like Mandela, he was a Healdtown 'old boy'.)

In 1982 these security measures relating to political offences, detention without trial, and the banning of persons and organizations were consolidated in a new Internal Security Act,[85] which retained the principal features of the existing security legislative apparatus. Most important, section 6 of the Terrorism Act was retained in section 29 of the Act.

Security laws of this kind, which were part of the ordinary law, obviated the need for emergency measures. In effect, they created a permanent state of emergency. The 156-day state of emergency declared in 1960, following the shootings at Sharpeville, had led to a loss of confidence in the South African economy and the government was determined to avoid this happening again. It was far better to deal with political dissent by means of security laws permanently on the statute book than by special emergency legislation which alarmed foreign investors. It was not until 1985 that a state of emergency was declared again.

In 1983 the United Democratic Front (UDF) was formed to oppose the Tricameral Parliament, which co-opted coloureds and Indians into the parliamentary system. The UDF, a federation of over seven hundred affiliated organizations closely linked to the banned ANC, resorted to strikes, stay-aways and consumer boycotts in the townships in the Eastern Cape and Transvaal in the mid-1980s. In 1985 the government declared a state of emergency in thirty-six magisterial districts. This was briefly lifted but then reimposed for the whole country from 1986 to 1990.[86] The UDF was declared a banned organization in 1988. Wide powers were conferred on the security police to ban meetings and to arrest persons. Persons were detained for long periods and subjected to vicious torture. In Port Elizabeth, in a case brought by the Centre for Applied Legal Studies, a court restrained the police from torturing detainees. In 1985 the government provided information that nearly eight thousand persons had been detained in the emergency. Thereafter it refused to give information on detentions as it claimed that this information was being used by political opponents for propaganda purposes. The Detainees' Parents Support Committee, which monitored detentions until it was banned in 1988, estimated that twenty-five thousand persons were detained in 1986. The state of emergency was only lifted in June 1990, after President De Klerk had announced the end of apartheid.

Despite the fact that the arsenal of laws at the disposal of the apartheid government provided procedures for suppressing dissent and dealing with opponents of the regime extra-judicially – such as by banning and detention without trial – the government persisted in bringing most of those accused of committing acts against the security of the state to trial. Only in the 1980s did extra-judicial execution of militants at the hands of the security police become part of the state's repressive machinery. Thus trials under the security laws – political trials[87] – were a regular feature of the apartheid legal order.

There were several reasons, from the government's perspective, for putting political opponents on trial before the ordinary courts of the land. Firstly, it demonstrated a commitment to the rule of law. Secondly, it gave the government an opportunity to show white South Africans what was being done to subvert their security and how the government was coping with the protection of the security of the state.

The first attempt at a show trial, the Treason Trial, which ran from 1956 to 1961, ended in the acquittal of all accused on the ground that the prosecution had failed to show that the policy of the Congress Alliance was to overthrow the state by violent means or replace the existing order with a communist state. After this setback the government chose to charge militants under the recently enacted Sabotage Act and Terrorism Act, which defined the proscribed criminal act in broad terms and, in addition, contained rules of evidence and procedure favourable to the prosecution, particularly relating to the burden of proof.

Trials under the security laws were initially held in the cities in order to provide maximum publicity to the crimes of the accused. The Old Synagogue in Pretoria was a popular venue as its large hall lent a touch of theatre to the proceedings. But as defence lawyers succeeded in destroying state witnesses and presenting the cause of the accused in a favourable light, the government changed its strategy. Firstly, it sought to prevent foreign funding for defence lawyers by banning the Defence and Aid Fund under the Suppression of Communism Act in 1966.[88] When this failed to prevent the flow of funding from abroad for defence lawyers, the government transferred major security trials to remote country towns, such as Delmas in the Eastern Transvaal, far from the glare of the media and political supporters.

South Africa's divided legal profession presented problems for proper legal defence in trials under the security laws. Attorneys (solicitors), who managed such trials and instructed advocates to appear in these trials, were vulnerable to pressure from both government and their ordinary clients. Consequently, few were prepared to handle such cases and it was left to a small group of attorneys such as Raymond Tucker, Joel Carlson, Shun Chetty and Priscilla Jana to manage such trials. Advocates (barristers) were less exposed to pressure. In most countries, however, the top trial lawyers generally refuse to defend persons charged with unpopular crimes, of which crimes against the state are the most obvious example. In apartheid South Africa this did not happen. Many of the leading advocates, with major commercial law practices, such as Sydney Kentridge, Isie Maisels and Rex Welsh, appeared as defence counsel in political trials. Other advocates, such as George Bizos, Denis Kuny and Ernie Wentzel, developed a professional expertise in political trials that greatly embarrassed state prosecutors. Moreover, the availability of funding from abroad ensured that most persons charged with serious crimes under the security laws were properly defended.[89]

The fact that trials under the security laws were adequately funded and properly defended meant that public interest law institutions, such as the Legal Resources Centre and the Centre for Applied Studies, were not called upon to provide defence in security trials. On occasion, advocates from these institutions did appear as counsel in such trials, but the institutions themselves were not involved. I was employed as counsel in several security trials – notably the trial of SWAPO leaders and the Bophuthatswana treason trial of *State* v. *Banda* – but my role was confined to advising on or arguing points of international law. I never acted as ordinary counsel for a whole trial under the security laws. These trials lasted for many months, sometimes years, and my post as professor of law at Wits and director of the Centre for Applied Legal Studies precluded me from such a long-term engagement as counsel.

This meant that my main role in respect of the security laws and their implementation was that of critic – and advocate for the repeal of these laws. Section 6 of the Terrorism Act[90] was the principal target of my criticism, as it was the law under which some forty-seven hundred persons were detained and subjected to both mental and physical torture. It was, as I stated in my book *Human Rights and the South African Legal Order*, the 'symbol of repression in South Africa as it departs so radically from the accepted notions of criminal justice'.[91]

In 1969 Winnie Mandela and twenty-one others were held for several months under section 6 of the Terrorism Act. They were then charged under the Suppression of Communism Act for engaging in activities on behalf of the banned African National Congress. After several witnesses called to give evidence for the prosecution refused to do so, and had alleged that they had been ill-treated while in police custody, the prosecutor withdrew the charges against the accused. This was because the evidence of brutal police interrogation seriously embarrassed the government. This resulted in their being found not guilty. They were, however, immediately rearrested and again detained under the Terrorism Act.

At a protest meeting held at Wits over the detention of 'the 22' in May 1970, I stated in respect of section 6 of the Terrorism Act:

> I do not like to use the term 'law' to describe this provision because it totally lacks any element of justice, fairness or morality. It is an aberration of law. It is the type of law which was enunciated by Hitler and which, after World War II, was denied the name of law by the Nuremberg Tribunal and the German courts themselves.
>
> All South Africans should be concerned about section 6 and the rule of law. But we know this is unlikely. Most South Africans are too timid, too affluent or too apathetic to do anything about a principle which does not relate to our two South African idols – money and sport. So students must fill the vacuum left by their elders. They must act on behalf of South African society in this travesty of justice.[92]

I recalled that a number of detainees had died under mysterious circumstances and demanded that the government establish an open judicial commission of inquiry into the implementation of the Terrorism Act. This call was endorsed by the *Rand Daily Mail.* In an editorial it declared in respect of my account of deaths in detention and allegations of torture, 'It is an ugly record. Ugly enough to more than justify Professor Dugard's call for a full public examination of the methods of interrogation used by the security police.'[93]

'The 22' were later charged with similar offences under the Terrorism Act but a plea of double jeopardy – a plea that they had already been acquitted of this crime – succeeded and they were again acquitted.[94] Their freedom was illusory, for immediately after their release they were served with banning orders under the Suppression of Communism Act.

In 1971 Ahmed Timol fell to his death from the tenth floor of police headquarters at John Vorster Square in Johannesburg while he was in detention under the Terrorism Act. Did he jump to avoid further torture? Was he deliberately pushed by his interrogators? Or was he dropped by them in error as they were holding him by his ankles from the window? An inquest magistrate subsequently found that no one was to blame for his death, in effect returning a verdict of suicide.

Protests were held throughout the country. The public protest meeting held in Durban was effective in respect of promoting public awareness, but it had serious consequences for freedom of speech for academics. At this meeting Professor Barend van Niekerk declared that the purpose of section 6 of the Terrorism Act was to procure evidence by way of torture and called on judges to reject all evidence obtained from witnesses who had been held under the Terrorism Act. For this statement he was convicted of contempt of court by the Appeal Court in Bloemfontein, on the ground that his statement was designed to interfere with the course of justice by calling on judges to reject all evidence obtained from detainees irrespective of its intrinsic merits.[95] The judgment sent out a clear message to academic critics: restrain your criticisms of the security laws. In an article in the *Sunday Times*, I argued that the judgment of the Appeal Court made it impossible to remind judges of the Nuremberg principles according to which a law ceased to be a law if it was the antithesis of justice. I continued that the judgment meant 'if decapitation were introduced for abusive language it would be unlawful to appeal to judges to refuse to apply the law'. Did judges really need this protection from the memory of Nuremberg? I asked.[96]

The inquest into the death of Ahmed Timol was followed by the trial of his friend Mohamed Salim Essop, who had been been arrested together with Timol, brutally tortured and hospitalized. Essop, a Wits student, and three others were tried by Judge J.H. ('Lammie') Snyman and sentenced to five years' imprisonment, the minimum sentence required by the Terrorism Act. In passing sentence, Judge Snyman castigated unnamed legal academics for misleading students by their harsh criticisms of the security laws into believing that they were morally justified in breaking the law.[97] These 'politically-minded academic lawyers', he stated, had evoked 'contempt for the real law of the country' by condemning the Terrorism Act as being in violation of the rule of law.[98] This was a clear reference to Barend van Niekerk and me, for we had already been named by a National Party member of Parliament as being responsible, together with

Helen Suzman, for encouraging student protests and undermining respect for law and order.[99]

Detention without trial and its necessary corollary, torture, continued to flourish until the end of apartheid, either under the consolidated Internal Security Act of 1982 or under the emergency measures of the late 1980s. But in the 1980s a new security measure made its appearance: assassination. Shadowy security police units, understandably believing that their political superiors wished certain persons to be 'eliminated', resorted to assassination. Several of my friends were killed by police operatives in this way. David Webster, an anthropologist at Wits, who had been active in the Detainees' Parents Support Committee, was shot outside his home in Johannesburg in May 1989. Anton Lubowski, an advocate from Windhoek and a leading member of SWAPO, with whom I had worked closely on human rights issues, was killed in Windhoek in September 1989. Jeanette Schoon, with whom I had worked at the Institute of Race Relations, was killed by a letter bomb together with her six-year-old daughter in Lubango, northern Angola. Matthew Goniwe, whom I had defended on a charge under the Suppression of Communism Act in Transkei in 1976, was killed outside Port Elizabeth in June 1985.

The security laws failed in their task of maintaining security. But they succeeded in terrorizing a country and its people.

12

Police

South Africa under apartheid was a police state. The police force was not, however, an all-white body. About half the force was black, but the top leadership positions were in the hands of whites.[100] Broadly, the police force was divided between the ordinary police force, which investigated crime and maintained order, and the security police, who were responsible for the preservation of the apartheid state by enforcing the security laws. In practice this distinction was not rigidly maintained. The 'ordinary' police force was responsible for enforcing the pass laws, which meant that it was employed to roam the white suburbs in large trucks to arrest blacks unable to produce a proper pass. As the pass laws were the most visible sign of racial oppression for most blacks, the ordinary police were viewed as agents of the apartheid state. This perception was endorsed by the fact that the ordinary, uniformed police force was also used to suppress political demonstrations and protests. The failure to distinguish ordinary policing from policing designed to preserve the apartheid state meant that the police force as a whole was seen as the agent of apartheid. Consequently, those opposed to apartheid had no confidence in the police and tended to see them as a hostile force.

As in most police states, the police generally kept a low profile and were not to be seen on the street, particularly on the white street. But when they were needed to enforce the law, they emerged in great numbers. Protests in the black townships were brutally repressed, and student protests at Wits often degenerated into police raids on campus with batons, whips and tear gas.

The security police were ever present but seldom seen. Informers – spies – were rife, particularly at Wits. At one stage there were spies from three branches of intelligence – the security police, the Bureau of State Security and military intelligence – embedded in the Wits student leadership, each reporting to his master without knowledge of each other's role. And, of course, spies doubled up as agents provocateurs. Inevitably, revealing spies became the concern of many. On occasion genuine student activists were wrongly suspected of being spies and this led to a mood of confusion and distrust among students.[101] I had a student in my international law class, Derek Brune, who was a prominent radical member of the Student Representative Council.[102] I remonstrated with him for failing to attend tutorials, believing that a student radical might learn from my classes. Later his cover was blown and it appeared that he was an agent for the security police. He went on to serve the security police in Namibia. After independence he switched sides and worked for the newly independent government of Namibia. Such conduct simply confirmed Hannah Arendt's thesis of the banality of evil.[103]

Student spies were harmless in the sense that they had no executive powers. The security police themselves were, however, more fearsome. Many told of torture at their hands. And detainees died in detention. The killing of Steve Biko and Neil Aggett while in detention sent out a message to all: no one was safe in the hands of the security police.

I tried to keep my distance from the police, both uniformed and security. But it was not always possible.

In July 1972 I wrote an article in the magazine *New Nation* about the disproportionate force used by police against student demonstrators at Wits. I explained the antagonism between police and student in the following way:

> Ideologically and emotionally, the police have every reason to dislike students. Their profession is one in which obedience is placed above 'reasoning why' – with the result that they are particularly prone to government propaganda, which in recent years has equated student demonstrators with terrorists and communists. Many of the police come from underprivileged homes where educational opportunities are lacking. This leads them to resent affluent and privileged students. The police see themselves as defenders of white civilization and students as the enemy of the State. Students see the police as the outward and visible sign of a corrupt system. It does not require much insight to realise that they are two factions which should be kept apart.

The article was picked up by the Afrikaans newspaper *Die Vaderland*, which in a front page article in bold letters proclaimed the article as a smear on the police. 'The implication is clear,' it stated, 'the police come from bad homes and are uneducated.'[104]

I immediately wrote a letter to *Die Vaderland* protesting that it had misinterpreted my article. It was not intended to be insulting, I wrote, but simply meant as a sociological explanation for why the police used excessive force against students.[105] But this was of little avail. Our family was subjected to a concerted campaign of harassment that was described by the Afrikaans newspaper *Rapport* as 'terror'.[106] Although one newspaper suggested that a radical right-wing guerrilla group was responsible, Jane and I suspected that the campaign was orchestrated by the police. In any event we took precautions by barricading the windows of Jackie's and Justin's bedrooms to protect them.

This harassment had both a frightening and, in retrospect, humorous side. Early morning phone calls threatened me with dire consequences if I did not leave the country. In response we disconnected our phone and boarded up our windows lest a bomb be thrown at them, as had happened to other critics of the regime. Less threatening, but more annoying, were the unsolicited loads of coal and sand delivered COD – cash on delivery – and dumped in our driveway; the unordered taxis that arrived at our front gate; and the advertisement placed in *The Star* for the rent of our house at a ridiculously low rental. This advertisement, which inflated the number of rooms in our house and added a swimming pool to its attractions, not surprisingly resulted in a stream of persons knocking at our front door demanding to rent our house. Such harassment was apparently the strategy of the police for dealing with those they did not like. Professor Kobus van Rooyen, chairman of the Publications Appeal Board, had his house advertised for sale at a third of its market value after the board had refused to ban the movie *Cry Freedom*, about the life and death of Steve Biko, in 1988.[107]

Death threats, by phone or by letter, were a regular occurrence. Generally, I took the view that anyone who would threaten to kill me had no intention of carrying out his threat. Sometime in the mid-1970s, however, Jane and I both received a spate of threatening postcards, directed at ourselves and our children. As I believed these threats emanated from the police, I phoned the head of the security police, Brigadier Johan Coetzee, and asked him to call off the police. Of course, he denied police involvement but promised to send a senior officer in the regular police force to investigate my complaint.

Warrant Officer Van Rensburg accordingly arrived to take a statement. He then proceeded to visit Jane on several occasions to discuss who might be making death threats and why. Jane soon realized that he was from the security police and not the regular police force. Consequently she refused to serve him tea in our house as she felt the presence of a security officer who had probably tortured people would contaminate the house. This resulted in her holding discussions with him in the garden. These discussions, Jane told me, became very heated when she berated him for working for the apartheid state and warned him of the consequences that might follow in a democratic South Africa. At one of these meetings he expressed an interest in the garden and asked Jane about a particular garden shrub and where he might find it.

A few months later, there was a stand-off between security police and students at Wits when the police sought to invade the offices of the Student Representative Council. The vice-chancellor asked me to mediate and, when I arrived at the scene, I saw Warrant Officer Van Rensburg at the head of the police force. He hailed me as an old friend, saying, 'John, you remember that garden shrub your wife told me about? Please tell her I have managed to find it.' Needless to say, my credibility with Wits' radical students suffered drastically.

The bugging of phones was widespread. Jane and I knew that our phone was bugged when we had a phone installed in a new house within twenty-four hours at a time when most people waited for several months. This meant that we were careful what to say when we made calls. That our phone was bugged was confirmed when my old university friend Marius Schoon, who was house-arrested to our house after serving a twelve-year sentence for sabotage, was staying with us. One day when I tried to make a phone call I was put through directly to police headquarters.

Bugging led to paranoia on the part of many. Every click or irregular noise on a phone was attributed to security police bugging. Whites who had no political connection and who refused to associate themselves with anti-government speech or action were often convinced that their phones were being tapped. One heard such claims made with regularity at dinner parties in Johannesburg's Northern Suburbs by people who had no anti-apartheid involvement whatsoever. It made them feel important and was advanced as a justification for doing nothing. But such claims could not always be dismissed.

Many who were paranoid about police surveillance had good cause to fear. Joel Carlson, my instructing attorney in the SWAPO case, believed that there were bugging devices everywhere. If he wished to tell me something sensitive, he would take me into the garden and tell me not to stand near any tree or shrub lest it be bugged. There was a broken-down car in the street outside his house, which he was convinced contained a monitoring system to bug his house. He called the traffic authorities repeatedly to remove the car without any success. I thought he was simply being paranoid. The day after Joel fled the country to seek asylum in the United States, the car disappeared. Paranoia was often justified.

Police surveillance was a regular topic of conversation. At parties attended by a banned person – that is, a person prohibited from attending social gatherings – the prospect of a knock on the door added a touch of excitement to the evening.

We, whites on the left, were prepared to risk police action, particularly when we knew it did not carry serious consequences with it. We broadly knew how much we could risk in a state characterized by arbitrary police action. But the overwhelming majority of whites were not prepared to take any risks. They refused to criticize the government publicly or privately, stayed well clear of protest action and, if they were politically aware, were careful to confine their political activities to those of recognized white political parties.

Generally, whites preferred not to know what was happening in South Africa lest it have consequences for them. The reputation of the police force succeeded in producing compliance in white South African society. Most whites believed that the law imposed more restraints on personal freedom and freedom of speech than it did. This was safer. The success of a police state depends not upon the limits imposed by law and police action but on the limits perceived by the silent majority. Their acquiescence is assured by their perception of what they may not do.

In 1984 I was arrested at a demonstration and detained in police cells for several hours. Demonstrations against government action along Jan Smuts Avenue on the perimeter of Wits University were a regular feature of university life. While the assembly of persons out of doors was prohibited by the Internal Security Act of 1982, it was generally accepted that no unlawful assembly or gathering took place if protesters stood at least ten metres apart with placards denouncing the government. One afternoon I was participating in a demonstration called by the Black Sash, the South African Council of Churches and the Detainees' Parents Support Committee (DPSC) to protest against detentions without trial, and advised protesters not to stand too close to each other. Suddenly a posse of policemen arrived in police vans and arrested thirty-five protesters, including Max Coleman of the DPSC and me. We were taken to the Hillbrow police station and held in cells for about four hours before being released on warning to appear in court the next day on charges under the Internal Security Act.[108] The following day the case was postponed pending further investigations. Later the prosecution was dropped, no doubt because the state realized that it had been a lawful protest.

Jane and I were placed under intense police surveillance as a result of my friendship with Marius Schoon with whom I had been a fellow student at Stellenbosch's Wilgenhof residence. Initially Marius had been an ardent supporter of the government but gradually he changed his views to a moderate anti-government position. We belonged to a discussion group that debated contemporary issues and over the weekends we frequently climbed the mountains surrounding Stellenbosch. After he left university Marius moved further to the left, becoming an active member of the Congress of Democrats, and in 1964 he and two other activists were persuaded by an agent provocateur to plant a bomb at the Hillbrow police station. The bomb failed to explode. He was arrested and sentenced to twelve years for the crime of sabotage. While he was in prison, his wife Diana committed suicide and his parents died. I visited Marius irregularly while he was in prison in Pretoria, and Jane and I also spent time with his daughter Jane.

When Marius was released in 1976, he had nowhere to live and asked to stay with us. At the time we realized that this act of friendship would be misconstrued as support for Marius's political beliefs, but we took the view that friendship should prevail over fear of what the authorities might think. Jane and I believed that he would be with us for a couple of weeks, which would allow him time to find his own accommodation. As was the rule with the release of political prisoners, Marius was served with a banning order that confined him to our house from 6 pm to 6 am. It was interesting having Marius with us and hearing his amusing anecdotal experiences of his new-found freedom. Banks and shops found it difficult to deal with someone who had been in limbo for twelve years and spoke unashamedly about his prison years. But two weeks passed and the security police refused to vary his house arrest order to allow him to move. I pleaded with Brigadier Johan Coetzee of the security police, as our house was really too small to accommodate him and he had found a cottage in which to live. But the security police refused to allow Marius to leave for six weeks. No doubt they wished to inflict as much inconvenience as possible on all of us.

As a former political prisoner, Marius was unable to find employment. I visited him in the cottage of a friend to which he had been house-arrested after he left us. There he told me of his friendship with Jeanette Curtis, also a banned person, with whom he was by law not allowed to communicate. Later they married, fled the country and joined the ANC in Botswana where they stayed until they received a tip-off that their lives were in danger from the South African security police. While he was in Botswana, I wrote to him about my attempt to persuade the British government to grant him asylum in the UK. When they left Botswana, Marius and Jeanette moved to Angola. There a bomb intended for Marius, delivered by Craig Williamson of the security police, killed Jeanette and her daughter. Marius returned to South Africa in 1990 and died in 1997. He unsuccessfully contested the granting of amnesty to Craig Williamson before the Truth and Reconciliation Commission.

In 1982 a mysterious pamphlet titled '… And just who is professor Dugard?' from a group calling itself 'Delta 4' was widely distributed to the media and the general public. After a comprehensive and accurate account of my academic qualifications, it declared that 'one might almost be fooled into regarding dear John as a pillar of our society'. But, it continued, 'there is another side to John Dugard. A sinister side which remains secret. One may almost say a hidden agenda which rules his life. And this is his involvement with and support for the policies of the South African Communist Party (SACP) and African National Congress (ANC).' The pamphlet then recounted statements that I had made criticizing the government and calling for captured members of the ANC to be treated as prisoners of war and not criminals, which supposedly provided evidence of my support for the SACP and ANC. It concluded by stating that 'Dugard's support for the ANC and SACP is not surprising. It stems from his friendship with the white communist Marius Schoon … When Schoon got out of prison in 1976 he went to live with Dugard. Dugard also tried, unsuccessfully, to allow Schoon to settle in the UK … Schoon remains in secret contact with Dugard … Surprised? Remember Dugard is not alone – he is a member of the ANC's secret fifth column in our country.'

That this document emanated from the security police became apparent when police archives were opened after the fall of apartheid. These revealed that I was on a list of 'politically sensitive persons to be kept under investigation'. An operational analysis of the 'Schoon Network' commissioned by Captain Craig Williamson, dated 8 September 1980, said of me:

> He is an agent of influence in bringing the South African legal system into disrepute in the sense that all his activities have propaganda value for the Left. In addition he had clandestine contact with the ANC/CP as the letter below demonstrates,[109] but the precise nature and scope of his relationship with the ANC/CP is not known. It is suggested, from the correspondence and from the present roles of Schoon and Dugard, that Dugard's clandestine relationship with Schoon and therefore the ANC/CP persists. Dugard could be assisting the ANC/CP in requests for information, and could even be acting on suggestions from the ANC/CP.[110]

Although I voted for the Progressive Party and advised Helen Suzman, I was not a member of any political party or movement. I believed that a professor of law doing the kind of work in which I was engaged should remain independent. Ideologically I was best classified as liberal (with a small 'l') or social democrat. Certainly I was never a member of the ANC or SACP. No one ever tried to recruit me for either of these parties because, I suspect, I was known to be an independent liberal. So the security police got it wrong. Certainly the ANC never believed that I was in any way affiliated with it after 1990 when I was repeatedly passed over for appointment to meaningful office in post-apartheid South Africa by the ANC government.

13

The death penalty

The death penalty was a central feature of the apartheid state's system of criminal justice. Until 1958 there were three capital crimes – murder, treason and rape. Only in the case of murder where the court found no extenuating or mitigating circumstances to be present was the death penalty mandatory. After 1958 a number of other crimes were made punishable by death: robbery and housebreaking with aggravating circumstances, kidnapping, sabotage and participation in terroristic activities.

The death penalty was part of criminal justice before 1948 but was imposed with increased vigour after apartheid was instituted. During the 1960s the annual toll of the gallows exceeded a hundred and Barend van Niekerk, South Africa's foremost abolitionist campaigner, estimated that South Africa accounted for 47 per cent of the world's executions.[111] In 1987, 164 persons were executed in South Africa, which placed South Africa second only to Iran in the number of executions.

Most of those executed were convicted of murder, and most were black. Of some three thousand persons executed after 1910, only about a hundred were white. No white man was ever hanged for the rape of a black woman and only a handful were hanged for the murder of a black person. Conversely, blacks convicted of the murder or rape of whites were generally hanged. Racial discrimination in the imposition of the death penalty was obvious, but in 1970 Barend van Niekerk was prosecuted for contempt of court arising out of an article in the *South African Law Journal*,[112] which examined the evidence supporting the discriminatory imposition of the death penalty. Although Van Niekerk was acquitted on the ground that he lacked the necessary intention for the crime of contempt of court, the presiding judge took the opportunity to rebuke him for writing an article which lowered the esteem in which the judiciary was held.[113] Although this prosecution succeeded in stifling debate about the death penalty, the article did succeed in reducing the number of executions.

Race was not the only factor that made the imposition of the death penalty arbitrary. Most persons charged with capital crimes were unable to afford counsel and were defended by young, inexperienced lawyers appointed by the trial court in co-operation with the Bar Council. Consequently legal defence provided in capital cases was seldom of the standard of that in other criminal proceedings where the accused was able to instruct his lawyer of choice. In addition, most capital trials involving black accused required the services of an interpreter who interpreted the testimony of witnesses from one of the African languages into English or Afrikaans. Inevitably error crept into the nuances of language, often with disastrous results for the accused. My own experience as a young advocate at the Durban Bar made me fully aware of these failings in the administration of justice. I had defended some seventy persons charged with capital crimes, of whom nine had been sentenced to death, at a time when I lacked any experience as an advocate. And I had a client who was sentenced to death and executed after a dispute about the correct interpretation of his evidence.

The death penalty was rarely imposed for a political crime, such as treason, sabotage or terrorism, or a politically motivated crime, except where it was accompanied by murder. John Harris, a member of the African Resistance Movement, was executed in 1965 for placing a bomb at the Johannesburg main railway station which killed an innocent bystander.[114] Solomon Mahlangu was hanged in 1979 for the death of two civilians killed in a police chase after he had returned from military training in Angola. Andrew Zondo was executed in 1986 for detonating a bomb in a shopping centre, killing three adults and two children. And there were others. But in most cases either the judge, as in the Rivonia trial, or the executive, as in the 1969 trial of the SWAPO leadership, was sensitive to the likely international consequences of executing a high-profile political offender and preferred a sentence of life imprisonment.

I gave expert evidence in several cases in South Africa and Namibia on the trend in international law to treat members of liberation movements as prisoners of war rather than as ordinary criminals, in order to make judges aware of the international implications of the death sentence. In most cases this argument succeeded but not in the case of Thelle Simon Mogoerane, Jerry Joseph Mosololi and Thabo Marcus Motaung,[115] charged with attacking a police station, who had the misfortune to appear before one of South Africa's most notorious 'hanging judges', David Curlewis. Judge Curlewis made it clear that he was not interested in international law and that he found my evidence a waste of time by placing his head between his hands on the bench and feigning sleep while I was testifying. They were duly sentenced to death and executed.

The abolitionist cause was never popular as most whites saw the death penalty as a necessary protection against the perceived savagery of blacks. In 1969 Ellison Kahn of Wits, an ardent abolitionist, and Barend van Niekerk launched the Society for the Abolition of the Death Penalty in South Africa (SADPSA). In the same year Helen Suzman proposed a private member's motion in Parliament,[116] calling for the appointment of a commission of inquiry into capital punishment, but no other MP was prepared to support this motion. SADPSA was revived in 1988 by the Centre for Applied Legal Studies, in response to the execution of 164 persons in 1987 and a cause célèbre involving the sentencing to death of six persons for their participation in a riot resulting in the killing of the deputy mayor of Sharpeville,[117] in which Edwin Cameron played a major role in securing a reprieve. This new concern resulted in a drop in the number of executions to 53 in 1989 and the imposition by the government of a moratorium on hangings in 1990. The death penalty was not abolished by South Africa's post-apartheid Constitution. However, in one of its earliest decisions, *S* v. *Makwanyane*, the new Constitutional Court unanimously held the death penalty to be unconstitutional.[118]

14

Censorship

There were a host of laws imposing prohibitions or restraints on freedom of expression in apartheid South Africa. Together these laws created a culture of political conformity in white society. The freedom to express dissenting political views was severely curtailed by the Suppression of Communism Act of 1950, renamed the Internal Security Act in 1976, when it was amended to cover all forms of subversion. In introducing the amendment the minister of justice stated that 'All communists are subverters, but all subverters are not communists and we would like to reflect this in the Act.'[119] The ideology of communism that it was forbidden to advocate in terms of this law included any doctrine 'which aims at bringing about any political, industrial, social or economic change' or 'which aims at the encouragement of feelings of hostility between the European and non-European races' by 'the promotion of disturbance or disorder, by unlawful acts or omissions'.[120] Although it was a criminal offence to advocate communism so defined, few prosecutions were brought. Instead the government preferred to ban persons suspected of promoting this form of political change by executive order, which meant that they might not be quoted at all – in addition to being prohibited from attending meetings of more than two persons. Newspapers that were deemed by the government to advocate 'communism' might also be silenced by the executive, as was illustrated by the 1977 banning of *The World*, the newspaper with the largest circulation among blacks. And, of course, political organizations, such as the South African Communist Party, that promoted 'communism' were proscribed. The promotion of feelings of hostility between the races was also prohibited and punishable,[121] but this law was interpreted to cover only incitement to racial hostility by blacks and not the inflammatory racist comments by whites which were part of accepted political rhetoric.

The common law crimes of contempt of court and criminal defamation were used to silence academic critics – as shown in chapter 6 – and the press. I recall a case in 1979 in which the editor of the *Sunday Express*, Rex Gibson, and journalist Jennifer Hyman were prosecuted for contempt of court and criminal defamation arising out of an article that criticized courts for allowing inexperienced advocates, appointed by the state, to represent political detainees. As I had made a statement quoted in the article claiming that many state-appointed advocates were unqualified to provide proper legal defence in complicated security trials, I was called to testify. The case was heard by Judge John Milne, the foremost liberal judge on the Natal Bench, and prosecuted by Cecil Rees, whom I had confronted as a junior advocate in my days at the Durban Bar. In the course of my evidence I mentioned that there were many complex repressive and discriminatory laws to be interpreted in a security trial. This incensed Rees, who claimed that there were no such laws on the South African statute book and demanded that I identify any of them. I had recently completed writing *Human Rights and the South African Legal Order* and the full arsenal of the laws of apartheid was fresh in my mind. I began to list these laws, only to be interrupted by a loud complaint from Rees to Judge Milne 'that the witness is making a political speech'. Milne quietly replied that Rees had asked for such information and ruled that I be allowed to continue with my litany of the laws of apartheid. Rees was livid. Rex Gibson and Jennifer Hyman were acquitted.

There was a separate legal regime for the censorship – banning – of literary, political, scientific and artistic publications and of movies. This regime underwent several changes during the apartheid era. Before 1963 censorship was effected by a variety of statutes which provided mainly for the banning of imported works and resulted in the banning of such literary works as D.H. Lawrence's *Lady Chatterley's Lover*, Nabokov's *Lolita*, Steinbeck's *The Wayward Bus* and Henry Miller's *Tropic of Cancer.* In 1963 a law[122] was passed to create a Publications Control Board which was charged with the task of deciding on the compatibility of publications, films and plays with standards of indecency and obscenity. In the ten years of its existence this board prohibited over eight thousand publications, including works by some of South Africa's best-known writers, such as André Brink's *Kennis van die Aand*. The government's objection to this scheme was that it provided for a right of appeal to the Supreme Court, which set aside a number of bannings on the grounds that they misjudged contemporary standards of indecency and obscenity. Consequently in 1974 a new law, the Publications Act,[123] was introduced.

Under the new scheme anonymous lay committees, meeting in secret, were empowered to ban the distribution and possession of publications (excluding newspapers) and films considered to be 'undesirable' on the ground that they were 'indecent or obscene', blasphemous, ridiculed any section of the inhabitants of the Republic, were harmful to race relations or were 'prejudicial to the security of the state, the general welfare or the peace and good order'.[124] Appeal against the decision of such a committee lay to the Publications Appeal Board (PAB), a non-judicial body, but there was no appeal to a court of law.

The first chairman of the PAB was a retired judge, J.H. ('Lammie') Snyman, with whom I had clashed over the application of the Terrorism Act. He brought with him a reputation for allegiance to the government and narrow-mindedness. That this reputation was deserved was soon apparent when the Appeal Board upheld the ban on an Afrikaans literary masterpiece, *Magersfontein, O Magersfontein!* by Etienne Leroux. Appearing before him was not a pleasure, as I discovered when I appealed against the banning for both distribution and possession of a publication of the Institute of Race Relations on *Detention without Trial in South Africa 1976–7*, which had been banned because its portrayal of the torture of detainees (including Steve Biko) allegedly gave support to the Communist Party and the ANC and harmed South Africa's reputation. My argument that sensory deprivation was a form of torture, and that it was this practice and the deaths in detention rather than the publication that harmed South Africa's reputation, was not well received.[125]

In the light of the appointment of Judge Snyman as chairman of the PAB, the standards applied and the arbitrary nature of the whole system, most writers and publishers decided not to appeal to the board lest this be seen as lending legitimacy to the system. Also, the high cost of litigation and the small return that might be expected from the unbanning of a book deterred appeals. The result was that appeals were rare and the decisions of the anonymous committees went largely unchallenged.

The Centre for Applied Legal Studies embarked on a challenge to the system, firstly, by publicizing and scrutinizing the standards applied, and secondly, by providing free legal services to writers and publishers.

The hitherto unpublished reasons advanced by the PAB for its decisions were compiled by Louise Silver in a *Digest of Decisions of the Publications Appeal Board*. Merely by publishing the outrageous reasons advanced by the board for banning publications brought the whole system into ridicule. For instance, the publication of the reasons advanced by the PAB for finding the depiction of nudity in a publication obscene, because it revealed the shadow of a nipple or the hint of pubic hair, spoke for itself. There was no need for comment on such reasoning.

Our second strategy was to argue appeals without fee before the board.

Gilbert Marcus, Edwin Cameron and I appeared regularly before the Appeal Board on behalf of publishers, film producers and writers. By insisting that the board be guided by established common law principles and the jurisprudence of foreign courts, particularly the US Supreme Court, we succeeded in compelling the PAB to adopt a more transparent and coherent approach to its decision-making. There is no doubt that we were assisted in this task by the appointment of Professor Kobus van Rooyen as chairman of the board in 1980. Van Rooyen,[126] who had served as an acquiescent deputy to Lammie Snyman, was a professor of criminal law at the University of Pretoria. I knew him fairly well at the time as an academic colleague and as the son of a colleague of my father in the inspectorate of black education.

Unlike his predecessor, Van Rooyen proved to be receptive to the arguments that CALS lawyers raised, and we had an extraordinarily high success rate, securing the release of books, films and journals. Writers who had resisted appeal to the PAB on the ground that they did not wish to give legitimacy to the system requested their publishers or producers to appeal on their behalf. In this way I was able to secure the release of Sipho Sepamla's *A Ride on the Whirlwind* (1981), set during the 1976 student rebellion. The books of African writers were particularly prone to censorship. It seemed that the committees simply banned works by African writers without reading them. I successfully appealed against the ban imposed on the entire Heinemann African Writers Series by calling my Wits colleague, the writer Es'kia Mphahlele, to testify about the literary merits of African writing. Critics of the system were reluctantly obliged to admit that there was merit in appealing to the PAB.

The strongest critic of the censorship system was a good friend – the Nobel laureate Nadine Gordimer – who took a very firm position on appeals to the board. It was not a court of law, had no legitimacy and should not be given credibility by invoking it, she insisted. I argued with her that the Appeal Board should be used, particularly after it acquired a progressive chairman, as this would put the book or film back into circulation. She was adamant in her refusal to co-operate with the PAB. 'Nadine,' I would say, 'it is fine for you to adopt a high-handed approach because your books that are banned in South Africa (as many were) are published abroad and read there. But what about black and Afrikaans writers whose books are only published locally? When their book is banned, that is the end of the book.' This argument failed to convince her.

In the 1980s the BBC made a six-part film of Nadine's short stories in *Six Feet of the Country*, but predictably this series was banned for viewing in South Africa. Nadine called me about this. 'John,' she said, 'you know that in principle I cannot and will not appeal the banning of *Six Feet of the Country*.' I waited for her to continue. 'But would you be prepared to appeal on behalf of the producer?' We both laughed. She was clearly embarrassed. I took the ban on appeal and it succeeded. *Six Feet of the Country* was released and Nadine was happy. Despite this, she remained opposed to working with the PAB.

Nadine was a strong-minded woman with a sharp intellect whose writings captured the very essence of apartheid South Africa. We wrote a monograph together on *What Happened to Burger's Daughter, or How South African Censorship Works*,[127] in which we examined the reasons advanced for the banning of her 1979 book *Burger's Daughter*, which portrayed a South African family that supported the South African Communist Party. Modelled as the characters were on Bram Fischer and his daughter Ilse, the book was banned on the grounds that it propagated communist doctrines and threatened the security of the state. The ban was, however, set aside by the Appeal Board after several months.

While I focused mainly on appeals in respect of literary works, Gilbert Marcus argued a number of important appeals affecting political matters. In 1983 Van Rooyen asked Gilbert to argue the ban on possession of pamphlets containing the Freedom Charter of 1955. When Gilbert's arguments succeeded in having the Freedom Charter unbanned, the security police angrily reproached Kobus for having appointed a 'communist' to argue the case.[128] Gilbert was also successful in having the popular newspaper *New Nation* unbanned during the state of emergency. This time the government's anger was directed at Van Rooyen himself when the minister of home affairs, Stoffel Botha, proclaimed, 'Van Rooyen, fuck the reasons for your judgment.'[129]

There was an exceptional side to CALS's association with the PAB. This was the only occasion on which we worked *within* the political system to advance human rights. This was made possible by Kobus van Rooyen, who was committed to administering the system of censorship in such a way that it did not encroach unreasonably on freedom of expression. Under his leadership the PAB was prepared to be guided by arguments premised on evidence of changing standards of indecency, obscenity and state security. He led the PAB away from the narrow, Calvinist philosophy of Lammie Snyman into a relatively enlightened system that accorded with contemporary literary standards. Sadly, the role he played has not received the credit it deserves.[130]

Books were mainly banned for distribution, and sometimes possession. Prosecution for production of an undesirable work was extremely rare. On one such occasion I represented an avant-garde Afrikaans writer, Dan Roodt, who was prosecuted for publishing a radical literary journal called *Taaldoos*.[131] The offensive article that led to the prosecution was a satire directed at the sexual proclivities of the Springbok rugby team, for whom more satisfaction was derived from feeling each other under the showers after the game than the game itself. I attempted to defend Roodt by explaining that he was a serious literary scholar influenced by Michael Foucault. Experts on literary theory, such as Professor Gerrit Olivier of Wits, were called in his defence. But the magistrate was unconvinced by this show of literary erudition and convicted Roodt, a conviction that was upheld on appeal. Roodt received only a suspended sentence, but I had the distinct impression that the appeal judge was so angered by the satire directed at one of South Africa's most holy institutions – the Springbok rugby team – that he was inclined to send Roodt to prison. After the political transformation Roodt, ever provocative, emerged as a spokesman for the extreme Afrikaner right wing.

Self-censorship was a major problem. The editors of newspapers and other publications worked closely with their legal advisers to ensure that they did not transgress any of the myriad laws restricting freedom of speech. Inevitably editors erred on the side of caution and in so doing engaged in self-censorship. The Prisons Act,[132] which made it an offence to publish information about the treatment of prisoners, for instance, discouraged the press from commenting on prison conditions – particularly after the trial in 1969 of the editor of the *Rand Daily Mail*, Laurence Gandar, and journalist Benjamin Pogrund for publishing a series of articles exposing brutal prison conditions.[133]

It was an offence under the Prisons Act to publish photographs of a prisoner. The result was that pictures of Nelson Mandela and other political prisoners were prohibited in South Africa while they were widely displayed abroad, particularly in the 'Release Mandela' campaign. I was involved in a dispute in the late 1980s between the former editor of *Drum* magazine, Jim Bailey, and one of South Africa's leading photographers, Jürgen Schadeberg, over the publication of a picture of Mandela as a boxer taken before he went to prison. Jim had been advised, correctly, by his lawyers that it was unlawful to publish such a picture under the Prisons Act. Schadeberg and I argued that pictures of Mandela were common currency abroad, that the South African authorities would be too embarrassed to prosecute the publication of a picture of Mandela, and that we should take the risk of publishing. We prevailed over Jim and Mandela's picture was duly published. As we had forecast, there was no response from the authorities.

15

Judging the judges

Justice in South Africa was administered by magistrates and judges. Magistrates were appointed from the ranks of the civil service. They were bureaucrats whose first allegiance in practice was to the government. While they administered the law competently in the magistrate's courts in disputes with no political connection, they could not be expected to behave independently in the application of the laws of apartheid. Judges who presided over civil and criminal law matters in the provincial divisions and the court of appeal of the Supreme Court occupied a different status. With few exceptions they were barristers in private legal practice appointed by the executive but with tenure until the age of seventy. Inevitably the government took care to appoint judges who it believed were sympathetic to its policies or, at least, would not challenge the apartheid system. Judges prided themselves on their detachment from the executive and their independence. Indeed, the government protested the independence of the judges more vigorously than the judges themselves. The ultimate interpretation and application of the law was in their hands and the reputation of South Africa's system of justice was measured by their performance. It was essential therefore that the government could boast that the law was applied in a completely independent fashion by an independent judiciary as this conferred legitimacy on the system.

There were some hundred and twenty judges of the Supreme Court at the end of the apartheid era and fourteen judges of appeal. Judges in the provincial divisions sat alone or in courts of three or five judges, while the Appellate Division usually sat with five judges. Judges had jurisdiction over major civil disputes and serious crimes, particularly those that carried the death sentence. Only judges might impose sentence of death. Judges were all white males for most of the apartheid era. Only in the last decade was a woman appointed. No black lawyer was ever appointed as a judge although there was no law prohibiting such an appointment. The majority of judges were drawn from the Afrikaans community. Most judges, whether Afrikaans- or English-speaking, were conservative by nature and outlook, but a minority, comprising both Afrikaans-speaking and English-speaking judges, were of liberal outlook.

The South African judiciary was modelled on the English judiciary. Judges did not wear wigs, but in most other ways they followed the traditions and dress code of the English judiciary. Like England, South Africa had a divided legal profession, with only barristers – called advocates – entitled to appear before the judges of the Supreme Court. Attorneys, or solicitors, who dealt directly with the public, enjoyed a right of audience only in the magistrate's courts. Only advocates might be appointed as judges.

South Africa, like the United Kingdom, recognized the supremacy of Parliament. This meant that, unlike American judges, South African judges had no power to review and set aside legislation enacted by Parliament. The Tricameral Constitution of 1983, like its predecessor, expressly declared that 'no court of law shall be competent to inquire into or pronounce upon the validity of an Act of Parliament'.[134] But there was room for judicial creativity in the interpretation of statutes, the review of executive action and subordinate legislation (enacted by authorities other than Parliament), and the development of common law. In such cases the judicial process was essentially a choice between competing interpretations and principles. And, of course, judges exercised a choice in fact-finding when they were required to choose between conflicting evidence. This creativity was recognized in cases not involving 'political' issues, that is, most of the work of the judiciary. However, when the repressive and discriminatory laws of apartheid were in issue, or when the person accused was alleged to have violated one of the laws of apartheid, both judges and government tended to deny that judges had any choice, any room for manoeuvre. In such cases, they claimed the judicial decision was purely mechanical: judges were merely applying the law of the land, the law of a sovereign Parliament in accordance with their oath of office. In this way they were absolved of moral responsibility.

For the first fifteen years of the apartheid era, the myth of the mechanical judge who bore no responsibility for applying the laws of apartheid was maintained. Of course, during the constitutional crisis of the 1950s involving the removal of the coloured voters from the common voters' roll there was much debate about the powers of the judiciary, and judges were praised or criticized depending on the position they took. But that was an overtly political issue involving the composition of Parliament, and the moral choice that judges made was obvious. In cases dealing with the interpretation of the laws of apartheid, there was, however, little critical comment on judicial decisions.

The situation changed radically in 1966 after the appearance of the article by Tony Mathews and Ronald Albino in the *South African Law Journal*[135] examining decisions of the Appeal Court on the interpretation of the detention-without-trial laws, which put in question the impartiality and integrity of the judiciary. Predictably, both government and judiciary were outraged by this article. Next came the article by Barend van Niekerk on the implementation of the death penalty, also published in the *South African Law Journal*,[136] which found that statistics showed clearly that the death penalty was applied in a discriminatory manner against blacks. This resulted in the prosecution of Van Niekerk for contempt of court.[137]

In 1971 I delivered my Wits inaugural lecture as a professor in which I examined decisions of the courts in matters of race and security and concluded that judges were influenced by an inarticulate premise based on racial and social prejudices.[138]

The fourth act of academic revolt was that of Barend van Niekerk again. In 1972, at a public protest meeting in the Durban City Hall against the implementation of the detention-without-trial laws, which had resulted in a number of deaths, he castigated judges for failing to condemn the Terrorism Act, which authorized indefinite detention without trial, and called on them to 'kill' the law by refusing to admit evidence that had been procured under this law. For this Van Niekerk was tried and convicted of contempt of court. This conviction was upheld by the Appellate Division,[139] presided over by Chief Justice Ogilvie Thompson, who made it clear in remarks to members of the Johannesburg Bar shortly afterwards that he was furious over the criticism directed at courts by academics and was determined to stop it.

But now the genie was out of the bottle. Academic criticism of the courts could not be stopped by the contempt-of-court power. The close examination of judicial decisions on matters affecting race and security became part of academic discourse and publication, albeit by only a small number of academics. Books and law review articles began to appear examining the manner in which judges had exercised their choice in the interpretation of statutes.[140] Judges were identified as pro-executive or 'liberal', depending on their interpretation of the law.

Other issues concerning the judiciary that had hitherto been taboo were also now raised. While it was well known to practising lawyers that some judges were more inclined to hang than others, it now became commonplace to discuss the identity of hanging judges. After all, statistics showed that only about a quarter of the judges had imposed sentence of death and that some three judges had been responsible for most of the death sentences. Another issue that had previously been kept out of debate was the manner in which the chief justice of the Appellate Division, Pierre Rabie, had carefully allocated cases with a political colour to judges who could be relied on to find in favour of the government. I drew this to the attention of the 1983 Hoexter Commission of Inquiry into the Structure and Functioning of the Courts.[141] Judge Hoexter expressed his concern about this matter, but the practice continued in the Appeal Court until the retirement of Judge Rabie in 1989.

The government was not happy about this development, to put it mildly. This questioning of the independence of the judiciary meant that the government could no longer invoke judicial decisions upholding the repressive and discriminatory laws of apartheid as impartial and objective interpretations of the law, thereby providing legitimacy to the system. In 1988 I was rebuked for this by President P.W. Botha in response to a letter I had written to him complaining about the government's threat to introduce legislation to overrule the decision of the Appeal Court in the *Moutse* case. He wrote:

> First of all I wish to reiterate the Government's high regard for the abilities, independence and proud traditions of our judiciary ... The reputation of our courts certainly concerns us all. On many occasions criticism has been levelled against our courts and the Appellate Division in particular: some judges have been branded as politically partisan and executive-minded in their approach, while some benches have been labelled conservative, as opposed to libertarian. It is sometimes even asked suggestively why so-called political trials are only heard by certain judges. Such unjustified and destructive criticism does nothing to enhance the reputation of our courts. On the contrary, it is calculated to achieve exactly the opposite here and abroad – a matter which surely deserves your consideration as well.[142]

Although judges had ceased to be a protected species, most remained impervious to academic criticism and continued to interpret the law generously in favour of the government. A small group of judges, however, became concerned about the question whether their presence as judges lent legitimacy to the apartheid regime. Where the law or the facts were unclear, these judges now distanced themselves from the executive and interpreted the law in favour of individual liberty and racial equality. This was particularly apparent in Natal where a number of judges, led by the judge president of the Natal Division, John Milne, asserted their independence with new vigour. So much so that whenever it was possible, counsel brought challenges to the law in Natal. This was apparent during the state of emergency in the 1980s when the Supreme Court of Natal became the preferred forum for challenges to the law.

A new question concerning the judiciary now arose, and this was whether the limited power that judges had to interpret the law benevolently justified 'good judges' remaining in office. In 1983 Raymond Wacks, a former student of mine at Wits, who had succeeded Barend van Niekerk as professor at the University of Natal, after the latter's untimely death, delivered his inaugural address in which he called on liberal judges to resign because the effect of their remaining on the bench was to legitimize an illegitimate system.[143] In essence he argued that the limited power of judges to do good was outweighed by the evil that their presence on the bench brought by providing legitimacy to a wicked legal system. I challenged him, arguing that a 'moral' judge could do more good by remaining on the bench and interpreting the law benevolently when possible than by withdrawing from the system and leaving it to 'wicked' judges to administer the law.[144] In support of my argument I cited a comment of my colleague at Wits, Etienne Mureinik, who stated, 'If we argue that moral judges should resign, we can no longer pray, when we go into court as defence counsel, or even as accused, that we find a moral judge on the Bench.'[145]

As was to be expected, my views were greeted with approval by the small band of 'moral' judges on the bench. But to my surprise I now found that I had become popular with more neutral judges who had previously dismissed my harsh criticism of the bench. They were pleased that someone of my stature had defended their decision to remain on the bench. And to my still greater surprise several of these judges now joined the camp of the 'moral judges'.

The best barometer of changing judicial attitudes at the time was provided by the Mount Grace seminars sponsored by the Centre for Applied Legal Studies.

In 1982 I was invited to participate in the Aspen Institute seminar on Justice and Society, held in Aspen, Colorado, and moderated by Harry Blackmun of the US Supreme Court and Norval Morris, professor of criminology at the University of Chicago. The seminar, made up of judges, human rights activists (such as Neelan Tiruchelvam, the Tamil director of the International Centre for Ethnic Studies in Sri Lanka, who was killed by a Tamil Tiger suicide bomber in 1999), academic lawyers, journalists and lawyers in private practice, discussed some of the great moral issues that lawyers, philosophers and writers had confronted. For instance, to prepare us for the debate on the question whether an unjust law should be obeyed, we were required to read Herman Melville's *Billy Budd*, the story of a young English seaman tried and convicted by the ship's captain, despite his belief that Budd was innocent, and executed in order to maintain discipline at sea during the Napoleonic Wars. It is a book that starkly raises the question of obedience to an unjust law. The idyllic setting for the seminar and the ample time allowed for informal discussion over meals and afternoon outings seemed to liberate lawyers from their normal routine and allow them to consider issues often seen to be too academic, or perhaps too challenging.

Could the Aspen experience be used in South Africa? I asked myself. Would it be possible to bring judges and human rights lawyers together in a secluded setting to discuss the real issues facing the law in South Africa, such as the legitimacy of a legal system premised on discrimination and repression, the role of the judge and lawyer in such a system, the problems facing black lawyers in a racist society, the failure of South African law to meet international human rights standards, whether South Africa should aspire to an entrenched Bill of Rights, and so on. Two obstacles presented themselves immediately: firstly, the venue, and secondly, the participation of judges.

The first obstacle was soon overcome. After some searching, Laura Mangan of CALS 'discovered' a small country hotel near to the village of Magaliesburg, situated some thirty or forty kilometres from Johannesburg. Mount Grace, as the hotel was known, was able to accommodate some forty guests, the ideal size for a seminar.[146]

The second obstacle, judicial participation, promised to be more difficult. Richard Goldstone, a 'moral judge' from the Transvaal Provincial Division and a good friend, agreed to participate but predicted that only four or five judges would ever accept an invitation to such a seminar. Richard was proved to be very wrong.

The first seminar, titled ' Access to Justice', was held at Mount Grace one weekend in 1984, under the auspices of the Centre for Applied Legal Studies, with thirty-two participants comprising ten judges, seven advocates, eight attorneys and seven academics. Those invited were expected to read a number of carefully selected law review articles on justice in general and the South African situation in particular. Each topic was briefly introduced and then opened up for debate. Everything was off the record. No minutes were kept and we were all sworn to observe 'Chatham House rules' – that is, no comments to the press and no attribution of views to particular speakers. Sessions were limited in time and ample opportunity was provided for walks in the countryside, volleyball and good meals with an unlimited supply of wine. At that time, all judges were white. However, care was taken to invite the handful of black advocates and attorneys engaged in human rights litigation.

One of the black lawyers who participated in the first seminar was Godfrey Pitje, president of the Black Lawyers Association, who as a young lawyer working in the law office of Mandela and Tambo had resisted the order of a magistrate to sit at a separate table reserved for black lawyers. The decision of the Appellate Division upholding this visible assertion of racial separation and inequality in the administration of justice was one of the most clearly racist decisions of that court.[147] Pitje's presence at this, and subsequent, seminars was a stark reminder of the manner in which judges had collaborated in the construction of the apartheid legal order.

The first seminar was a success. Discussion ranged over a wide number of topics seldom discussed by judges among themselves, let alone with non-judges. No subject was viewed as taboo. New friendships were made. Many judges confessed to me privately that they had never before met socially with a black lawyer.

The Centre for Applied Legal Studies held eight Mount Grace weekend seminars between 1984 and 1991. Over the years more than fifty judges attended the seminars, including a number who were seen as part of the judicial establishment and not known for their sympathies towards human rights activism. I even heard complaints from some judges that they had not been invited. Indeed, many judges viewed an invitation to a Mount Grace seminar as a privilege. What we had not foreseen was that judges would welcome the opportunity to discuss matters that troubled their consciences with activists in a private off-the-record setting. Later seminars included judges and academics from abroad, including Professor Louis Henkin and Jack Greenberg of the Columbia Law School, US federal judges Nathaniel Jones, Marvin Frankel and Leon Higginbotham, Professor Michael Reisman of Yale Law School and Canadian judge Louise Arbour, who later became UN high commissioner for human rights. South Africa's judges seemed to appreciate exchanging ideas with foreign lawyers, who were less aggressive than their South African counterparts. These lawyers did, however, raise the issue of how South African judges were viewed abroad and of the importance of following international standards of justice.

In the late 1980s there was much public debate about new constitutional models. Mount Grace provided judges with an opportunity to discuss issues such as a Bill of Rights and judicial review, in a private setting. Many judges made it clear that they were unhappy about the system under which they operated and how they would prefer to be able to apply a Bill of Rights.

The Mount Grace experience served to demonstrate the value of communication between judges and human rights lawyers. Before Mount Grace some successful judges had seen human rights lawyers as activists determined to destroy the legal system rather than as lawyers concerned about respect for the rule of law. Human rights lawyers, for their part, had all too often seen judges as reactionaries determined to uphold the apartheid state. The Mount Grace seminars made us realize that we shared a common concern for decent legal standards of which we as lawyers could be proud. We might employ different methods to achieve our goals, but ultimately the goals were not very different.

The Mount Grace seminars had a sad ending. In 1991 the Legal Resources Centre held a meeting at Mount Grace which was bugged by the security police. Arthur Chaskalson and I had a meeting with the manager of Mount Grace to discuss this matter. The manager, a former Rhodesian, was quite open with us. 'You know how powerful the security police are and how difficult it would have been for us to refuse,' he said. I was not surprised as I had always assumed that all our meetings at Mount Grace were bugged. That was part of the South African way of life at that time. This revelation, however, made it impossible for us to continue to meet at Mount Grace, as participants wanted some assurances that their views would not be shared with the security police. Many of the judges and lawyers who attended the Mount Grace seminars were to become judges in post-apartheid South Africa.

16

Constitutional debate

Debate over South Africa's constitution was as old as the Union of South Africa itself and, after 1961, that of the Republic of South Africa.

In 1909, when the four former British colonies met to consider the constitution for the Union of South Africa, there were competing visions of how South Africa might best be governed. Some delegates at the National Convention responsible for drafting the constitution, mainly from Natal, wanted a federation, but most supported a centralized system of government. There were lone voices in favour of a Bill of Rights, but this was not a popular cause. There was general support among the delegates for a constitution modelled on that of the United Kingdom, with a sovereign Parliament, no entrenchment of individual rights, and no power conferred on the courts to review Acts of Parliament.[148] The South African constitution of 1909 was, however, a distortion of the Westminster parliamentary system. Parliament was to consist of white members, elected by white voters. The Cape Province was an exception until 1956, for in 1909 the right of qualified non-white voters who had enjoyed the franchise in the Cape Colony was entrenched in the constitution. But African voters were disenfranchised in 1936 and coloured voters in 1956, after a bitter constitutional struggle. The South African Parliament therefore was one in which whites made laws for all the people of South Africa, but in which the majority of the people were not represented. This meant that the foundation of the British system of the supremacy of Parliament – that Parliament represented the will of the people of Britain exercising universal suffrage – was ignored in South Africa.

Although South Africa, like the other British dominions of Australia, Canada and New Zealand, enjoyed de facto independence from Britain after 1910, most white South Africans saw the country as lacking full independence while it retained the British King or Queen as constitutional head of state. So it was that in 1961, following a referendum for whites only, South Africa elected to become a republic, and shortly afterwards to leave the Commonwealth. This brought little change to the system of government. Parliamentary supremacy, exercised by an all-white Parliament, was retained.

In 1983 Parliament changed its structure to accommodate two additional chambers, one for coloureds and another for Indians. But the Tricameral Parliament brought little change. Ultimate power remained with the white chamber in the new Parliament, with coloureds and Indians enjoying token representation while the African people, forming 70 per cent of the population, were completely excluded. They were to exercise their political rights in ethnic legislatures set up in each independent or self-governing Bantustan. Proposals in 1983 for a Bill of Rights were firmly rejected.

The 1983 constitution initiated a new debate about the need to provide constitutional protection for human rights. While most lawyers and critics advocated a Bill of Rights that protected individual civil, political and, possibly, socio-economic rights, the apartheid regime insisted that a Bill of Rights should protect group rights, with the rights of the white group given special protection. At this time I began to raise the question of the wisdom of allowing the existing high courts, which had been discredited under apartheid, to supervise a Bill of Rights and proposed that consideration be given to the establishment of a constitutional court along the lines of such courts in Western Europe.[149]

In 1989 the ANC in exile published its *Constitutional Guidelines for a Democratic South Africa*. These guidelines declared that the constitution of a democratic South Africa should include a Bill of Rights, based on the Freedom Charter, which envisaged the protection of both civil and political and socio-economic rights. Nothing was said about how this Bill of Rights was to be protected.

Until the mid-1980s constitutional debate took place mainly in South Africa itself, among politicians, scholars and civil society. With the ANC and other organizations prohibited from participating in this debate, it meant that the views of the liberation parties were unheard. The exchange of views was aggravated by the perceived prohibition on meetings with the ANC abroad. There were many ways in which the government could have, and in all probability would have, punished South Africans who travelled abroad to hold discussions with members of the ANC. Passports might easily have been withdrawn and a prosecution could possibly have been brought for furthering the aims of the ANC. This was a real, not imagined, threat. This meant that meetings with members of the ANC abroad were carried out with great circumspection. In 1981 I was invited as the first white South African resident to attend a meeting of the Africa-America Institute in Williamsburg, Virginia, and met with Thabo Mbeki and other members of the ANC. One night we gathered in my hotel room for drinks and discussed matters that could in no way be construed as subversion. But afterwards I felt that I had been very daring.

Things began to change in the mid-1980s. In 1986 Pieter de Lange, the head of the Broederbond, met with Thabo Mbeki at a conference in New York. Then in July 1987, the Institute for a Democratic Alternative for South Africa (IDASA), led by the former leader of the Progressive Federal Party, Frederik van Zyl Slabbert, and Alex Boraine, organized a meeting of mainly Afrikaner intellectuals with Mbeki and other leaders of the ANC in Dakar, Senegal, to discuss strategies for bringing about fundamental change in South Africa. This meeting was denounced by President P.W. Botha, but it was difficult for him to take punitive action because at this stage members of South Africa's National Intelligence Service were already holding secret talks with members of the ANC abroad.[150]

During the late 1980s there were a number of meetings of South African businessmen and academics with leaders of the ANC abroad. Lawyers were also part of this process. In 1989 Professor Ronald Dworkin, Oxford University's professor of jurisprudence, asked me to help organize a meeting of South African judges and lawyers and members of the ANC constitutional committee at Nuneham Park near Oxford. The organization of this meeting went well and several judges, including Chief Justice Michael Corbett, agreed to participate. Then, when news of this meeting leaked out, the minister of justice, Kobie Coetsee, issued an order prohibiting judges from attending. Corbett had no alternative but to withdraw, as did some other judges. But many did attend, and a number agreed to come at the last minute when fellow judges withdrew. Those who participated included John Milne, John Didcott, Johann Kriegler, Les Rose Innes, Hannes Fagan, Edwin King and Andrew Wilson – all Mount Grace participants. It was clear that many South African judges were no longer prepared to take orders from the minister of justice. The South African-based contingent included public interest lawyers, legal academics and practitioners while the ANC was represented by Kader Asmal, Albie Sachs, Penuell Maduna and Brigitte Mabandla. And, of course, Ronald Dworkin succeeded in stimulating and directing the course of the debate. We held frank and open talks in an idyllic environment on what form a future South African constitution should take and how lawyers might contribute to achieving this goal.

Later, in August 1989, I participated in a meeting in Lusaka of a delegation from Lawyers for Human Rights led by its president, Jules Browde, and director, Brian Currin, and the ANC leadership comprising Oliver Tambo, Thabo Mbeki,

Joe Slovo, Penuell Maduna, Jack Simons, Brigitte Mabandla, Pallo Jordan and Zola Skweyiya. This meeting was probably more significant than that of Nuneham Park because it provided the political leaders of the ANC with the opportunity to express their views on structures of government, the courts and the protection of human rights.

The meetings at Nuneham Park and Lusaka gave the constitutional debate a touch of reality that was lacking in such debates in South Africa itself. At both these meetings I was impressed with the commitment of the ANC to a constitutional democracy that included a Bill of Rights.

17

Apartheid, international law and the international community

South Africa employed a highly legalistic approach to the United Nations and the international community during the apartheid era. International law was used as a shield to protect it from a hostile world determined to impose upon South Africa the post-World War II values of respect for human rights and promotion of self-determination. This was true in respect of both South West Africa and South Africa itself.

The legal basis for international intervention in the case of South West Africa was clear, as we have seen. South Africa's legal opposition to international intervention in respect of South Africa itself was more defensible. The legal basis for United Nations (UN) opposition to apartheid was the provisions in the Charter of the UN committing member states to the principle of self-determination of peoples and the promotion of 'respect for, and observance of, human rights and fundamental freedoms for all without distinction as to race, sex, language or religion'.[151] These provisions were, however, contradicted by article 2(7) of the Charter, which declared that 'nothing contained in the present Charter shall authorize the United Nations to intervene in matters which are essentially within the domestic jurisdiction of any state'. Understandably, South Africa argued that article 2(7) prevailed over the vague, aspirational human rights provisions in the Charter and that South Africa's domestic affairs were beyond the reach of the UN. So confident was it in the correctness of its argument that it proposed that the matter be referred to the International Court of Justice for an advisory opinion. The refusal of the General Assembly to comply with this request confirmed South Africa's view that it was on sound legal ground in denying the right of the UN to intervene in its domestic affairs.

In 1948 the UN began a process of providing substance to the human rights provisions in the Charter. In December 1948 it adopted the Universal Declaration of Human Rights in a non-binding resolution; and thereafter it promoted a number of binding treaties dealing with specific human rights. South Africa, under the newly installed apartheid government, made it clear that it had no intention of accepting any obligation under the Universal Declaration of Human Rights when it abstained from voting on the resolution together with the Soviet Union, its satellites and Saudi Arabia. Furthermore, it refused to sign any of the UN's human rights treaties. This meant that South Africa was not bound by the International Convention on the Elimination of All Forms of Racial Discrimination (1965), the International Covenant on Civil and Political Rights (1966), the International Covenant on Economic, Social and Cultural Rights (1966) and the Convention against Torture (1984). In particular it was not bound by the 1973 Convention on the Suppression and Punishment of the Crime of Apartheid, which declared apartheid to be a crime against humanity and criminalized the main features of apartheid.

International law is founded on the consent of states. States are bound only by rules of international law to which they have expressly consented in treaties or by rules to which they have implicitly consented by their practice or acquiescence – what is known as customary international law. South Africa was clearly under no obligation to comply with the human rights treaties to which it was not a party. Moreover, it made it clear that it refused to consent to evolving customary international law rules by persistently objecting to such rules. In these circumstances South Africa was able to argue that it was not bound by human rights treaties and the new rules of customary international law on non-discrimination, human rights and self-determination.

These arguments were not untenable. They were premised on a sound interpretation of international law even if they reflected an old-fashioned view of international law that largely preceded the UN Charter and the recognition of respect for human rights as part of the new world order. This was probably the reason why the UN preferred to oppose apartheid through the political organs of the UN and not to have recourse to the International Court of Justice for an advisory opinion on the illegality of apartheid. In this respect the UN followed a different course from what it had pursued in the case of Namibia, where the law was firmly on its side.

The UN had a different interpretation of international law premised on human rights. It saw the human rights provisions in the Charter as imposing an obligation on South Africa to promote human rights and not to deliberately pursue policies that supported racial discrimination and political repression. The prohibition on intervention in a state's domestic affairs, it argued, could not shield a state from scrutiny of its human rights practices. Moreover, the prohibitions on racial discrimination and serious human rights violations such as torture were recognized as peremptory norms binding on all states without the need for their consent. It rejected the claim that a policy of imposed Bantustanization could be portrayed as an exercise in self-determination.

This interpretation of the law commanded large majorities in both the Security Council and the General Assembly and provided the legal basis for punitive measures. In 1977 the Security Council imposed a mandatory arms embargo on South Africa,[152] and in 1985, in a non-binding resolution, it urged states to suspend all new investments and guaranteed export loans in and to South Africa and to prohibit the sale of computer equipment that might be used by the army and police.[153] Starting in 1962,[154] the General Assembly called on states to break off diplomatic ties with South Africa, boycott all South African goods, impose an arms embargo on South Africa, refuse landing and passage facilities to South African aircraft, and suspend all cultural, educational and sporting exchanges with South Africa.

Other international organizations and states followed the United Nations. The Organization of African Unity, the Commonwealth and the European Community imposed different sanctions on South Africa, and individual states enacted legislation to prohibit trade. Many withdrew or refrained from entering into diplomatic relations with South Africa. In 1986 the US Congress passed the Comprehensive Anti-Apartheid Act, which imposed limited economic sanctions on South Africa and suspended the landing rights of South African Airways on US territory. Cultural and sporting associations and foreign universities ended all contacts with South Africa. South Africa was forced to withdraw from the Commonwealth and several UN specialized agencies,[155] and was expelled from others.[156] Attempts to expel it from the UN itself failed, but South Africa's credentials were rejected by the General Assembly and it was prohibited from participating in the work of that body.

The response of civil society was equally, if not more, effective. Led by the Anti-Apartheid Movement, consumers in many parts of the world boycotted South African wine, fruit and other produce. Entertainers, sportsmen and women, and academics who visited South Africa were shunned at home. Pension funds were persuaded to cease investing in companies that did business in South Africa and, finally, banks were pressured into refusing to make loans to the South African government.

18

Apartheid ends

On 1 February 1990 I was asked to speak to a group of visiting American foundation officers on the future of South Africa. My particular mandate was to predict what newly elected President De Klerk would say in his speech on the occasion of the opening of Parliament the next day – 2 February. There was much speculation in the press about the direction he would take. Would he announce that the government was determined to continue its *kragdadige* (strong-arm) policies or would he perhaps adopt a more moderate policy than his predecessor, P.W. Botha? In my speech I dismissed suggestions that he would pursue a conciliatory approach. I reminded my audience of a similar occasion in August 1985 when P.W. Botha was expected to proclaim a softening of apartheid and political reforms but had instead declared, in what was dubbed the 'Rubicon speech', that the government would not deviate from its course and would instead pursue a *kragdadige* line. I predicted that De Klerk would deliver another hardline speech.

I was wrong, completely wrong. When I listened with Jane to De Klerk's speech the next day, I found it hard to believe what I heard. The ANC, PAC and SACP were to be unbanned; emergency restrictions were to be lifted; and political prisoners, including Nelson Mandela, were to be released. President De Klerk called for negotiations, in which Mandela would play a prominent part, aimed at achieving 'a totally new and just constitutional dispensation in which every inhabitant will enjoy equal rights'.[157] Such a dispensation, he continued, would include a democratic constitution, universal franchise and equality before an independent judiciary. Apartheid was dead.

A number of reasons have been advanced for De Klerk's decision. The failing economy and the refusal of foreign banks to continue lending; township unrest; the end of communism in the Soviet Union and, with it, the inevitable weakening of the ANC abroad; economic, cultural and sports sanctions; foreign disinvestment; and the Damascene conversion of De Klerk himself from a believer in apartheid to believer in a democratic South Africa. The psychological impact of isolation upon white South Africans receives little attention today but it was undoubtedly a factor that made white South Africans receptive to the abandonment of apartheid. White South Africans deeply resented the exclusion of South Africa from international sport, the refusal of entertainers to visit South Africa and the severance of ties with foreign institutions, including churches and universities. They found it disturbing to be given a cold and, at times, hostile reception on travels abroad. The pariah label inevitably had a profound effect on a sports-obsessed and travel-driven people. None of these factors alone can account for the end of apartheid. It was undoubtedly a combination of these and other forces that made it impossible for apartheid to continue.

The influence of international law should not be overlooked. International human rights law, the repudiation of race discrimination and the labelling of apartheid as a crime against humanity had destroyed the legitimacy of apartheid and provided the basis for the political, economic, sporting and cultural isolation of South Africa. International law had created South Africa as a pariah state. Although opinion is divided on the extent to which sanctions and international pressure premised on the violation of international law contributed to the end of apartheid, there can be no doubt that they were important factors.[158] For years I had taught and written that apartheid violated international law and that this had serious consequences for South Africa. It was good to be proved right.

The end of apartheid brought with it hopes for a new South Africa, one in which the colour of one's skin would not determine one's position in society; and one in which the wealth of the land would be shared more equitably. I realized full well that my own position in society would change. I would cease to be part of a small group of advocates for human rights and democratic values and would soon be replaced by exiles from abroad and newly freed black activists who would seek to promote some of these values in the context of the struggle for power.

Also, I would cease to be an expert in a branch of the law that most lawyers had carefully avoided. Apartheid and, with it, the apartheid legal order had come to an end. I had lost one of my two areas of expertise. Fortunately, I had always maintained my professional interest in international law. Now I would be free to return to my first professional love.

Perhaps the most memorable consequence of the end of apartheid was my meeting with Nelson Mandela – or Madiba as he was often called. I did not meet Mandela[159] before he was imprisoned. I came to know his wife Winnie through

Joel Carlson, who was her attorney when she was detained and prosecuted in the period 1969–71. While she was in banishment in Brandfort, a desolate village in the Orange Free State, she contacted me with a strange request. 'The Old Man wants you to help our daughter Zindzi become a lawyer.' Zindzi was a bright young woman with a mind of her own who was determined to succeed in life, but not as a lawyer. I had many discussions with Zindzi about her studies and her work for Operation Hunger at the Institute of Race Relations. And I reported back to Winnie, and through her to Madiba, on the progress I had made – or, rather, I had not made. I did not succeed in persuading Zindzi to become a lawyer. Instead she became a successful businesswoman and, later, ambassador. But this failure did ensure that I made contact with Madiba himself.

In 1985 I received a letter from Madiba, written from Pollsmoor Maximum Prison,[160] in which he told me that the family had decided that Zindzi should study at the University of Cape Town and not Wits. He expressed the hope that I would understand this decision. Zindzi, he said, had told him of my interest in his family and the advice I had given her. 'I sincerely hope that one day I will be able to thank you face to face.' Then he turned to Healdtown and enquired whether the Mr Dugard who was principal of the Training School was my father. 'I will be happy if you tell me that you were once at Healdtown because in that case we would have some common link which is worth preserving.' I replied that I considered myself to be a Healdtown old boy too. I then gave him some news about his old law school, Wits, and told him how pleased I was that it was now admitting black students.

Madiba carried out his promise to thank me face to face. A few weeks after his release in 1990, I received a call from Cassim Saloojee, with whom I had worked closely at the Institute for Race Relations and who was now a prominent member of the ANC, informing me that Madiba wished to see Jane and me. We met him at the Mandela home in Orlando, Soweto. It was a moving experience, and not what we had expected. Madiba told us that he wanted to thank both of us for helping his family while he was in prison. In a meeting which continued for over an hour, he explained in the most intimate manner the dilemma he had faced as a political leader, husband of a young wife and father of two young daughters. He had been compelled to choose between pursuing his role in the political struggle and his responsibilities as a husband and father. 'Had he made the right decision?' he frequently asked himself in prison. It had made it easier for him to know that his children were being cared for. It was clear that he was still troubled by the decision he had made.

I met Madiba several times thereafter during the political transition, but then the intimacy had gone. He was the politician, the leader of the nation.

The last occasion on which I met him was in March 1999 when he received an honorary degree at the University of Leiden. When he recognized me in the academic procession, he broke with protocol to greet me on the podium. This small gesture did much for my reputation at Leiden.

19

Transition, the constitution and its institutions

The 1990s saw many changes in both my personal and professional life. As this is not an account of my personal life, I will say little about it, except that in 1991 Jane and I were divorced. At this time Jackie was a political science student at Wits and Justin was doing his military service. Military service was no longer what it had been under apartheid and Justin spent his service in the air force in Pretoria, mainly in the catering department, which prepared him for his later career as chef and restaurant manager.

De Klerk's speech of 2 February 1990 ushered in a period known as the transition to democracy, which saw the release of political prisoners, the return of exiles and constitutional negotiations that ultimately led to the first free elections of April 1994 and the adoption of a new constitution for a democratic South Africa. The transition also witnessed violent activities throughout the country, arising from the conflict between the ANC and the Inkatha Freedom Party, the actions of the Afrikaner Weerstandsbeweging (AWB) and the clandestine operations of a mysterious 'Third Force' responsible for the assassination of anti-apartheid activists. During this time my principal professional concerns were the transformation of the University of Fort Hare, unravelling the mysteries of the Third Force, constitutional negotiations and the creation of the Truth and Reconciliation Commission.

Fort Hare

Fort Hare, situated in the Eastern Cape near the town of Alice, was established in 1916 as a university catering mainly for black students. Its alumni included many leaders of post-colonial Africa such as Julius Nyerere, Kenneth Kaunda, Seretse Khama and Robert Mugabe, and most of South Africa's black leadership, notably Oliver Tambo, Nelson Mandela, Robert Sobukwe, Govan Mbeki, Desmond Tutu and Mangosuthu Buthelezi. In 1959 it lost its autonomy when it was brought under the direct control of the apartheid regime and restricted to admitting only Xhosa students following the enactment of the Extension of University Education Act of 1959. For me, Fort Hare had special significance because it was situated near my birthplace of Fort Beaufort and Healdtown, and because my father had served on its council in the mid-1950s.

In March 1990, shortly after De Klerk's speech to Parliament, I was appointed to the council of the University of Fort Hare, together with people such as Archbishop Tutu, Professor Francis Wilson, Advocate Lewis Skweyiya and Govan Mbeki, with the mandate of transforming the university. This involved taking not only policy decisions on the nature and direction of the university but also decisions on its general administration, from appointing senior officers and dealing with complaints from staff, students and workers to disciplinary and budgetary matters. There was a sense on the part of the council that we were really contributing to the reconstruction of a once great university, that we were part of the building of the new South Africa. I remained a member of council until 1998.

The Independent Board of Inquiry into Informal Repression

In 1989 Frank Chikane, the secretary-general of the South African Council of Churches, survived an assassination attempt carried out by the apartheid regime. The police broke into his suitcase at Jan Smuts Airport, when he was about to fly to Namibia, and laced his underpants with paraoxon, a poisonous insecticide. Poisoned, he survived only by immediately flying on to the United States for treatment. In response, Chikane initiated the establishment of the Independent Board of Inquiry into Informal Repression (IBIIR), whose task it was to investigate and monitor the activities of mysterious death squads. So I became a member of this board, which included Archbishop Tutu, Frank Chikane, Max Coleman, Sheena Duncan (head of the Black Sash), Laurie Ackermann (a former judge, then a professor of human rights at the University of Stellenbosch), Brian

Currin (director of Lawyers for Human Rights) and Peter Harris (a human rights attorney who was responsible for carrying out most of the decisions of the IBIIR).[161]

Created in the 1980s, and responsible for the killing of many activists as well as the bombing of the offices of the South African Council of Churches in 1988, these police death squads, which came to be known as the Third Force, continued to operate after De Klerk's speech in February 1990 and threatened the transition to democracy. Both the identity and the structure of these units were unknown at the time of the establishment of the IBIIR. It was later revealed that two bodies were responsible for the killing and terrorization of opponents of apartheid, the Civil Cooperation Bureau (CCB), which operated under Military Intelligence, and a police unit operating from the farm Vlakplaas near Pretoria.

The IBIIR investigations centred on the revelations of Captain Dirk Coetzee, a renegade senior police officer from Vlakplaas, about the murder of anti-apartheid activists. Although these revelations were disbelieved by commissions of inquiry established by President De Klerk, they were later accepted by the Truth and Reconciliation Commission and the courts.

The shadowy world of a police force reluctant to give up power was difficult to penetrate. More onerous was the task of persuading members of the old apartheid regime charged with investigating allegations of clandestine police involvement in assassinations to make findings against their own colleagues.

The death squad at Vlakplaas came to be synonymous with its most notorious member, Eugene de Kock, nicknamed 'Prime Evil' by the press. De Kock made a full disclosure of the crimes in which he had been involved before the Truth and Reconciliation Commission and was sentenced to 212 years in prison in 1996. Undoubtedly De Kock became a scapegoat for both his commanding officers and his political superiors who had condoned and probably endorsed the activities of the Vlakplaas unit. In 2015 he was released on parole after seeking forgiveness from the families of those he had killed.[162]

Truth, Reconciliation and Amnesty

Before 1990 it was assumed that if the liberation movements succeeded in overthrowing the apartheid regime by military means, the leaders of the regime would be tried in the same way that Nazi leaders had been tried at Nuremberg. The spectre of Nuremberg was held out as a threat by the liberation movements in exile. The foundation for such trials had been laid out in the 1973 International Convention on the Suppression and Punishment of the Crime of Apartheid, which declared apartheid to be a crime against humanity and provided for individual criminal responsibility for those guilty of committing the crime of apartheid. Although the convention was primarily designed to authorize the trial of apartheid criminals outside South Africa during the apartheid era, it was also seen as providing the basis for trials before an international tribunal after the demise of apartheid. This plan was thwarted by F.W. de Klerk's abandonment of apartheid and initiation of negotiations for a democratic South Africa. The question now was what was to be done with those members of the apartheid regime and the liberation movements who had committed terrible crimes such as murder, torture and forced disappearance. And was the crime of apartheid – the imposition of a regime of systematic oppression and domination by one racial group over another – to be punished?

In the early days of the debate that arose, I publicly advocated the Nuremberg option and the prosecution of leaders of the apartheid regime for both the crime of apartheid and murder, torture and forced disappearances, in the belief that this alone would break South Africa's connection with its past. Undoubtedly I was influenced by the philosophy of the German jurist Gustav Radbruch, who had argued that the laws of Nazi Germany were so evil that they failed to qualify as law, with the result that those who had enforced them could not raise the defence that they had acted in accordance with the law. The Nuremberg option was, however, impossible in a situation involving a negotiated settlement. Consequently, in 1992 I advocated a softer line, suggesting that while it was still in power, the National Party should establish a commission tasked with examining crimes that had been committed during the apartheid era and identifying those responsible. Those who had committed crimes would not be punished. Publicity and public shaming would be their sole punishment. Their crimes would be forgiven in a spirit of reconciliation but not forgotten.[163]

The question of how to approach the crimes of the past became a crucial issue in negotiations, one which threatened to derail the whole process. Although the National Party was prepared to release political prisoners and to grant immunity from prosecution to ANC exiles, the ANC was not willing to allow the government to grant amnesty to its own security forces, arguing that this was a matter to be dealt with in the constitutional negotiations.

Politically there were only two options open to the negotiators: unconditional blanket amnesty, which was favoured by the National Party, or conditional amnesty. The latter was chosen. The Interim Constitution, adopted by the Multi-Party Negotiating Process at the World Trade Centre, made no provision for amnesty. However, in the period between the approval of the draft constitution by the multi-party conference and its adoption by Parliament at the end of 1993, the ANC and the National Party, meeting behind closed doors, hammered out a deal on amnesty in a postscript to the draft constitution. This postscript, which came to be known as the 'postamble' of the Interim Constitution, committed post-apartheid South Africa to a policy of reconciliation and understanding and not vengeance. The 'postamble' provided that 'In order to advance such reconciliation and reconstruction, amnesty shall be granted in respect of acts, omissions and offences associated with political objectives and committed in the course of conflicts of the past'. In order to give effect to this decision, Parliament was instructed to enact legislation to provide for the mechanisms by means of which amnesty would be dealt with.

The next year saw a wide-reaching debate about how reconciliation and amnesty were to be achieved. The Institute for a Democratic Alternative for South Africa (IDASA), under Alex Boraine, took the lead in this debate. Conferences were held to discuss the experience of countries such as Chile and Argentina with truth and reconciliation and to consider how these models could be used by South Africa. There was general agreement that a commission should be established to allow victims of apartheid to tell their stories and to provide an opportunity for the perpetrators of crimes to confess and seek forgiveness, but opinions were sharply divided over the question of amnesty. Who was to be given amnesty and how this matter was to be regulated became the subject of fierce debate. The minister of justice, Dullah Omar, engaged with IDASA in drafting legislation to give effect to the 'postamble'. I participated in this exercise together with Alex Boraine, Professor C.A. Norgaard (of the European Commission on Human Rights), the political philosopher André du Toit, Arthur Chaskalson, Albie Sachs and Mohamed Navsa (of the Legal Resources Centre). Amnesty presented the greatest problem. Although it was agreed that a special amnesty committee should be empowered to grant amnesty for acts constituting a 'gross violation of human rights' where the applicant had made a full disclosure of all the relevant facts, difficulties surrounded the question of how to decide whether an offence was 'associated with a political objective' and committed in the course of conflicts of the past. Drawing on the principles of extradition law on the subject of political offences,[164] agreement was reached on the criteria to be employed for deciding whether an offence had been committed with a political objective. These included the motive of the offender, whether the offence had been committed in the course of a political uprising or disturbance, the gravity of the crime, and whether it was directed at a political opponent.

In 1995 Parliament enacted the Promotion of National Unity and Reconciliation Act,[165] which provided for the establishment of a Truth and Reconciliation Commission (TRC) appointed by the president to conduct hearings and investigations into gross violations of human rights committed between 1960 and 1993.This was assisted by an amnesty committee, a quasi-judicial body entrusted with the task of considering and, where appropriate, granting amnesty to applicants. Presided over by Archbishop Tutu, the TRC heard testimony from both victims and perpetrators of gross violations of human rights, and the amnesty committee granted many applications for amnesty.

Whether truth and reconciliation was a success or not remains a matter of debate in South Africa. It certainly healed many of the wounds in South African society and paved the way for a new South Africa. But it failed to address the criminality of apartheid itself, as the imposition of a policy of systematic oppression by one racial group over another was not treated as a crime for which amnesty had to be sought. Radbruch's philosophy was ignored. The apartheid legal system was not repudiated as unworthy of the name law. Consequently cabinet ministers and senior bureaucrats who had managed population removals, the pass laws and the invasion of neighbouring states went free. Only the foot soldiers of apartheid in the security forces who had committed murder and torture were required to seek amnesty.

South Africa's amnesty runs counter to prevailing international opinion – and law – which refuses to recognize impunity for serious international crimes. Many members of the security forces were granted amnesty for crimes that would qualify as crimes against humanity, and still many more remain unpunished as a result of a policy of non-prosecution of members of the military forces who refused to apply for amnesty. Can society tolerate a situation in which such persons and those responsible for directing the system of apartheid remain unpunished? I do not profess to have the answer.[166] The matter was brought home to me when I was at a restaurant in Johannesburg and looked up to see Craig Williamson sitting at the opposite table. Williamson, a former student at Wits and security police agent, had been responsible for killing my friend Jeanette Schoon and her young daughter. Was I supposed to forgive and forget?

Constitutional Negotiations

De Klerk's speech of 2 February 1990 triggered a season of constitutional conferences at which the form and nature of the new constitutional order were debated. Universal franchise and a Bill of Rights were accepted as basic features of such an order, but there was disagreement over such matters as whether South Africa should be a federation or have a central government, whether there should be proportional representation or whether the old constituency system should be retained, whether the Bill of Rights should be confined to civil and political rights or extended to include social and economic rights, whether property rights should be entrenched, and whether the Constitution should be protected by a Constitutional Court with testing power or by the ordinary courts of the prevailing system. Constitutional law, which had hitherto been avoided as 'politically dangerous' by many scholars, suddenly became the main preoccupation of both academic lawyers and legal practitioners. The standard of debate at conferences organized by IDASA, the Five Freedoms and the universities was high as participants drew on comparative law and the experience of other countries in the search for an ideal constitution.

I debated a number of issues at these conferences. An engagement with the Communist Party leader, Joe Slovo, recently returned from exile, on 'Security Legislation under a New Constitution' became heated when he advocated the banning of racist parties, such as the Conservative Party, while I maintained the traditional liberal position that all views were to be protected by a freedom of speech clause in a new constitution.[167] It was a pleasure to debate with Joe, who was able to advocate radical positions in a warm and pleasant manner. Although he had been in charge of ANC military planning, he was certainly not the ogre that he had been portrayed during the apartheid era.

An issue on which lawyers were strongly divided was the question of which court should be entrusted with enforcing the Constitution and the Bill of Rights. Many lawyers, and most judges, favoured retaining the existing courts for this purpose but making sure that these became representative of South African society. Others, of which I was one, advocated the creation of a special constitutional court that represented a break with the past and comprised judges reflecting the racial diversity of South Africa and professionally qualified to pronounce on constitutional issues.

In December 1991 the constitutional debate at conferences was superseded by the creation of a structure for constitutional dialogue between the main political parties, known as the Convention for a Democratic South Africa (CODESA). In 1992, as violence continued to grip the country, CODESA broke down following major disagreements between the ANC and National Party over both the process for creating a new constitution and its content. At this point I was invited to participate in a conference held at the Friedrich Naumann Foundation conference centre in Sintra, Portugal, hosted by IDASA, to consider the way forward. The conference brought together a strange mix of South Africans from different backgrounds and of different political persuasions and included Van Zyl Slabbert, Alex Boraine, Nthato Motlana, Jon Qwelane, Franklin Sonn, Colin Eglin, Rudolf Gouws and Helen Zille. In common we were persons outside the constitutional negotiations but with some influence on public opinion. We discussed what might be done to restart negotiations and what form the ultimate constitution might take. We were full of ideas and were able to advance conflicting views without acrimony as we had no constituencies to which we were accountable. But I cannot say we achieved anything. Certainly, our deliberations had little, if any, influence on the course of events in South Africa. But, perhaps, this was all part of a process that would lead to something.

In April 1993 a fresh attempt was made at negotiations through the Multi-Party Negotiating Process (MPNP), in which twenty-six parties initially participated. Inevitably, the process was dominated by the ANC and National Party. This was clear from Cyril Ramaphosa's famous definition of 'sufficient consensus' in the MPNP: 'if we [ANC] and the National Party agree, everyone else can get stuffed'.[168] The critical forum was the Negotiating Council whose work was facilitated by technical committees with the task of advising the council on matters such as fundamental rights, constitutional affairs and the repeal of discriminatory laws and legislation impeding free political activity. The MPNP was guided by a planning committee led by Mac Maharaj of the ANC and Fanie van der Merwe of the National Party. It was the same Fanie van der Merwe who had led the investigations of the Schlebusch Commission in 1972 and had interrogated me on intercepted correspondence.

I was nominated to serve on the committee dealing with fundamental rights but, so I heard, was vetoed by both the ANC and the National Party. Instead I was appointed as member, and chair, of the committee charged with the task of identifying discriminatory statutes and those that impeded free political activity. Pius Langa, chair of the National Association of Democratic Lawyers (NADEL), who later became chief justice, was also a member of the committee.

I had serious misgivings about the mandate of the committee. It was an impossible task to identify all the laws on the South African statute book that were discriminatory or impeded free political activity. For decades, going back well before the advent of apartheid, successive parliaments had enacted laws of this kind. Some of the laws were obvious, such as the Population Registration Act, providing for race classification, the Group Areas Act, providing for separate but unequal residential areas, and the Internal Security Act, which authorized restrictions on freedom of speech and association. But there were other laws which appeared harmless on the surface but which placed restrictions on freedom of political activity or discriminated on grounds of race. In any event, we asked, what was the purpose of such a list of offensive statutes? Those that were obviously repressive or discriminatory could easily be identified and should be repealed as soon as possible. The others should be repealed over time. Without a political will to enforce such laws, there seemed to be no hurry in repealing them. In any event it was anticipated that a Bill of Rights would be adopted and any law in violation of such a Bill of Rights would be declared invalid by the courts.

So our committee decided that a higher code – a Bill of Rights – setting out the standards by which the validity of repressive and discriminatory laws would be measured should be adopted instead of trying to identify all the offensive laws. The Negotiating Council was not satisfied with this approach and instructed the committee to draw up a list of inhibiting and discriminatory legislation and to draft a code by which the validity of laws was to be measured. The committee did so and then effectively dissolved.

The Negotiating Council was still unsatisfied and appointed an ad hoc committee to investigate this matter afresh. Clearly the ANC saw it as politically important that the full horrors of the statute book be displayed. Nothing came of this as it became clear that the Interim Constitution would contain a Bill of Rights with a set of standards by which the validity of laws was to be judged. The principal offensive statutes identified by our committee were repealed before the Interim Constitution came into effect. This task is still unfinished. There are many obscure statutes that restrict fundamental freedoms or discriminate on grounds of race. When, and if, these laws are challenged, they are set aside by the courts, but the legacy of apartheid is still to be found in the South African statute book.

The MPNP and the bodies that it spawned ultimately succeeded in drafting an Interim Constitution,[169] which was approved by Parliament and provided the basis for South Africa's first democratic election held on 27 April 1994. Predictably the ANC won the election, securing 62 per cent of the national vote, while the National Party received only 20 per cent. Some in the ANC were disappointed that the party did not receive two-thirds of the national vote as this would have given it a free hand in the drafting of the final constitution. But Mandela himself wisely commented that he was relieved, as this would have resulted in 'an ANC constitution, not a South African constitution'.[170]

The Interim Constitution included a set of thirty-four Constitutional Principles with which the 'final' Constitution was to comply. The National Assembly and the Senate doubled as a Constitutional Assembly charged with the task of drafting the final Constitution. This assembly was divided into theme committees, supported by technical committees. One theme committee – number 4 – was charged with the task of drafting a Bill of Rights and was to be guided by the Constitutional Principle that read: 'Everyone shall enjoy all universally accepted fundamental rights, freedoms and civil liberties, which shall be provided for and protected by entrenched and justiciable provisions in the Constitution.'

I was appointed to serve on the technical committee for the drafting of a Bill of Rights, together with Sandy Liebenberg, Halton Cheadle and Ig Rautenbach. Halton, of course, I knew well as a colleague at CALS and a friend; Ig I also knew well as a colleague at the Rand Afrikaans University; but Sandy I had not met previously. I do not know how we were chosen as none of us lobbied for membership of this committee. I understood that I had been nominated by the Democratic Party, Sandy and Halton by the ANC, and Ig by the National Party. But party association ended for us all on nomination. We worked together as a team and took little account of party positions, although we were obviously aware of the expectations of various parties. We were all persons with independent minds, determined to draft a Bill of Rights for the South African Constitution which contained universally accepted fundamental rights.

Our first loyalty was to the fundamental human rights declared in international and regional human rights conventions. Inevitably we had recourse to national constitutions, notably those of Germany, Canada, the United States and India. We were also obliged to consider the suggestions made by civil society in meetings held throughout the country and in the thousands of written submissions solicited from the general public. We did consider them but it soon became apparent that different interest groups, which had little interest in human rights as they were universally understood, had canvassed hard among their followers to secure massive write-ins for their views. Support for the death penalty featured prominently among the submissions from the general public. Animal rights activists also produced a large write-in for animal rights, which we dismissed largely because they were not universally recognized. This process of consultation with the general public gave the Bill of Rights political legitimacy and lent support to the view that it was an indigenous instrument and not simply a copy of international human rights conventions.

The Constitutional Assembly had a generous budget and our committee met regularly in Cape Town and in pleasant venues in its wider precincts. For instance, one weekend was spent drafting in a hotel near Franschhoek. Overcome with the beauty of our surroundings, we drafted what became section 24 of the Constitution, declaring the right to have 'the environment protected for the benefit of present and future generations'. An innovative provision, not to be found in international human rights conventions, was the prohibition of discrimination on grounds of 'sexual orientation'. This prohibition, contained in section 9(3) of the Constitution, placed South Africa in the forefront of the struggle for gay and lesbian rights. Later, as the rest of Africa embarked on homophobic campaigns, South Africa, inspired by its Constitution, pursued a different path and adopted legislation to recognize same-sex marriages.

The property clause was, and still is, the most controversial provision in South Africa's Bill of Rights. Proposals to our committee ranged from the omission of such a clause to an absolute protection of the right. The compromise solution took the form of a lengthy provision asserting the right to property subject to expropriation for a public purpose, accompanied by compensation. Restitution was provided for in respect of those who had lost land as a result of discriminatory legislation under previous regimes.

Bills of Rights do not uniformly guarantee social and economic rights. Many provide protection for civil and political rights only. The principal distinction between the two sets of rights is that civil and political rights in large measure place restraints on government and prescribe negatively what government may not do. For instance, government is prohibited from torturing, detaining without trial, failing to conduct fair criminal trials, and suppressing freedom of speech. Social, economic and cultural rights, on the other hand, require government to take positive action to achieve something – such as to provide education, health care, food, water and social security. While a court may have no difficulty in deciding whether a government has violated a civil or political right by, for example, practising torture or denying a fair trial, it will be confronted with a different situation where it is required to rule on whether a government, having regard to its resources, has done enough to promote education or health care. For this reason it is said that while civil and political rights are justiciable, in the sense that they are subject to judicial determination, social and economic rights are non-justiciable.

There was considerable opposition to the inclusion of social and economic rights from both within the Constitutional Assembly and without. In the Assembly, both the Democratic Party and the National Party had reservations about socio-economic rights while the Chamber of Mines, Free Market Foundation and the Institute of Race Relations made submissions opposing the inclusion of these rights. On the other hand, the ANC and civil society were strongly supportive of such rights. Within the technical committee there was no disagreement. We all agreed that socio-economic rights should be included on the ground that they were 'universally accepted fundamental rights'. However, we recognized that they 'should not place an obligation on the state that cannot be fulfilled in terms of its resources and capacity'; and that the legislature should have primary responsibility for implementing the rights although the courts would have the power of review.[171] In the end we approved clauses providing for access to adequate housing, health care, food, water, social security and education, which rights the state was required to take steps to progressively realize within its available resources.

At the time I expressed the view that the ANC would rue the day it had supported socio-economic rights as it would be charged with the task of implementing them when in government. Subsequent events have confirmed this. The ANC government has failed to deliver on the commitments to social and economic rights in the Constitution, and this has resulted in a number of cases before the Constitutional Court admonishing the government.[172] But, more important, the socio-economic provisions in the Bill of Rights represent a commitment which the people of South Africa may invoke as a lodestar for their demands for social and economic equality.

I had a special interest in the international law provisions in the Constitution dealing with the relationship between international law and domestic law. Although not a member of the committee charged with this matter, I was kept abreast of developments and provided advice and comment on the subject. I was therefore pleased to be invited to participate in discussions on the final draft on these provisions at a meeting held in stately Ditchley Park in England. These provisions declare that customary international law is part of South African law and that legislation is to be interpreted to accord with international law. The South African Constitution of 1996 is one of the most international law-friendly constitutions in the modern world, contrasting sharply with the apartheid legal order in which international law was viewed as a hostile legal system.

The new Constitution[173] was adopted by the Constitutional Assembly and approved by the Constitutional Court in 1996. It was a massive collective exercise and many had a hand in the drafting process. For me it was dream come true. Whenever I have reason to consult the 1996 Constitution, I recall the days when South Africa was without a Bill of Rights, Parliament was supreme, discriminatory and repressive legislation prevailed, and international law was ignored. South Africa has good cause to be proud of its Constitution, which ranks among the most progressive in today's world.

The Constitutional Court

Before 1990 I had not considered a judicial appointment. I could not in all conscience apply the law of apartheid and, of course, there was no way that the National Party government would appoint me. But the creation of the Constitutional Court changed everything.

Since the early 1980s I had advocated the creation of a constitutional court with the power to review legislation in a new South Africa. This was despite opposition from most lawyers, who believed that it would be wiser to maintain the existing Appellate Division as the supreme court, but with power of judicial review. Essentially this was a debate between those who wished to make a clean break with the past as a result of the poor performance of the judiciary under apartheid and those who believed that continuity of the existing judicial structure would create stability. At an early stage during the constitutional negotiations it became clear that the former view would prevail and that a new constitutional court would be established with judges who had opposed the apartheid system, drawn from the ranks of both practising lawyers and legal academics. This gave rise to speculation as to who might be appointed to such a court, which became more intense after the adoption of the Interim Constitution providing for the creation of an eleven-member Constitutional Court.

The Constitution provided for the appointment of a president of the Constitutional Court and four sitting judges by the president of the country. Six other judges were to be appointed by the president, after consultation with the newly appointed president of the Constitutional Court. These six were to be drawn from a list of candidates, compiled by the Judicial Service Commission, comprising representatives of the legal profession and members of Parliament representing different political parties. The Judicial Service Commission was required to recommend ten persons, with due regard to considerations of race and gender, to the president to enable him to make his choice. From the outset I indicated I was interested in appointment to the Constitutional Court.

In June 1994 President Nelson Mandela appointed Arthur Chaskalson as president of the Constitutional Court. This came as no surprise: Arthur had distinguished himself in the field of human rights as director of the Legal Resources Centre. This was followed by the appointment of four sitting judges. There were over a hundred nominees for the remaining six seats but this number was whittled down to a shortlist for interviews by the Judicial Service Commission. I was one of those interviewed. The interview went exceptionally well and my name was one of ten forwarded to the president on the recommendation of the commission. I was not one of the six selected.

I was disappointed, but not really surprised. I accepted that if the Constitutional Court was to have credibility and legitimacy, it would need to have women and black members. Race and gender were essential considerations in the selection process and I had urged the creation of a constitutional court precisely to ensure that women and black persons might be included. Moreover, political rewards were inevitable. There was another factor which counted against me. I had been the pre-eminent critic of the judiciary during the apartheid years. If the new Constitutional Court was to have the support of the existing judges, appointed by the apartheid regime, it would be wiser for it not to include someone who had accused judges of siding with the executive and supporting apartheid. That this was a consideration was hinted to me by Arthur Chaskalson in a conversation we had shortly before the election when he told me that he had refused to write a foreword for this reason for Rick Abel's book *Politics by Other Means: Law in the Struggle against Apartheid 1980–1984*, which critically examined the decisions of judges in a number of cases handled by CALS and the LRC. Forewords were instead written by Nelson Mandela, Geoff Budlender, assistant director of the LRC, and me. At the time I did not pay sufficient attention to this incident, but as the selection grew closer I realized that Arthur had been warning me that this might become a consideration.

The Constitutional Court has proved to be one of the most successful institutions of the 1996 Constitution. It has established respect for human rights as the focal point of its jurisprudence and it has given significant judgments in the fields of civil and political, social, economic and cultural rights.[174] It has succeeded in restoring public confidence in the courts of South Africa.

Human Rights Commission

The Human Rights Commission was created by the Interim Constitution (and confirmed by the 1996 Constitution) to protect and promote human rights. Comprising eleven members, it was to be appointed by the president, on the advice of a joint committee of both Houses of Parliament, with the approval of both Houses. I was nominated for membership of the commission, was interviewed by the joint committee and was informed that I was appointed. This did not surprise me as, somewhat arrogantly, I believed that having narrowly missed appointment to the Constitutional Court, I could not fail in my bid for membership of the commission. But it was not to be. After the commission had been constituted, President Mandela decided that Helen Suzman, who had not sought nomination, should be a member. He therefore phoned Tony Leon, leader of the Democratic Party, the official opposition in Parliament, and informed him that it would be disproportionate for the 'liberal camp' to have more than one candidate and that I should stand down – or rather be stood down, for I was not consulted on this matter – in favour of Helen. Reluctantly Tony agreed. I was pleased at Helen's appointment, but I could not understand why both Helen and I could not have been appointed to the commission, with her as representative of the Democratic Party and me as an independent liberal voice. In his autobiography, *On the Contrary*, Tony Leon wrote of this episode:

I never discerned why government was so resolute on not appointing Dugard, hardly a DP partisan such as Suzman. It might have been those racial, gender or quota-filling requirements which soon – on an ever accelerating basis – became the *raison d'être* for all public appointments. Or perhaps senior ANC figures bore some personal animus towards the mild-mannered, distinguished professor. The mystery has never been explained, and Dugard was to be a double-casualty of the democratic transition to which he had so resolutely dedicated himself.[175]

20

New pastures

When it became clear that I could not expect to play a part in the building of South Africa's human rights institutions, I turned once more to international law. An initial boost was given to my new career as an international lawyer when I was invited by Cambridge University to be the Arthur Goodhart Visiting Professor of Legal Science for the academic year 1995–6. At the same time, on the suggestion of James Crawford, the newly appointed professor of international law at Cambridge, and Eli Lauterpacht, my former academic supervisor at Cambridge, I was appointed as director of the Lauterpacht Centre for International Law.

My daughter Jackie accompanied me to Cambridge, to read for the MPhil in political science, and together we stayed in the spacious residence that was part of the Goodhart endowment. Although the Goodhart Chair was for one year only, I was asked to stay on at the Lauterpacht Centre for a further year.

Shortly before I left South Africa in 1995, I was elected, as the first South African member, to the Institute of International Law, an association of international lawyers with a restricted membership. The institute, founded in 1873 and awarded the Nobel Peace Prize in 1904, conducts studies of particular topics of international law to guide the development of international law. On the basis of my membership of this body, and my position as director of the Lauterpacht Centre, James Crawford suggested that I consider election to the International Law Commission (ILC).

The ILC is a body established by the UN to codify and develop international law. It comprises thirty-four members elected by the General Assembly representing the five regional groups recognized by the UN – Western Europe (including the United States, Australia, Canada and New Zealand), Eastern

Europe, Africa, Asia and Latin America. Some eight commissioners represent African countries. Members of the commission hold office on a part-time, unpaid basis for five years but may be re-elected. The ILC, which meets for ten weeks each summer in Geneva, prepares draft treaties on particular branches of international law and forwards these drafts to the Sixth Committee (Legal Committee) of the General Assembly. This body decides whether to transform the draft into treaty form, in which case it becomes binding on states as a treaty, or to leave the draft as a restatement of customary international law.

In order to stand for election to the ILC, it was necessary to be nominated by one's government. For this purpose I approached Kader Asmal, a good friend and a cabinet minister in the new South African government. He agreed, and persuaded Thabo Mbeki and Alfred Nzo, the foreign minister, to make this nomination. So I went to New York to campaign for the ILC elections in the General Assembly in October 1996 with the full backing of the South African Permanent Mission to the United Nations in New York. I was duly elected as a member of the African group in the commission.

When I was about to leave Cambridge in 1997, I was approached by the University of Leiden to enquire whether I would be interested in the position of professor of international law at that university. Clearly membership of the ILC was an important consideration for Leiden. I said that I was committed to staying in South Africa but agreed to be interviewed. After the interview, conducted by a committee presided over by Judge Rosalyn Higgins of the International Court of Justice, I was offered the post. I considered it seriously. Leiden was a fine university, and being in Leiden would give me access to the world of international law. But I declined: I was committed to staying in South Africa.

Back in South Africa, I settled in again at Wits. I was determined to become involved in the practice of international law and so I approached Aziz Pahad, deputy minister in the Department of Foreign Affairs, about the possibility of a consultancy in the department. This was a time when government departments were employing consultants very freely and so I became optimistic about such an appointment. Nothing materialized and I began to wonder whether I had made a mistake in turning down the Leiden offer. Then an event occurred that helped me to make up my mind. I had long had an interest in international criminal law. I had written extensively on issues such as the creation of an international criminal court and the extradition of fugitive offenders, and I had lectured on the subject at Cambridge and Wits. In the early 1990s the UN had established ad hoc international criminal tribunals for the former Yugoslavia and Rwanda, and this led the international community to embark on the establishment of a permanent international criminal court. A conference to draft a statute for such a court was planned to be held in Rome in mid-1998. South Africa, then in the heyday of the Mandela presidency with its distinct human rights policy, was one of the chief proponents of this venture and a member of a group termed the 'like-minded states' that took the lead in the planning of this conference. A key position in the Rome conference was that of chair of the drafting committee, and my name was put forward by the group of like-minded states. This nomination was, however, vetoed by Dullah Omar, the new minister of justice, with whom I had worked in the apartheid years and whom I regarded as a friend.

In 1998, shortly after the decision not to allow me to participate in the Rome conference for the creation of the International Criminal Court, I was asked by the University of Leiden to reconsider my decision and was offered the post on a five-year contract with the possibility of reappointment to the age of seventy. There were many reasons for accepting the offer. I could go no further in South Africa and soon I would be forced to retire from Wits with no pension.[176] I was not keen to practise as an advocate as my main expertise was in international law, which could not support a practice at the Bar. I was an expert on the law of apartheid, which, thankfully, no longer existed. I was the foremost critic of judicial reasoning, but felt constrained from criticizing judicial friends applying a Constitution that I had helped to draft and of which I approved. So I accepted Leiden's offer and set about making plans to leave in August 1998. Most friends seemed to understand my predicament. No one tried to persuade me to stay. There was no counter-offer from Wits.

I left on a high note. Ismail Mahomed, the chief justice of the Supreme Court of Appeal, spoke at a farewell function held at Wits. Ismail was an emotional man who was not afraid of hyperbole. In his speech he said of me:

> He brought a new focus to the training of lawyers and the practice of the law; and when South Africa was ready properly to respond to the very deep conflicts between the law and the practices which it had sustained for so long and the ideals and values which had informed the civilization from which it had evolved, John Dugard had prepared a whole generation of lawyers with a new mindset.

In an editorial the Johannesburg *Sunday Times* wrote: 'we agree with the judges who spoke at his farewell: South Africa has failed Dugard, one of the most influential legal scholars in recent years. And in failing him we have failed ourselves.'[177]

In November 1998, shortly after I arrived in Leiden, I was appointed as senior counsel ('silk') by President Mandela.

I was sixty-two when I left South Africa, an age at which most contemplate retirement. Instead I was to become a professor in a university whose non-Anglo-American ways were strange to me, in a foreign country that I had only previously visited briefly. I was required to reinvent myself as a full-time international lawyer and to live in a strange environment.

The first year that I lived in Leiden was not easy. But then in September 1999 I met my present wife Ietje Barbas, a friend of Richard and Noleen Goldstone. I moved to The Hague and we were married in 2003. Through Ietje, I have become part of Dutch society, and, at the same time, of Europe. She speaks Dutch, English, Portuguese and French like a native, so Europe ceased to be a foreign continent. I have become a part of Ietje's family and I have learnt to like The Hague, a small city with all the advantages of city life, beautiful parks and a nearby beach.

I taught international law – in English – at Leiden for eight years, mainly in the master's programme, consisting of small groups of students from all parts of the world. After I retired from Leiden at the end of 2006, I was appointed as a part-time professor in the Centre for Human Rights of the University of Pretoria and spent three fulfilling months there each year for five years.

21

The International Court of Justice

The two primary legal institutions in the United Nations system are the International Court of Justice (ICJ) and the International Law Commission (ILC). The former is designated by the Charter of the United Nations as 'the principal judicial organ of the United Nations'[178] and adjudicates disputes between states in accordance with the rules of international law, while the ILC is responsible for developing the rules of international law through the process of codification. In practice, judges of the ICJ are often elected from the ranks of the ILC, which is seen as a stepping stone to the court.

In the previous chapter I told of my election to the ILC, on which I served three five-year terms from 1997 to 2011. During this time I was appointed as special rapporteur, a position which required me to research and report on a particular subject to guide the ILC in its codification exercise. The subject of my special rapporteurship was diplomatic protection, the right of a state to protect a national against a state responsible for injuring such a national abroad. In successive drafts prepared for each session of the ILC, I sought to inject a human rights perspective into the subject, emphasizing that diplomatic protection is one of the methods employed by international law to protect human rights. This project culminated in a set of draft articles dealing with the conditions and procedures for protecting nationals injured abroad. The draft articles serve as a restatement of international law and have been invoked by international tribunals as a reflection of international law.

I suppose most international lawyers secretly aspire to become a judge of the ICJ in same way that most lawyers in national systems see appointment as a judge as their ultimate ambition. During the apartheid years I knew that I had no prospect whatsoever of becoming a judge of the ICJ as there was no way in which a South African national would be considered for appointment to this court. The end of apartheid brought little change to this perception, but when I became a member of the ILC I began to contemplate such a possibility.

The International Court of Justice, situated in The Hague, is the oldest and most prestigious international court in the world. It hears disputes between states and gives advisory opinions at the request of the political organs of the UN. The court comprises fifteen judges, with three positions reserved for African judges. Judges hold office for nine years and are elected by the General Assembly and the Security Council of the UN, voting separately. Judges are nominated by an independent national group and not by government. This is designed to eliminate or reduce the political factor in the election. Before making a nomination the national group is required 'to consult its highest court of justice, its legal faculties and schools of law'.[179]

In 2001 the South African national group, comprising Chief Justice Arthur Chaskalson, Deputy Chief Justice Pius Langa, Professor Thandabantu Nhlapo and Professor Medard Rwelamira, considered the applications for nomination to the ICJ. As required by the Statute of the ICJ, the national group consulted widely among the legal profession, law schools and civil society, before unanimously nominating me as the South African candidate for the ICJ election to be held in October 2002. This nomination was supported by the national groups of Australia, the Netherlands and Sweden.

Protocol required that the Department of Foreign Affairs transmit the nomination to the secretary-general of the United Nations, but it refused to do this. When Arthur Chaskalson insisted, the department reluctantly transmitted my nomination, by which time my principal rival, Abdul Koroma of Sierra Leone, had been campaigning for several months.

Elections in the UN system are tough and highly politicized. In practice, governments support their candidate for elected offices by exchanging reciprocal agreements with states to support each other's candidates and by lobbying support. Candidates also spend time at the UN headquarters in New York campaigning with the assistance of their own government's diplomats. Without the full support of a candidate's diplomatic mission, he or she cannot succeed. No candidate unsupported by his or her mission has ever won an election in the UN.

I had every reason to expect support from the Department of Foreign Affairs after my nomination had been lodged with the UN. But it was not to be. For some reason, still unknown to me, the Department of Foreign Affairs refused to support me in any way but at the same time failed to inform me that it would not do so. I made every effort to find out what the department's position was, but all such requests were either brushed aside with the promise of future support or simply unanswered. Although President Mbeki promised that support would be forthcoming, it became clear that the minister of foreign affairs, Nkosazana Dlamini-Zuma, had decided not to support me.

In October, with the election scheduled for later that month, I went to New York for two weeks still hoping that I would receive the support of the government. I was welcomed by the head of the South African Mission, Ambassador Dumisani Kumalo, whom I knew well from previous visits to New York. He was at his wit's end about whether to support my candidature as he had received no instructions from Minister Dlamini-Zuma despite daily requests. I attempted to lobby delegates on my own behalf without the assistance of the South African Mission. They responded warmly and promised to give my candidature serious consideration as soon as they received official notification from Pretoria of its support. No such notification came. As was to be expected, I lost the election to Abdul Koroma. I did, however, have the dubious distinction of being the only candidate who has ever conducted an election campaign on his own in the UN without the support of his government.

All in all, it was a humiliating and costly experience. Despite requests, I did not receive an explanation from the foreign minister for her decision not to support me.[180] I still speculate about the reasons for this treatment. There was no question of personal animosity as I had never met Dlamini-Zuma. Race was a possible explanation. But this explanation cannot be reconciled with the endorsement I received from the government for three elections for the ILC. This leaves the problem of independence as the most likely explanation. I suspect that the government did not want a judge on the International Court who could not be relied on to decide in accordance with its own foreign policy expectations. In 2002 the government had already abandoned the human rights-oriented foreign policy of Mandela in favour of one that gave support to African governments irrespective of their human rights record. With my human rights record I could not be trusted.

Undeterred, I again sought nomination for the International Court in 2008, when the next election for an African place on the ICJ was held. Again, the national group, this time under Pius Langa, endorsed my nomination. But this time Minister Dlamini-Zuma had the decency to write to me to say that the government had decided not to support me.

There are fifteen permanent, full-time judges on the International Court in disputes between states. Surprisingly, if a judge is a national of one of the parties to the dispute, she or he may continue to sit as a judge. If the other party to the dispute has no national on the court, it may appoint a judge itself, known as a judge ad hoc, to sit on that particular case. If neither state has a national judge on the court, both may appoint judges ad hoc. This strange practice has its origin in international arbitral practice in which it is the custom for states to nominate arbitrators to serve with the independently appointed arbitrators.

Judges ad hoc serve as full and independent members of the court and participate in all its hearings, deliberations and decisions as equal members. Usually states appoint their own nationals to serve as judges ad hoc but this is not always done. In some instances states appoint non-nationals whom they regard as qualified to sit on the case to ensure that their side of the dispute is properly understood by the court.

Although I was prevented from becoming a permanent judge on the International Court, I have had the good fortune to serve intermittently as a non-permanent judge – judge ad hoc – on this court from 2000 to 2018. From 2000 until 2006 I was judge ad hoc appointed by Rwanda in a dispute between the Democratic Republic of the Congo and Rwanda in which the DRC alleged that Rwanda had engaged in acts of genocide in the eastern DRC. In 2006 the court found by a substantial majority, in which I concurred, that it had no jurisdiction to hear the case.[181] From 2004 to 2008 I was judge ad hoc in a dispute between Malaysia, which had appointed me, and Singapore on the sovereignty over a cluster of islands in the Straits of Singapore near Malaysia. By twelve votes to four the court found that the principal island, Pedra Branca/Pulau Batu Puteh, belonged to Singapore. I dissented on this decision.[182] In 2010 Costa Rica instituted proceedings against Nicaragua for carrying out activities in an area near to the San Juan River dividing Costa Rica and Nicaragua over which Costa Rica claimed sovereignty. I was appointed as judge ad hoc by Costa Rica. In 2011 Nicaragua counter-claimed that the road Costa Rica was building in its own territory along the San Juan River near the disputed area was causing environmental damage to the river, which falls within Nicaragua's sovereignty. These two cases were joined by the court. Then followed several hearings involving requests for interim measures to protect each party's interests. Only in 2015 did the court decide, unanimously, that Nicaragua had violated the territorial sovereignty of Costa Rica, that Costa Rica had breached its obligation to conduct an environmental impact assessment before embarking on the construction of the road along the San Juan River, and that Nicaragua had failed to prove that Costa Rica's road had caused significant transboundary harm to it.[183] In February 2018 the court ordered Nicaragua to pay compensation to Costa Rica for expenses it had incurred in monitoring Nicaragua's actions and for harm caused to its environment. I agreed with the court's finding on compensation for the expenses incurred but disagreed with the court on the amount of damages awarded for environmental harm.

In 2012 I was awarded the Order of the Baobab (gold), South Africa's highest civilian award for community service, for my work in the fields of human rights and international law. Six South African universities have conferred honorary degrees on me – KwaZulu-Natal, Cape Town, Nelson Mandela University, Pretoria, Witwatersrand and Stellenbosch.

PART THREE

Palestine

I have been engaged in reporting or advising on human rights situations in several countries outside southern Africa. The violation of human rights in all these countries – Iran, Egypt, Northern Ireland, Malawi, the United States and occupied Palestine – has been severe, involving police brutality, political repression, torture and unfair trials. But only in occupied Palestine has a form of apartheid been the issue. This explains why occupied Palestine has been singled out for this study of apartheid, together with apartheid in South Africa and Namibia.

Part Three begins with a history of Palestine; it sets the scene for an examination of Israel's policies and practices in occupied Palestine, which after many years of study and observation I have concluded might be described as akin to apartheid as practised in southern Africa. This part traces the evolution of my experiences over a period of more than twenty years that led to this conclusion. It examines the hallmarks of apartheid as practised in southern Africa that prevail in occupied Palestine and the response of the international community.

Many prefer to confine apartheid to southern Africa under the rule of the racist National Party. The 1973 International Convention on the Suppression and Punishment of the Crime of Apartheid did not restrict its prohibition on apartheid to the race policies of southern Africa. In 1998, four years after the end of apartheid in South Africa, the Rome Statute of the International Criminal Court confirmed that apartheid is a crime against humanity wherever committed. This means that it is no longer possible to seriously argue that apartheid was a peculiarly South African phenomenon.

This is an account of apartheid in occupied Palestine: the West Bank, East Jerusalem and Gaza. It makes no attempt to address the question whether apartheid is applied by Israel within Israel itself.

22

A brief history of modern Palestine, 1917–2000

This history begins with the Balfour Declaration of 1917 and ends in 2000. In 2001 I became involved in Palestine as commissioner and special rapporteur for the United Nations, an involvement that is described in subsequent chapters together with the main events that have occurred since 2000.

The history of Palestine is disputed, divisive and emotional. No history can hope to satisfy all. However, in this brief chapter an attempt will be made to provide a fair account of this history,[1] relying mainly on indisputable facts and those on which there is general consensus. Opinions are reserved for later chapters.

Before World War I, Palestine as we know it today was part of the Ottoman Empire and had been part of that empire for nearly four hundred years. When Turkey joined the Central Powers of Bulgaria, Austria-Hungary and Germany in World War I, Britain and France set about undermining the Ottoman Empire by entering into agreements with Arab leaders to secure their support in exchange for independence after the war. In an exchange of letters between the British high commissioner in Egypt, Sir Henry McMahon, and King Hussein, the sharif of Mecca, in 1915 and 1916, the British government conveyed its intention of supporting the independence of Arabs in the Middle East on condition that they assisted in fighting the Turks. That the British were not to be trusted in their promise to the Arabs was made clear when in 1916 the Sykes–Picot Agreement was entered into between Sir Mark Sykes of Britain and François Georges-Picot of France in which they agreed to divide Turkey's former possessions in the Middle East between Britain and France, with the exception of Arabia (today's

Saudi Arabia), whose independence was to be recognized in the event of an Allied victory. No mention was made in either the McMahon–Hussein correspondence or the Sykes–Picot Agreement of Zionist aspirations for establishing a Jewish homeland in Palestine.[2]

The World Zionist Federation had been established in 1897 under the leadership of Theodor Herzl. Zionists favoured the creation of a separate home for the Jews but initially were divided on the location of such a home. Many favoured Palestine but others were prepared to settle for Uganda or elsewhere. In Britain, support for a Jewish home in Palestine was passionately and effectively pursued by Chaim Weizmann, a Russian Jewish scientist who became a naturalized British subject. Weizmann co-opted Lord Walter Rothschild, a prominent banker and the leader of British Jewry, and together they succeeded in persuading the British government to support the idea of a Jewish homeland in Palestine. This support took the form of a letter, dated 2 November 1917, addressed to Lord Rothschild and published in *The Times* by the British foreign secretary, Arthur Balfour. This letter, which has come to be known as the Balfour Declaration, and which Israel claims justifies the creation of the state of Israel, declared:

> His Majesty's Government view with favour the establishment in Palestine of a national home for the Jewish people, and will use their best endeavours to facilitate the achievement of this object, it being clearly understood that nothing will be done which may prejudice the civil and religious rights of existing non-Jewish communities in Palestine, or the rights and political status enjoyed by Jews in any other country.[3]

There were ulterior political motives for this declaration. Lord Balfour saw it as a way of diverting would-be Jewish immigrants to Britain to another country, and the British government saw it as a way of securing the support of Jews in Russia and the United States for Britain's war effort.

The intended division of the Ottoman Empire between Britain and France after World War I did not materialize. The Russian Revolution and America's entry into the war produced a climate that was antagonistic to annexationist claims of the kind formulated in secret treaties, such as the Sykes–Picot Agreement. Now self-determination, democracy and the protection of minorities were proclaimed as the true aims of the Allied cause. In 1918 President Woodrow Wilson enunciated his famous Fourteen Points, which expounded a new world order based on self-determination, and in the same year South Africa's Jan Smuts published a pamphlet entitled *The League of Nations: A Practical Suggestion* which proposed a system of mandates, in terms of which the colonies of Russia, Austria-Hungary and Turkey would be placed under the tutelage of 'advanced' states accountable to the League of Nations. Smuts carefully excluded Germany's African colonies from the system, but his plan was adopted by Woodrow Wilson and extended to all former colonies of the defeated states. It was this international scheme that was applied to both South West Africa and Palestine.

The mandates system was provided for in the Covenant of the League of Nations. Article 22 declared:

> To those colonies and territories which as a consequence of the late war have ceased to be under the sovereignty of the states which formerly governed them and which are inhabited by peoples not yet able to stand by themselves under the strenuous conditions of the modern world, there should be applied the principle that the well-being and development of such peoples form a sacred trust of civilization and that securities for the performance of this trust should be embodied in this Covenant.

'Advanced' nations were entrusted with the task of administering these territories, to be known as mandates, in order to give effect to this 'sacred trust'. They were accountable to the Council of the League of Nations for their administration. A distinction was drawn between the developed former colonies of the Turkish Empire – Palestine, Iraq, Syria, Lebanon and Transjordan – and the less developed former colonies of Germany in Africa, including South West Africa, and the Pacific Ocean. The former possessions of the Turkish Empire were designated as Class A mandates because they were well advanced and could be provisionally recognized as independent nations with less administrative assistance than the former German colonies, which were designated as Class B and Class C mandates. (The mandate for South West Africa is discussed in Chapter 3.)

In 1922 Britain was appointed as mandatory power over Palestine, Transjordan and Iraq while France became mandatory over Lebanon and Syria. (Initially Britain administered Transjordan and Palestine together, but later Transjordan became a separate mandate.) The mandate agreement for Palestine repeated the language of the Balfour Declaration in its preamble. This stated that Britain as mandatory should be responsible for putting into effect the Balfour Declaration 'in favour of the establishment in Palestine of a national home for the Jewish people, it being clearly understood that nothing should be done which might prejudice the civil and religious rights of existing non-Jewish communities in Palestine'. This, continued the preamble, constituted recognition of the 'historical connection of the Jewish people with Palestine'. Article 2 of the mandate reaffirmed this in stating: 'The Mandatory shall be responsible for placing the country under such political, administrative and economic conditions as will secure the establishment of the Jewish national home, as laid down in the preamble, and the development of self-governing institutions, and also for safeguarding the civil and religious rights of all the inhabitants of Palestine, irrespective of race and religion.' Other provisions of the mandate provided for the facilitation of Jewish immigration 'while ensuring that the rights and position of other sections of the population are not prejudiced', and for freedom of conscience and worship, provided that there was no discrimination on grounds of race, religion or language. English, Arabic and Hebrew were to be the official languages of Palestine.

During the mandate period from 1922 to 1946, the British government, as mandatory power, faced an impossible task of trying to reconcile the conflicting commitments of establishing a national home for the Jewish people while at the same time respecting the civil and religious rights of the majority.[4] For in 1922 the population of Palestine was 752,048, of which only 83,790 were Jews. Britain did facilitate Jewish immigration with the result that by the end of the mandate in 1946 the Jewish population had risen from 11 per cent in 1922 to 30 per cent. In 1946 the population of Palestine was 1,952,920, of which 583,327 were Jews.

Jewish immigration and the sale of land to Jews were resisted by the non-Jewish Palestinians (Muslims and Christians) and resulted in serious clashes with the British administration. In 1936 an Arab revolt resulted in over three hundred deaths and many more wounded. A commission of inquiry known as the Peel Commission concluded that the mandate was unworkable as Arabs wanted national independence for Palestine and an end to Jewish immigration. The Peel Commission recommended the termination of the mandate and the partition of Palestine into an Arab state and a Jewish state. David Ben-Gurion, on behalf of the Jewish Agency, which represented Jewish interests in Palestine, accepted this proposal, but the Arab Higher Committee rejected it. Conflict continued with the British making a vain attempt to curb Jewish immigration, which in turn gave rise to Jewish terrorism carried out by the Irgun and Stern gangs.[5] So it was that when the League of Nations was dissolved in 1946 and replaced by the United Nations, the British government announced that it would terminate the mandate and hand the Palestine problem over to the United Nations. By this time the other A Class mandates – Lebanon, Syria, Iraq and Jordan – had become independent states.

The UN General Assembly was divided on how to resolve the Palestine problem. On 29 November 1947, the question of partition as a solution was put to the vote. By a vote of 33 (including France, the United States and the

Soviet Union) to 13 (including all Arab states), with 10 abstentions (including Britain and China) the General Assembly adopted Resolution 181(II) providing for the partition of Palestine into an Arab and a Jewish state, with an economic union between them, and the internationalization of Jerusalem under UN administration.

Resolution 181(II) was accepted by the Jews but rejected by the Arabs. This was not surprising as the partition plan offered the Jewish community (comprising 33 per cent of the population of Palestine) 57 per cent of the land and 84 per cent of the agricultural land.

The legality of Resolution 181(II) was and still is debated by international lawyers. Moreover, it was clearly impossible to implement it in the face of Arab opposition. Attention then returned to the possibility of a UN trusteeship agreement, and on 20 April 1948 the United States introduced the text of a draft Trusteeship Agreement for Palestine before the General Assembly which envisaged a single Palestinian state.[6] Time was, however, running out as Britain had announced that it would evacuate its administration at midnight on 14 May.

At midnight on 14 May 1948 Israel declared its independence unilaterally, invoking Resolution 181(II) in support of its independence. The new state was immediately recognized by President Truman on behalf of the United States, much to the surprise and consternation of the US State Department, which had warned against premature recognition.[7] Two days later Israel was recognized by the Soviet Union. In January 1949 David Ben-Gurion, head of the Jewish Agency, was elected as prime minister of Israel, and Chaim Weizmann was elected as president.

Israel's declaration of independence was followed by hostilities between the new state and the Arab states of Egypt, Jordan, Syria and Lebanon, which were brought to an end by the armistice agreements of 1949. These armistice agreements created a de facto border, known as the Green Line, between Israel and the remainder of Palestine, which resulted in the state of Israel occupying much more of Palestine than was envisaged by Resolution 181(II). On 11 May 1949, Israel was admitted to the United Nations, with Britain abstaining from voting in both the Security Council and the General Assembly. Although there is a debate about the legal basis for the creation of Israel, the better view is that it was created by secession from Palestine, as the territory of the new state was its armistice territory and not the smaller territory, with Jerusalem as an internationalized city, proposed by the partition plan of Resolution 181(II).[8]

The remainder of the mandated territory of Palestine was subjected to military occupation: Jordan occupied East Jerusalem and the West Bank while Egypt occupied Gaza. Egypt did not annex Gaza and made it clear that it administered the territory provisionally pending a peace settlement resulting in a Palestinian state. Jordan, on the other hand, purported to annex East Jerusalem and the West Bank, but this annexation was recognized only by Britain and Pakistan. For the United Nations, East Jerusalem and the West Bank remained under the temporary military occupation of Jordan, with a status akin to that of Gaza.

The 1948–9 conflict resulted in the displacement of three-quarters of a million Arabs, which amounted to about 85 per cent of the Palestinian population living in the territory that had become the state of Israel. This process of dispossession and expulsion, described by historians as ethnic cleansing,[9] is today known as the Nakba, or Catastrophe. Palestinians forcibly driven from their homes by Jewish militia sought refuge in refugee camps in the West Bank, Jordan, Syria and Lebanon. On 11 December 1948 the UN General Assembly adopted Resolution 194(III), which declared that refugees should be allowed to return to their homes 'at the earliest possible date' and compensation should be paid to those not wishing to return. To date, refugees have not been allowed to return nor have they been compensated. The issue of refugees is a highly emotional subject and one of the issues that will have to be resolved in any peace settlement between Israel and the Palestinians.[10]

In 1956 President Nasser of Egypt nationalized the Suez Canal. Israel joined France and Britain in a tripartite alliance to overthrow Nasser, which resulted in Israel occupying the Sinai Peninsula. The invasion was brought to an end by pressure from the United States, the Soviet Union and the UN. Reluctantly Israel withdrew from the Sinai but succeeded in securing the opening of the Straits of Tiran, which allowed shipping to reach the Israeli port of Eilat. After the conflict the UN established a peacekeeping force, the United Nations Emergency Force (UNEF), to police the Israeli–Egyptian border.

In 1967 relations between Israel and Egypt became strained as a result of Egypt's closure of the Straits of Tiran to Israeli shipping, the withdrawal of UN peacekeepers at the request of Egypt, and bellicose rhetoric from Cairo. On 5 June Israel launched an air attack against Egypt, destroying most of the Egyptian air force, which was followed by a ground offensive in Gaza and the Sinai. Jordan and Syria joined Egypt in the war against Israel. In six days Israel defeated all three states, and occupied the Sinai, Gaza, the West Bank, East Jerusalem and the Golan Heights. Did Israel act in pre-emptive self-defence or was Israel the aggressor, relying on the hostile climate in the region as a pretext for its attack on Egypt? There are conflicting accounts of the legality of the war,[11] and the jury is still out on this matter.

After the war, the UN Security Council adopted Resolution 242(1967), which emphasized the 'inadmissibility of the acquisition of territory by war' and called for the 'withdrawal of Israeli armed forces from territories occupied in the recent conflict', a resolution that was confirmed by Resolution 338(1973). The position in international law is clear: a state that occupies territory following a war may not annex that territory, irrespective of whether it acted as aggressor or in self-defence. Instead it must occupy the territory as belligerent occupant pending a peace settlement.

In 1973 Israel fought another war with its neighbours: the Yom Kippur War. On Yom Kippur, the Day of Atonement, the holiest day of the year for Jews, Egypt and Syria attacked Israeli positions in Sinai and Golan, with initial success. Israel recovered and drove both Egyptian and Syrian forces back into Egypt and Syria before peace was brokered by the UN.

In 1978 peace talks hosted and facilitated by President Jimmy Carter were held between Anwar Sadat of Egypt and Menachem Begin of Israel at Camp David.[12] These talks resulted in the Egypt–Israel peace treaty of 1979 in terms of which relations between Egypt and Israel were normalized and Israel agreed to withdraw its forces and settlers, numbering some forty-five hundred, from Sinai.

Israel annexed East Jerusalem in 1980 and the Golan Heights in 1981. Although these annexations have been condemned by the UN and are not recognized by any state – including the United States – they have been fully implemented, with the result that Israeli law applies in East Jerusalem and on the Golan Heights.

Israel continues to occupy the West Bank and Gaza as belligerent occupant. (The position of Gaza after 2005 is discussed in a later chapter.) Belligerent occupation is a regime recognized by international law to apply to territories occupied by a victorious state following an armed conflict. It prohibits annexation of the occupied territory and is intended to be of short duration. It permits the occupying power to administer the territory in accordance with the laws of the occupied territory subject to the requirements of international law and the security needs of the occupying power. Essentially its aim is to allow the victorious power to secure itself against a resurgence of armed conflict pending a peace agreement with the vanquished state. The rules governing belligerent occupation are to be found in customary international law, the Hague Regulations of 1907, and the Fourth Geneva Convention of 1949 and its accompanying First Protocol of 1977.

Although it is a party to the Fourth Geneva Convention, Israel argues that this is not applicable to the West Bank and Gaza because these territories were not under the sovereignty of Palestine before 1967 but were instead subject to the belligerent occupation of Jordan and Egypt. Israel does, however, claim to administer the occupied territories as a matter of policy in accordance with the humanitarian principles of the Fourth Geneva Convention.

Israel's main objection to the Fourth Geneva Convention is that it expressly prohibits the transfer of settlers from the occupying power into the occupied territory. Following its occupation of East Jerusalem, the West Bank and Gaza, Israel embarked on a policy and programme of establishing Jewish settlements in these areas. Settlements are today the major stumbling block in the way of a peaceful resolution of the conflict.

Palestinian resistance in the 1970s and early 1980s was carried on largely by the Palestinian Liberation Organization (PLO) under Yasser Arafat from bases in Jordan, Lebanon and, finally, Tunisia. The PLO, established in 1964 with the aim of liberating the whole of the mandate territory of Palestine from Israeli occupation by means of armed struggle, was made up of a coalition of Palestinian political parties of which Fatah, the Popular Front for the Liberation of Palestine (PFLP) and the Democratic Front for the Liberation of Palestine were the most important.

In 1982 Israel invaded Lebanon in order to expel the PLO from that country. After the PLO had left Lebanon for Tunisia, the Lebanese Christian militia, the Phalangists, attacked the Palestinian refugee camps of Sabra and Shatila, inflicting heavy losses in what was described as a massacre. This was made possible by Israeli forces under Ariel Sharon, then minister of defence. Sharon was compelled to resign after the Kahan Commission of Inquiry in Israel had found that he had given indirect assistance to the Phalangists.

From 1987 to 1993 there was a Palestinian uprising against the occupation, known as the First Intifada. Policies of house demolition, deportation and extra-judicial killings, coupled with frustration on the part of the Palestinian youth, resulted in this largely spontaneous and community-driven uprising. The First Intifada, which involved over 1,200 Palestinian and 200 Israeli deaths, took the form of strikes, boycotts of Israeli products, civil disobedience and demonstrations, sometimes involving stone-throwing. The Israel Defense Forces (IDF) used strong-armed methods, including beatings, shootings, tear gas and mass arrests, to suppress the uprising. The UN was powerless to intervene in the face of US vetoes in the Security Council.

The uprising lost its impetus when a conference to revive the peace process through negotiation was held in Madrid, co-sponsored by the United States and the Soviet Union, and attended by Israel, the Palestinians and several Arab states. This conference led to bilateral meetings between Palestinians and Israelis in Washington and Moscow. Israel's insistence that the Palestinian delegation be confined to representatives from the West Bank and Gaza and did not include members of the PLO made it impossible to achieve a major breakthrough.

Before 1993 successive Israeli governments refused to have anything to do with the PLO. Even the PLO's November 1988 Algiers Declaration, which proclaimed a Palestinian state in East Jerusalem, the West Bank and Gaza, recognized the existence of Israel over 78 per cent of Palestine and proposed a two-state solution, failed to persuade Israel to deal with the organization.

Everything changed in 1993 when Israel met secretly with the PLO in Oslo and adopted the Oslo Accords. A Declaration of Principles on Interim Self-Government Arrangements of 13 September 1993 was later signed at the White House by Israeli prime minister Yitzhak Rabin and PLO chairman Yasser Arafat in the presence of American president Bill Clinton. This declaration provided for the establishment of a Palestinian Interim Self-Government Authority 'for a period not exceeding five years, leading to a permanent settlement based on Security Council Resolutions 242 and 338".[13] At the same time the PLO recognized the right of the state of Israel to exist in peace and renounced the use of violence, while Israel recognized the PLO as the representative of the Palestinian people. Permanent status negotiations were to commence within three years and were to address the core issues of the status of Jerusalem, refugees, settlements, borders and security arrangements.[14] In September 1995 a further agreement known as Oslo II was signed in Washington to further the Oslo process.

The principal territorial feature of the Oslo process was the creation of three zones in the West Bank for the interim period. Area A, consisting of the densely populated Palestinian cities and towns, over which the Palestinian Authority exercises most governmental powers, comprises 18 per cent of the West Bank. Area B, comprising 22 per cent of the West Bank, consists of smaller Palestinian towns and villages and rural areas, and falls under Palestinian civil control and Israeli security control. The remainder of the West Bank constitutes Area C, which is entirely controlled by Israeli military forces. It consists of settlements, some Palestinian community areas, rural areas and territory adjacent to the 1967 border. In total Israel yielded nearly 40 per cent of the West Bank to Palestinian civil control. The result of this arrangement is a series of non-contiguous islands of Palestinian cities and towns surrounded by areas under Israeli military control, which requires Palestinians travelling from one city to another to pass through a multitude of Israeli military checkpoints. In Gaza Israel retained 35 per cent of the land containing Israeli settlements and the roads leading to them, and the rest was handed over to the Palestinian Authority. East Jerusalem as annexed territory fell under full Israeli control. Although movement between the West Bank and Gaza was severely restricted, the two were viewed as a single territorial unit for the purposes of a future self-governing Palestinian entity.

It was, in the words of one of Israel's negotiators, 'amazing' that nothing in the Oslo Accords prevented the expansion of settlements. According to Shlomo

Ben-Ami, this was because the Palestinian negotiators were based in Tunis and 'had no knowledge of the conditions on the ground. Local leaders who had been brought up under the occupation, and the arrogance and agrarian hunger of the settlers, would not have let this happen.'[15]

The Oslo process was not a success. In 1995 it was dealt a fatal blow when a Jewish right-wing fanatic assassinated Yitzhak Rabin, Israel's most credible supporter of the process, with whom Yasser Arafat claimed he had established a 'peace of the brave'. Subsequent Israeli prime ministers either lacked the commitment to implement Oslo (Shimon Peres and Ehud Barak) or were determined to obstruct its implementation (Benjamin Netanyahu). In January 1996 Palestine held presidential and legislative elections, which were won by Yasser Arafat and Fatah.

Both Israel and Palestine were dissatisfied with the Oslo regime. Israel complained repeatedly that the Palestinian Authority under Yasser Arafat failed to prevent acts of violence committed by Islamic Jihad and Hamas (which had been formed during the First Intifada). The Palestinians were aggrieved to discover that the construction of settlements continued unabated and found the checkpoints that regulated their movements between different Areas humiliating and harmful to the economy. Moreover, agreements reached with Israel under Oslo in respect of the economy, the transfer of territory and prisoner release were not honoured.

In the last months of the Clinton administration in 2000, serious attempts were made to implement a final status agreement. President Clinton called a meeting at Camp David in July 2000 in which he, Arafat and Barak participated. But the talks broke down, mainly on the issue of sovereignty over Haram al-Sharif, which accommodates the al-Aqsa Mosque, Islam's third most sacred site, and the Dome of the Rock. This site is also of special significance to Jews as it is said to be the place on which the Jewish Second Temple stood. For Jews it is known as the Temple Mount. Neither side was prepared to compromise on this issue. The Palestinians, and particularly Yasser Arafat, were blamed for the breakdown of the talks. This is a disputed assessment, although it had the support of both Ehud Barak and Bill Clinton.[16] The Palestinians had indicated a willingness to compromise on borders, the incorporation of most settlements into Israel, and the right of return of Palestinian refugees. They would not, however, agree to Israeli sovereignty over Haram al-Sharif/Temple Mount. Both sides were equally intransigent on this issue.

Negotiations between the Israelis, Palestinians and Americans continued after the failure of Camp David, as all parties were aware of President Clinton's determination to secure a peaceful settlement in the last months of his presidency.

Another meeting was held at Taba from 21 to 27 January at which refugees, security, borders and Jerusalem were discussed.[17] Parties came close to reaching an agreement but time ran out. President Clinton's term of office had come to an end and Barak faced an election in early February. On 6 February 2001 the Likud Party under Ariel Sharon defeated Ehud Barak. Sharon announced that high-level talks between the Israelis and Palestinians would be discontinued.

In the meantime, the Second Intifada had started. This Palestinian uprising, which was to put an end to any optimism for a peaceful settlement that might have been engendered by the Oslo Accords, is the focus of later chapters.

23

The pre-United Nations years, 1982–1998

I first went to Israel in 1982. It was a land familiar to me in many ways. The Bible had taught me about its early history and international law had introduced me to its more recent one. I had studied the mandates system of the League of Nations, the dispute over the 1947 Partition Plan and the creation of the state of Israel. I had followed the 1967 Six-Day War and the occupation of the Palestinian Territories. Israel's security laws were of special interest, for it was common practice among academic lawyers in South Africa to compare these laws with those of South Africa and Northern Ireland. In 1961 Prime Minister H.F. Verwoerd had dismissed an Israeli vote against apartheid in the UN, declaring that Israel had taken land away from the Arabs who had lived there for thousands of years and that 'Israel, like South Africa, is an apartheid state'. But this was not a commonly made or accepted comparison. Even in 1982 there was no serious suggestion that Israel's laws, policies or practices resembled the race laws of South Africa. Apartheid was a South African phenomenon and was not to be found in occupied Palestine and certainly not in Israel itself.

Like most white South Africans, I saw this history of the Middle East through the spectacles of Israel. I had marvelled at Israel's military prowess in the Six-Day War and condemned repeated acts of terror committed by Palestinians. David Ben-Gurion and Golda Meir were admired; Yasser Arafat was not. Friends had fought with the Israeli forces in the Six-Day War of 1967; sons of friends had fought with Israeli forces in the Yom Kippur War of 1973. Jane and I were very much part of the Johannesburg Jewish community and there were many discussions about Israel. We were exposed to the sharp division of opinion over the direction of Israel, particularly since the 1977 victory of the right-wing Likud Party under the premiership of Menachem Begin, which made it difficult to continue believing that Israel wanted a just peace with the Palestinians.

In the late 1970s the conflict in the Middle East became a real issue on the Wits campus as a result of the admission of Indian students, many of whom were Muslims. Rival militant Jewish and Muslim students clashed violently on campus on days commemorating Israeli triumphs and Palestinian tribulations. Wits had never seen anything like this. Radical and conservative student groups had previously confronted each other on South African political issues but had never come to blows. It now became difficult to lecture dispassionately on the international law aspects of the Middle East. Normally docile students became angry if they did not agree with the presentation of the legal arguments.

In June 1982 Israel invaded Lebanon; in September of that year Palestinians in the refugee camps of Sabra and Shatila were massacred by Christian Phalangist militiamen with the knowledge and connivance of the Israeli Defense Forces. At Wits there were nasty protests and counter-protests. The vice-chancellor of the university, Professor D.J. du Plessis, was assaulted when he tried to intervene between pro-Israel and anti-Israel student groups. And in the United States the Aspen Institute had a problem.

The Aspen Institute had organized a seminar on 'Monotheism, Past, Present and Future' in its Tradition and Modernization programme to be held in Jerusalem in December 1982. A number of prominent Arabs were among those who had agreed to participate. Then came the invasion of Lebanon and they all withdrew. The Aspen Institute was in a quandary as to whether to proceed with the seminar, but as arrangements were far under way it was decided to continue with the seminar and to invite others to join. Fresh from the Aspen Institute's Justice and Society seminar in Aspen, Colorado, I was invited at the eleventh hour to join. I had never been to Israel or Palestine before and I had never considered going there either. But the invitation was too good to refuse: ten days in the Middle East, all expenses paid, and the prospect of a stimulating meeting.

The seminar was held and the participants accommodated in the picturesque Mishkenot Sha'ananim conference centre. Built in 1860 in the first Jewish neighbourhood outside the Old City, it commanded a magnificent view of the walls of the Old City and the Jaffa Gate. There were some thirty participants in the seminar, mostly American, drawn from all walks of life. We had been required to do a considerable amount of reading on religions, cultural traditions and the problems that had been created in the Middle East by modernization. Discussions centred on these themes, but we were also introduced to the history and politics of the region. Israeli political figures that led the discussions on the politics of the Middle East included Shimon Peres, whom several of us in the seminar wrongly judged to be a political has-been. Because of the invasion of Lebanon we had no Palestinian speakers. We visited Christian, Muslim and Jewish holy sites, Yad Vashem, the Galilee, Bethlehem, Nazareth, the Negev, the Dead Sea, Masada and Jaffa. The history and physical beauty of the country were overwhelming. It became clear that neutrality was as little an option in the Middle East as it was in South Africa.

We drove through the West Bank but did not visit a Jewish settlement. The Palestinian issue was ever present in our discussions, but we saw everything from the Israeli perspective. I knew that I would be back. Already I was a captive of the region. I wanted to learn more about Israel and Palestine. In particular I wanted to know more about the Palestinians and their side of the story.

Soon after I returned to South Africa I applied to the Human Sciences Research Council for funding for a study on the international law implications of the Israel–Palestine conflict and the different perspectives in Israel and Palestine on the role of international law.[18] The grant included funding for a visit to the region to interview informed interlocutors.

I met many prominent Israelis, including Chief Justice Meir Shamgar, Joel Singer, legal adviser to the Israel Defense Forces, who was later to play a key role in the adoption of the Oslo Accords, and Shabtai Rosenne, legal adviser to the Foreign Ministry. A highly critical picture of Israel's policies was given by Meron Benvenisti, former deputy mayor of Jerusalem, who prophetically warned of the dangers of the creation of settlements. And then there were the South African academics David Kretzmer and Stanley Cohen, both of whom had left South Africa and settled in Israel for idealistic reasons, only to find that they were grappling with familiar problems in their new home. David's main field of study was the review of actions of the military authorities in the West Bank and Gaza by the Supreme Court. He argued, convincingly, that like the courts of South Africa, the Supreme Court of Israel had used the law as an instrument to rationalize and legitimize the policies of the Israeli government in the occupied territories.[19]

The Palestinian perspective was provided by Raja Shehadeh and his colleagues Charles Shammas and Jonathan Kuttab at the human rights NGO Al-Haq. In those days it was easy to drive from West Jerusalem, where I was staying, to Ramallah, where Al-Haq was situated. There were none of the checkpoints and roadblocks that would later make this journey of some twenty kilometres a nightmare.

Raja's family history was not unusual. His father Aziz was a successful lawyer in Jaffa, close to Tel Aviv. In 1948, as Israeli forces closed in on Jaffa, he left with his family to their summer house in Ramallah, believing that they would return after a few weeks, as Jaffa was scheduled to be part of Arab Palestine in terms of the 1947 Partition Proposal. They were never to return, as Jaffa became part of Israel.[20]

Raja, himself a lawyer, is today recognized as Palestine's foremost English-language writer. In 1982 he published *The Third Way: A Journal of Life in the West Bank*, which examined life under occupation in the West Bank from the perspective of a human rights lawyer. In many respects it mirrored my own writing with its concerns about how the fig leaf of law was used to conceal brutal violations of human rights. In *The Third Way* he provided a third option to passive submission to the occupation or taking up arms against it. This was confronting the occupation by working through the law. In essence this was the course followed by public interest lawyers in South Africa.

I had a tour of the settlements in the West Bank with journalist Danny Rubinstein. There could have been no better guide. Rubinstein understood full well the ideology that compelled settlement growth and predicted, correctly, that settlements would expand to become a colonial empire. I spent a night in a settlement near Hebron with the brother of a friend from Wits. He was a cardiologist who had given up the comforts of suburban Johannesburg to live with his family in an isolated settlement. It was a cold night, perhaps the coldest I had experienced in my life, and I marvelled at the commitment of settlers to the austere way of life some had chosen to live. Of course, many settlements were not like this – they were suburban homes with every comfort. The excitement of learning and comparing was replaced by despair. I found living in two competing worlds a painful experience. Spending time in occupied Palestine and then returning to the freedom of West Jerusalem was too much. I felt torn between the different narratives. I decided to leave a week early.

In December 1987 the First Intifada erupted.[21] Before the Intifada started I had accepted an invitation to a conference organized by Al-Haq in Jerusalem. With little knowledge of the gravity of the situation, Jane and I arrived in Israel. I had promised Jane a short tour of Israel and Palestine before the conference, and we hired a car and set off to see the two countries. Soon we realized that we were in the midst of civil conflict. In order to pass through Palestinian roadblocks we displayed a *keffiyeh* on the car's dashboard, which we hastily removed when we approached an IDF roadblock. We passed demonstrations and IDF checkpoints and were made acutely aware of the conflict. This was not what I had promised Jane.

We stayed in the American Colony Hotel in East Jerusalem, for me unquestionably the most wonderful hotel in the world from the perspective of style, comfort and intrigue. Our first night was spent in the Pasha room, which

I recalled having seen in a Peter Ustinov movie. From the excitement of being in such a splendid room we received a rude awakening when at 4 am the faithful were called to prayer from a muezzin situated close by.

The conference was a great success. Al-Haq had assembled leading Palestinian human rights lawyers and prominent international lawyers from many countries to address the international law aspects of the administration of occupied territories with special reference to Israel's occupation of Palestine. Sadly, none of the Israeli international lawyers invited to participate accepted the invitation. The three-day conference ended with a strong statement condemning the disproportionate use of force employed by the IDF in suppressing the Intifada.

I delivered a paper on the enforcement of international humanitarian law and human rights law in which I advocated an advisory opinion by the International Court of Justice which would recognise the illegality of settlements and the right of Palestinian self-determination. I also suggested that some of the measures used to compel South Africa to abandon apartheid be applied to Israel. Significantly, while I condemned the violation of human rights, I made no attempt to equate Israel's policies and practices with apartheid.[22]

In 1992 I returned to Palestine to undertake an assessment of the Quaker Legal Aid Center in Jerusalem. This was a highly successful centre, which engaged in human rights advocacy as well as providing legal aid to Palestinians. It was staffed by competent Palestinian lawyers, but was largely governed by the American Friends, and there were demands that its governance should be 'Palestinized' or 'indigenized'. I was tasked with the job of assessing the work of the centre and its relationship with other Palestinian NGOs and examining the feasibility of handing over governance to Palestinians. I recommended that this be done. Today it is the Jerusalem Legal Aid and Human Rights Center.

In December 1997 I was invited to a conference hosted by the Minerva Center for Human Rights of the Hebrew University of Jerusalem on aspects of international humanitarian law. It was a stimulating meeting attended by the leading Israeli international humanitarian lawyers, but with no Palestinian lawyers. Inevitably there was a lack of understanding of the Palestinian perspective and of the facts of the occupation as seen by Palestinians. It was too much like all-white South African conferences discussing apartheid.

On this visit I stayed in the guesthouse on the campus of the Hebrew University with a magnificent view of the Old City of Jerusalem with the Dome of the Rock glittering in the sunlight. When the conference was not in session I walked down the Mount of Olives to the Old City. This was a few years after Oslo and there was peace in the land. But it was not to last for long.

It was during this visit to Jerusalem that David Kretzmer arranged for me to meet Chief Justice Aharon Barak in Israel's splendid new Supreme Court. He warned me that Barak was likely to ask me about torture, and he was right. No sooner had we sat down than Barak began to question me about how South African judges had handled torture during the apartheid years. I told him that most judges had not taken a firm stand against accepting evidence obtained from detainees who had unquestionably been tortured. It was clear that Barak was deeply troubled. He was obviously aware – for it was common knowledge – that the Israeli security services employed methods of torture, such as severe shaking, sleep deprivation and compelling detainees to sit in the 'Shabach position', which involved sitting for a long time in a small chair tilted forward, with hands bound behind to the chair and head covered with a hood, and being subjected to loud music. He knew too that the security services believed that these methods were a necessary component of the interrogation process and were essential to the maintenance of Israel's security and the prevention of acts of terrorism. But at the same time he was acutely aware that they were unacceptable to a state that professed allegiance to democratic values and the rule of law. He spoke about the need to achieve a balance between the interests of security and respect for human rights, and expressed the determination to find such a balance, however unpopular it might be.

The following year the Supreme Court of Israel handed down its decision on torture,[23] written by Barak, which held that the government and the security services were not permitted to employ or to authorize methods of interrogation that involved shaking, sleep deprivation or the 'Shabach'. Considerations of necessity or the search for the 'ticking bomb' could not justify such measures. In placing a prohibition on these methods of interrogation, Barak declared: 'At times a democracy must fight with one hand tied behind her back. Despite that, a democracy has the upper hand since the preservation of the rule of law and the recognition of individual liberties constitute important components of her security stance. At the end of the day, they strengthen her and her spirit and allow her to overcome her difficulties.'[24]

I met Aharon Barak later when I was UN special rapporteur on human rights in Palestine. He was a warm and engaging man. I admired him as a judge. Judging in a society so riven as Israel and so obsessed with security was not easy. I was critical of many of his decisions, particularly those dealing with settlements and the wall. But he was a judge determined to search for justice, however unpopular his decision might be. His decision on torture and a later decision on targeted assassinations[25] provided evidence of his determination to balance Israel's security needs with justice. Sadly, Israel's security services paid little heed to these decisions.

24

The Second Intifada and the UN Commission of Inquiry

On 28 September 2000 Ariel Sharon, leader of the Likud Party, accompanied by a large party of Likud supporters, visited the Haram al-Sharif/Temple Mount. The ostensible purpose of the visit was to assert the right of Israelis to visit the Temple Mount, but it was generally believed that the main purpose was to show that under a Likud government the Temple Mount would remain under Israeli sovereignty. Reluctantly the government of Ehud Barak gave permission to Sharon's visit, to dispel any suggestion that it was prepared to compromise Israeli sovereignty over the Temple Mount. Fearing that the visit would raise tensions among the Palestinians, Arafat and other Palestinian leaders called on Sharon not to go.

As predicted, the visit was followed by protests and demonstrations in the Old City of Jerusalem, in which seven Palestinians were killed and some three hundred wounded. Spontaneous demonstrations erupted all over the West Bank and Gaza prompted not only by Sharon's visit to Haram al-Sharif but also by disillusionment over the Oslo Accords, the brutality and humiliation of the occupation, poverty and the miserable conditions in the refugee camps.

Whereas the First Intifada was a popular uprising characterized by demonstrations (sometimes accompanied by stone-throwing), acts of civil disobedience and boycotts, the Second Intifada became a low-level civil war. Both sides employed armed force of different kinds, resulting in thousands of deaths and injuries.[26] Neither side made a serious effort to distinguish between combatants and civilians in their actions.

On the Palestinian side, suicide bombings resulting in the deaths of many innocent Israelis, stone-throwing, armed force and rocket fire from Gaza joined protests and peaceful demonstrations as features of the uprising. Over a thousand Israelis were killed, of whom the majority were civilians.

The Israel Defense Forces (IDF), supported by settlers, responded aggressively. Ground forces confronted mass protests and demonstrations with live fire, supported by F16 fighter aircraft and Apache gunship helicopters. The Israeli human rights NGO B'Tselem estimated that from 2000 to April 2008 some 4,475 Palestinians were killed, of whom most were civilians. Thousands of Palestinians were arrested, detained and tortured. Over four thousand houses were demolished, agricultural land was stripped of trees and crops, free movement was seriously restricted by checkpoints and curfews, the coast of Gaza was blockaded, and hospitals and schools were attacked

Arguably the Second Intifada continued until January 2009 after Israel's destruction of Gaza in Operation Cast Lead. It did, however, lose much of its impetus in February 2005, when Mohamed Abbas, who had succeeded Arafat as chairman of the Palestinian Authority, signed a truce at the Egyptian resort of Sharm-el-Sheikh. A truce between the Palestinians and Israelis was impossible before this date as Sharon, who was elected as prime minister of Israel in February 2001, maintained his stubborn hostility towards Arafat and refused to speak to him, unlike his predecessor, Ehud Barak.

On 19 October 2000 the UN Commission on Human Rights in Geneva adopted a resolution[27] to establish a commission of inquiry to investigate violations of human rights and humanitarian law by Israel in the Occupied Palestinian Territories after 28 September 2000. I was unaware of the establishment of this commission as the media had instead focused attention on the creation of a fact-finding mission into the Second Intifada to be chaired by US Senator George Mitchell, which had been established by President Bill Clinton, President Hosni Mubarak of Egypt, King Abdullah of Jordan and UN Secretary-General Kofi Annan at Sharm el-Sheikh on 17 October 2000. The first I knew about the UN commission was a phone call I received from the Commission on Human Rights when Ietje and I were on holiday in India, asking me whether I would be prepared to be considered as a member. I do not know who had suggested me for this position, but I later discovered that Nabil Elaraby, Egyptian ambassador to the UN and a fellow member of the International Law Commission, had had a hand in it.

On 2 January 2001, I learnt that I had been appointed to the commission together with Richard Falk and Kamal Hossain. I knew Richard Falk well. We had first met in 1967 when he had been an observer at the trial of thirty-seven Namibians charged with terrorism in Pretoria. Later he had been instrumental in inviting me to teach at Princeton, where he was professor of international law. Richard was a creative and controversial scholar who had taken a principled stand on many issues, particularly the illegality of US intervention in Vietnam. Kamal Hossain was a former foreign minister of Bangladesh, who had been imprisoned during Bangladesh's war of independence. He had extensive experience as an arbitrator and was the Commission of Human Right's special rapporteur on human rights in Afghanistan. I had not previously met him.

UN rules require the consent of the state to whose territory a fact-finding mission is sent.[28] This meant that Israel was fully entitled to refuse permission to the commission to visit both Israel and the occupied Palestinian territory.

The Israeli government was concerned not only about the possibility of a hostile report but was also worried about the members of the commission. With no track record on the Middle East I was clearly the most acceptable member. Richard Falk had been highly critical of Israel in his writings and was seen by the Israelis to be a self-hating Jew. Kamal Hossain, despite his reputation as a moderate, was a Muslim from Bangladesh, who was therefore perceived to be inherently hostile to Israel.

To our surprise, the Israeli government decided to grant the commission access to Israel and Palestine. I suspect that its decision was largely based on the fact that it would have found it difficult to justify co-operation with the Mitchell Fact-Finding Mission if it had denied access to the commission of inquiry of the Commission on Human Rights. But there was to be no co-operation with the commission of inquiry on the part of the Israeli government. The commission was, however, adequately informed of the Israeli position through its submissions to the Mitchell Fact-Finding Mission, to which it had access, and by speaking to Israeli interlocutors. Although it refused to co-operate, the government of Israel did not in any way obstruct the commission in the performance of its work. It granted a visa to Dr Hossain. Neither Richard Falk nor I required a visa to enter Israel.

There was no way South Africa would have granted permission to a commission of inquiry established by the Commission on Human Rights to enter Namibia, also an internationalized and occupied territory. So the decision to allow our commission to enter Palestine did display a sensitivity to international opinion and a willingness to co-operate at a low level on the part of the Israeli government.

Fact-finding commissions are an essential component of the machinery for the enforcement of human rights. No action can be taken against a state for violating human rights, and no attempt can be made at conciliation without ascertainment of the facts of the conflict in question. But fact-finding bodies are not courts of law. They have no power to compel a recalcitrant government to testify or to explain its actions, no power to compel witnesses to give evidence, and there are no formal procedures for the examination of witnesses. They must seek evidence in other ways and from sources not usually used by courts of law. Victims and eyewitnesses may be questioned in order to establish the facts, and the scene of the crimes may be visited to allow inferences to be drawn about military operations. In order to obtain a full picture it would be necessary to consult NGOs that had made a careful study of the situation, journalists who had reported on the conflict, and government officials to whom reports had been made. Fact-finding bodies therefore use all available means to obtain the evidence needed to fulfil their task.

The human rights inquiry commission visited the Occupied Palestinian Territories and Israel in February 2001. As the Commission on Human Rights did not appoint a chair of the commission, it was left to the three commissioners to make this decision. Initially Kamal and I acted as co-chairs, but during the course of the visit it was agreed that I should be chair. The commission was accompanied by a staff of eleven persons made up of advisers, security officers, interpreters and secretaries.

The commission visited the major cities of occupied Palestine: Gaza City, Khan Yunis, East Jerusalem, Ramallah, Hebron and Bethlehem. It met with Palestinian political leaders and officials, religious leaders, UN officials, foreign diplomats, the Red Crescent and the International Committee of the Red Cross, journalists, lawyers, academics and NGOs. The most helpful were the staff of UNRWA – the UN Relief and Works Agency – which was responsible for the housing, education and welfare of refugees, and the NGOs, both Palestinian and Israeli. Although Palestinian and Israeli NGOs functioned separately, they shared the common goal of advancing human rights through fact-finding research and advocacy.

We met Yasser Arafat, who turned out to be very different from what I had expected. He was not the militant terrorist figure that the Western media had painted. Instead he appeared to be a sensitive man prepared to listen to his guests. As on the many subsequent occasions on which I met him as special rapporteur, we started off our conversation through an interpreter, but he soon dismissed the interpreter and conducted his conversation in English. He was not fluent in English and his vocabulary was limited, but he spoke adequate and lively English. In Gaza he gave us an emotional account of the events that had led to the Second Intifada, of the disproportionate measures employed by Israel to suppress the uprising, and of the hostility between him and Sharon, who had recently been elected prime minister of Israel and who refused to meet with him. Without talks, Arafat insisted, a peaceful resolution of the conflict was unattainable. After our meeting we left the room to face the TV cameras. I was surprised when I was descending the stairs to find a small hand holding mine and leading me to the media. It was Arafat. At that stage I was unfamiliar with Arab custom according to which it was not unusual for men to hold hands. But somehow Arafat's hand-holding had a special intimacy.

We received full accounts from our interlocutors of the excessive use of force employed by the Israel Defense Forces[29] in its suppression of the uprising, the expansion of settlements and discontent over the Oslo process. In addition, we spoke to victims of the violence and their families and to the wounded in hospital. On occasion we visited areas of conflict and destruction. We visited farms and villages near the Israeli settlement of Netzarim where houses and agricultural lands had been bulldozed into oblivion by Caterpillar vehicles, an essential weapon in the IDF arsenal. In Khan Yunis refugee camp we were caught in crossfire. Palestinians had fired at the nearby settlement of Neve Dekalim, provoking a barrage of gunfire from the IDF. We scuttled for safety to a nearby building, but several Palestinians youths were seriously wounded. Despite the care of our security advisers, fact-finding was not a safe exercise.

The report of the commission[30] focused mainly on the actions of Israel because of our mandate. The disproportionate number of Palestinians killed and injured, and the extensive destruction caused to homes and agricultural land, provided clear evidence that the IDF had used excessive force. Instead of using water cannons, tear gas and soft rubber bullets to quell demonstrations, the IDF had used lethal hard rubber bullets and live ammunition. Many of those killed were children. Some Palestinians were deliberately killed – executed – when they might have been arrested. Military necessity was no defence. So there was clear evidence of the violation of the right to life and limb, to freedom of assembly, to family life and to property. The impact on personal freedom and the economy of restrictions imposed on movement by checkpoints, closures and curfews featured prominently in the report. Settlements received particular attention as they were seen to be a major reason for discontent on the part of the Palestinians. The commission confirmed the illegality of settlements, and found that they had grown in number since Oslo, that settler violence had increased and that settlements were a continuous source of humiliation to Palestinians.

The commission was mandated by the Commission on Human Rights to examine only the violations of human rights by Israel in the Occupied Palestinian Territory. The evidence showed, however, that Palestinians were also guilty of human rights abuses and we believed that this could not be ignored. Consequently our report condemned atrocities committed by Palestinians, including suicide bombings, the lynching of Israeli military reservists in Ramallah[31] and the attacks on Israeli ambulances.

Although the commission found that Israel had seriously violated the human rights of Palestinians, and recommended measures that Israel should take to protect human rights, its tone was conciliatory, emphasizing that both Palestinians and Israelis 'have a yearning for peace and security, and that a pre-condition for achieving a just and durable peace is for every effort to be made on all sides to ease tensions, calm passions, and promote a culture of peace'.[32] The report called for negotiations and declared that a durable peace should be premised on the self-determination of the Palestinian people and the security needs of Israel.

The commission saw it as its main task to examine the evidence of violations of human rights law in the Second Intifada. It made no serious attempt to examine the structures of the occupation that had given rise to the Second Intifada. The Oslo Accords were only briefly considered. There was no characterization of the settlement enterprise as a modern form of colonization. Any suggestion that Israel might be practising apartheid in the Occupied Palestinian Territories was studiously avoided. In its search for the facts, its determination to limit its findings to violations of human rights norms, and its failure to consider the ideology that drove Israel's policies in the Palestinian Territories, the commission saw the trees but not the wood.

Looking back at our report, I find it strange that we did not consider the issue of apartheid in occupied Palestine. Richard Falk and I had both experienced and studied the apartheid system of South Africa and were fully aware of the features of that system. We knew that there were already characterizations of the occupation of Palestine as a species of apartheid – for instance, there was Uri Davis's *Israel: An Apartheid State*,[33] published in 1987. And we were aware that the Rome Statute of the International Criminal Court had recently defined the crime of apartheid and made it clear that the crime had application outside southern Africa. The only explanation I have for this omission is that we knew that to suggest that Israel was guilty of the reviled policy of apartheid would not be believed and would distract attention from the conciliatory recommendations of the report. It was therefore much wiser to concentrate on the violation of human rights and the illegality of settlements as unrelated phenomena without any attempt to see the two as the components of a system of apartheid.

The reports of fact-finding missions established by the Commission on Human Rights (and its successor, the Human Rights Council) seldom have a major impact on international politics. So it was with our report. The Mitchell Fact-Finding Mission report, which appeared on 30 April 2001, some six weeks after our report, received more attention because of the high profile of its members. But it was simply a blander version and there were indications that it had been influenced by our report. It called for an end to the violence, for the Palestinians to stop acts of terrorism and the Israelis to stop building settlements, and for the parties to resume negotiations. It had as little practical or political effect as did our report. The violence continued, as did settlement construction, and the Israelis and Palestinians did not resume negotiations.

25

Special rapporteur on human rights in Palestine

I was to be given a further opportunity to consider the question of apartheid in occupied Palestine. Following my term as chair of the commission of inquiry into the Second Intifada, I was appointed as United Nations special rapporteur on the situation of human rights in the Palestinian Territories occupied since 1967 with the mandate to investigate Israel's violations of international law and to report with conclusions and recommendations to the Commission on Human Rights in Geneva and to the Third Committee of the General Assembly in New York.

This position was to bring me into closer contact with Israel's policies and practices in the Occupied Palestinian Territory (OPT). However, in my early reports to the UN I persisted in viewing the situation in Palestine during the Second Intifada as one involving violations of human rights law and international humanitarian law. I saw the occupation as the source of the violence without considering the institutions, policies and practices that had transformed the occupation into a system of apartheid. That conviction came later. And when it did, I refrained for some time from invoking the apartheid analogy as I feared, with justification, that it would undermine the credibility of my reports in the West. Only in 2005 did I characterize the occupation as a form of apartheid. Before examining the law and facts that led me to this conclusion, I need to say something about the post of special rapporteur and how I carried it out.

Today there is intense competition for special rapporteurships of the Human Rights Council, which replaced the Commission on Human Rights in 2005, particularly that of the situation of human rights in the Palestinian

Territories occupied since 1967. There was little interest in the post in 2001. This was probably because the three special rapporteurs[34] appointed since the creation of the post in 1993 had all resigned after a few years in office, citing their dissatisfaction with the mandate, which was seen as too political and one-sided.

I was in Geneva in June 2001 to attend the annual session of the International Law Commission. I heard in the corridors of the UN that the Commission of Human Rights was in search of new special rapporteur for Palestine and I knew that my name had been mentioned. But I assumed that if I was being considered, I would be approached about my availability. So it came as a great surprise when on 22 June 2001 I was contacted by the chairman of the Commission on Human Rights, Mr Leandro Despouy of Argentina, with the news that I had been appointed as special rapporteur on Palestine with the unanimous support of all regional groups. I immediately said that I was surprised as I had not been consulted and that I did not think that I had time for the post. He then informed me that it would embarrass South Africa if I declined, as South Africa would host the World Conference against Racism in Durban later that year. This led me to assume that I had been nominated by the South African government and that it had lobbied for the appointment on my behalf. I was flattered to be approached and I felt some responsibility to do something positive for the Palestinians. So I accepted for a year to see how it went. Shortly after I accepted, I met the South African ambassador, George Nene, in the delegates' lounge of the UN and asked him if it was true that South Africa wanted me to take the post. He was visibly surprised and said that South Africa had no interest in the post and would not be upset if I were to refuse it.

Working for the UN was not easy. UN independent experts, as opposed to consultants and staff, are unpaid. As with members of the International Law Commission (ILC), special rapporteurs received only a subsistence allowance for days spent in Geneva or in the field. However, members of the ILC were treated with respect and accorded ambassadorial status. Not so with special rapporteurs. We were expected to take instructions from relatively junior bureaucrats in the Office of the High Commissioner and to defer to them.

As special rapporteur, I visited the OPT twice a year for about seven to ten days on each visit. I wrote reports on my visits, which I presented to the Commission on Human Rights in March in Geneva and to the Third Committee of the General Assembly in October–November in New York. Researching and writing the report was time-consuming with the result that I probably devoted at least three months to my work as special rapporteur each year. I had to combine this with my job as full-time professor at Leiden, my work as member and special rapporteur of the ILC, and the post of judge ad hoc in the dispute between the Democratic Republic of the Congo and Rwanda. One year after I had been working as special rapporteur, Ietje and I had a serious discussion about whether I should continue. I suggested to her that she accompany me on a visit to the OPT and that we consider the matter further after the visit. She came to the OPT, saw and experienced the situation, and then proclaimed that I could not in all conscience resign. Thereafter she accompanied me on one visit each year and became my staunchest supporter – and most critical adviser.

The Israeli government did not recognize my mandate. Consequently it refused to allow members of government to meet with me. But the Israeli ambassador to the UN in Geneva made it clear that as a South African, who did not require a visa, I was always welcome to visit Israel and the OPT. No obstacles were ever placed in the way of my visits. As a matter of courtesy, I always sent the ambassador a copy of my proposed itinerary. On several occasions Foreign Ministry officials helped us when we were obstructed by the IDF. That the Foreign Ministry was concerned about my safety was brought home to me when I received a letter of apology after I had nearly been hit by a tear-gas canister fired by the IDF while I was observing a demonstration against the wall at Bil'in, following a report in the Palestinian press that I had been injured. I assured the Foreign Ministry that I had not been injured and that I had assumed the risk of being tear-gassed by observing the demonstration from too close.

My mandate as special rapporteur was confined to the violation of human rights and international humanitarian law by Israel as the occupying power. This meant that I was not required to investigate or to report on the violation of the human rights of Israelis, the violation of the human rights of Palestinians by the security forces of the Palestinian Authority, or the conflict between Fatah and Hamas. Understandably this limitation was a source of regular criticism by Israel and the United States. I too was concerned about these limitations and on occasion I went beyond my mandate and condemned Palestinian suicide bombers and the firing of rockets by Palestinian militants from Gaza. I also condemned the actions of the Palestinian Authority, such as its execution of convicted criminals, and I could not remain aloof from the impact of the Fatah–Hamas split on human rights. These comments were not well received by Arab states or the Palestinian Authority.

I believed that my role was not merely to ascertain the facts and to report to the organs of the UN on my observations. In addition, it was my function to take the UN to the people of Palestine and to show them that the UN really cared about their plight – even if I often had serious doubts myself on this score. Consequently I did not confine myself to reading UN and NGO reports and to discussions with informed interlocutors in the Palestinian Authority, UN agencies and civil society. In addition I made sure that our small team met with farmers, businessmen, doctors, nurses, patients, lawyers, school teachers and school children, and many others who had suffered under the occupation and who had stories to tell.

We visited the major refugee camps of Jabalia, Balata and Aida and listened to the refugee narrative. We saw the damage caused to homes by the Israeli Defense Forces on their search and arrest raids into Balata. We spoke to the wounded in hospitals. We heard graphic accounts of torture from former detainees. We walked through destroyed homes and flattened agricultural lands. We saw centuries-old olive trees uprooted by settlers. We traversed the so-called security wall by UN vehicle and on foot and spoke to farmers denied access to their lands. On occasion we came close to the conflict itself. In Beit Hanoun, while visiting destroyed agricultural lands, we once came face to face with Israeli tanks with their guns pointed at us. Tear-gas canisters were fired at us in Bil'in. It was not a safe mandate.

Palestine is a small country, and over the years I visited every part of it, its cities, towns and villages, and its fields and mountains. We travelled from Jenin in the north to the Hebron Hills in the south; from Qalqilya in the east to Jericho in the west. We stayed for much of the time in the American Colony Hotel and came to know both the Old City and the neighbourhoods of East Jerusalem. When not in East Jerusalem, we stayed in Gaza City and visited the towns and villages of the coastal belt. Travel was not easy because of the myriad military checkpoints on the roads of Palestine that hindered UN vehicles and seriously obstructed Palestinian traffic, but this was part of the Palestinian experience.

I have spoken about 'my visits'. But I was part of a team that usually comprised Darka Topali, Andy Clinton, Ali Hotari, Ietje and me. Darka Topali is a Serb who preferred to call herself a Yugoslav. She had served as assistant to my three predecessors and the commission of inquiry into the Second Intifada, and knew the region and its players well. Andy Clinton, our security officer from the Office of the High Commissioner for Human Rights, who had previously served with the Canadian armed forces, combined an interest in our security with a deep concern for the OPT. In theory Ali Hotari, a Palestinian from Beit Hanina in East Jerusalem, was our driver, seconded by the UN Development Program, but in practice he was friend, navigator, translator and adviser. Without Ali, we would not have learnt about the lives and the pain of Palestinians and we would not have seen the full beauty of Palestine. He led our informal exchanges with Bedouins and farmers; remonstrated with soldiers at checkpoints; and navigated our way through the fields and towns. Our itineraries were planned by Darka and the Office for the Co-ordination of Humanitarian Affairs (OCHA) – the most hands-on UN agency in the region – whose staff and local NGOs acted as guides, commentators and interlocutors.

We heard the official perspective on the occupation from members of the Palestinian Authority and the Palestinian Legislative Council, and from the mayors and governors of Palestine's cities. UN agencies explained their efforts to alleviate the suffering of the Palestinian people and to assist their development. We met with leaders of both Fatah and Hamas in order to make it clear that we were even-handed even if the UN was not. (The UN, under pressure from the United States, refused and still refuses to speak to Hamas.) Palestinian and Israeli NGOs were welcoming and informative. We visited the main Palestinian university campuses and met with the mufti of the al-Aqsa Mosque and the Latin Patriarch of Jerusalem.

In our journeying around Palestine we met many wonderful and impressive people, all with stories to tell about the hardships of the occupation, the brutality of the IDF and the indifference of the Palestinian Authority.

Yasser Arafat, confined by the IDF to the Muqata, his headquarters in Ramallah, for most of time I was special rapporteur, always had time to meet us. This was probably because the policy of the United States and Israel to isolate him meant that most foreign diplomats and leaders refused to meet with him. Visiting Arafat brought back memories of visiting political prisoners in Pretoria. Although he was always surrounded by security officials and advisers, the Muqata was his prison, for there was no doubt that Sharon was out to get him and he would risk assassination if he left the cramped quarters of the bomb-damaged Muqata. Looking tired and dishevelled in his uniform, nervously adjusting his *keffiyeh*, his eyes would light up when he saw us. He embraced me warmly, but it was clear that he was particularly glad to see Ietje and Darka. With an impish grin and a high-pitched voice he would regale us with the latest Israeli atrocities, starting each sentence with 'Can you believe it?' He always spoke warmly of Yitzhak Rabin and the 'peace of the brave' they had forged in 1993–4. The intense rivalry between him and Sharon was clear. He frequently reminded us that Sharon felt cheated that he had not been able to kill him in Beirut in 1982. No peace between the Israelis and Palestinians was possible with Arafat and Sharon in command. They hated each other too much. I learnt little new from Arafat and I did not always agree with him. But it was good to be with him. One felt in the presence of a person whom history had touched. Strangely, being with Arafat was like being with Mandela. They had both given their lives to the struggle of their people for liberation, their places in history were secure, but there was a sadness in their demeanour. The burden of history had taken its toll.

Yasser Arafat died in mysterious circumstances in November 2004. There are strong suspicions that he was poisoned by the Israelis but there is no proof to support this.[35] These suspicions have, however, been strengthened by the recent publication of *Rise and Kill First: The Secret History of Israel's Targeted Assassinations*, which describes attempts by Israel to assassinate Arafat.[36]

Arafat was succeeded by Mohamed Abbas, also known as Abu Mazen. I had not met Abbas previously, but soon after his appointment the new minister of foreign affairs, Nasser al-Kidwa, whom I had known as Palestinian ambassador to the UN in New York, arranged for me to meet him. I found it an uncomfortable meeting as he lacked the charisma of Arafat and seemed to be less interested in my views on the importance of a human rights dimension to Palestinian policies. Later, in June 2005, I met Ismail Haniyeh, the leader of Hamas in Gaza. He was warm, concerned about human rights, hopeful that the rift between Fatah and Hamas would be healed, and supportive of my mission.

I met Saeb Erekat, the chief negotiator of the Palestinian Authority, on many occasions. He was a forceful, articulate exponent of the Fatah position, who was bitterly opposed to Hamas and fiercely committed to finding a peaceful solution to the conflict. We had many discussions with him in Jericho, Ramallah and Jerusalem. He had a clear picture of the kind of Palestine that he wanted, one in which human rights were respected, economic prosperity prevailed, and religion did not determine the nature of the state.

Independent public figures provided a clearer picture of the present and future. Mustafa Barghouti and Hanan Ashrawi, both members of the Palestinian Legislative Council from Ramallah, and Eyad Sarraj, director of the Gaza Mental Health programme, were prepared to allocate some blame to the Palestinian Authority for its failures to promote the Palestinian cause but at the same time provided a critical and damning indictment of Israeli policies and practices.

As to be expected, lawyers were both friends and advisers. I valued the guidance of Raja Shehadeh, lawyer turned writer, and of the directors of the two leading Palestinian public interest NGOs, Raji Sourani of the Palestinian Centre for Human Rights and Shawan Jabarin of Al-Haq. In Israel, I could turn to David Kretzmer, Daphna Golan and Michael Sfard[37] for a critical assessment of the occupation.

Although the Israeli government refused to meet me, on occasion it arranged for me to meet with Israelis to put the Israeli position to me. One such person was an Israeli man who had lost a child to Palestinian suicide bombers. He was a sensitive man who understood the aspirations of the Palestinian people but found it impossible to forgive those who had taken the life of his child. It was an emotional meeting. He listened intently when I told him that I had spoken to Palestinian parents who had suffered in the same way. But I could see that he was unwilling to share his grief with the other side. I was later informed that there was a group of Israeli and Palestinian parents whose children had been killed by senseless acts of suicide bombers or the IDF and who found that meeting each other went some way to healing their emotional wounds.

26

Human rights and international humanitarian law

It was easy to assess Israel's compliance with its obligations in human rights law and international humanitarian law in my reports to the UN because both the law and the facts were clear. Unlike South Africa, which had refused to sign any human rights treaty and denied that it was bound by human rights law, Israel is a party to all major human rights and humanitarian law treaties and professes to be an adherent of international human rights law. The facts too are clear. Evidence of the violation of human rights law and international humanitarian law in the Occupied Palestinian Territory (OPT) is contained in the reports of UN fact-finding missions, NGOs and special rapporteurs, in books and the press. Israel's failure to respect the principles of international humanitarian law in its bombing of Gaza in 2008–9 and 2014 was vividly displayed on television screens throughout the world. Video recordings capture the actions of IDF soldiers engaged in the enforcement of the occupation. The past twenty years have witnessed an explosion of official and non-official fact-finding missions, media coverage and private video recordings. The world is a much smaller place than it was thirty years ago, and it is impossible today to conceal or cover up the violation of international humanitarian law and human rights law. Israel is more exposed to public scrutiny than South Africa ever was.

Israel's actions in occupied Palestine are to be judged by the standards imposed by a number of human rights conventions and rules of international humanitarian law, which in most cases Israel accepts are binding upon it. Israel became a party to the International Convention on the Elimination of All Forms of Racial Discrimination in 1979. This convention obliges it to prohibit all forms of racial discrimination and apartheid in territories under its jurisdiction. In 1991 Israel ratified the International Covenant on Civil and Political Rights and the Convention against Torture. Together these conventions oblige Israel to recognize and respect, without discrimination on grounds of race, the right to life, freedom from torture, from cruel, inhuman and degrading treatment, arbitrary arrest and detention, due process of law, the right to family life and freedom of movement in respect of all territories under its jurisdiction. Israel is also a party to the Convention on the Rights of the Child. Israel's argument that these conventions apply only within Israel itself and not the Occupied Palestinian Territory has been dismissed by both the bodies monitoring these conventions and the International Court of Justice.[38]

International humanitarian law – the law governing the treatment of combatants, prisoners and civilians in time of war or armed conflict and the limits imposed on states in the conduct of such hostilities – is to be found in the rules of customary international law and the Geneva Conventions of 1949. Of particular importance is the Fourth Geneva Convention Relative to the Protection of Civilian Persons in Time of War of 1949, which prescribes the law applicable in the case of a military occupation and imposes obligations on parties in respect of the treatment of civilians in occupied territories. Israel accepts that it is bound by the rules of customary international law on this subject and became a party to the Fourth Geneva Convention in 1951. However, it argues that the Fourth Geneva Convention does not extend to the Occupied Palestinian Territory because it applies only to the occupation of an independent, sovereign state and Palestine was not such a state at the time of its occupation in 1967. This objection has, however, been overruled by the International Court of Justice.[39]

The rules of international humanitarian law on occupation are designed to ensure that, notwithstanding the security needs of the occupying power, the day-to-day lives of civilians in the occupied territory should continue normally. In today's world this means that civilians must have adequate food, shelter, electricity and water, that municipal services such as sewerage will continue, that the sick will have access to adequate care, and that education will not be obstructed. Israel has largely delegated this responsibility to the Palestinian Authority and international donors but ultimately, as occupying power, it is obliged to ensure that the daily lives of the occupied people – the Palestinians – are disrupted as little as possible. The Fourth Geneva Convention in addition contains certain prohibitions that limit the powers of the occupying power to assert its security needs. Of particular importance are the provisions which prohibit collective punishment and all measures of intimidation or terrorism; wilful killing and torture or inhuman treatment; unlawful deportation and detention; the denial of a fair trial; and the wanton destruction or appropriation of property not justified by military necessity. In order to prevent the occupying power from colonizing an occupied territory, article 49(6) provides that an occupying power shall not transfer parts of its own civilian population into the territory it occupies.

Two cardinal principles govern the customary law of armed conflict: the principle of proportionality, which requires parties to an armed conflict to avoid or minimize collateral or excessive damage to civilians; and the principle of distinction, which requires parties to an armed conflict to distinguish between military objectives and the civilian population, and to refrain from indiscriminate attacks that fail to make such a distinction.

The public record shows that Israel has violated many of the rules and principles of both human rights law and international humanitarian law. Israel has been responsible for the deaths of thousands of Palestinians in the course of its Gaza wars and the suppression of protests. It proudly claims to be an abolitionist state, but its targeted assassination of militants,[40] of which there were over five hundred during the Second Intifada, suggests an impatience with judicial procedures and a determination to find other means to dispose of militants. Certainly this method of eliminating militants initiated by Israel has avoided the condemnation of the carrying out of the death penalty that occurred in South Africa. To aggravate the situation, targeted assassinations have often been accompanied by 'collateral damage' to civilians. Forty per cent of those killed in targeted assassinations during the Second Intifada were innocent bystanders.[41] In July 2002 a prominent figure in Hamas, Salah Shehada, was killed by a helicopter gunship in Gaza, and at the same time fifteen members of his family and neighbours were killed and a hundred and fifty neighbours injured. The indiscriminate killing of civilians in the Gaza conflicts has characterized the actions of the Israeli Defense Forces.

Although the Supreme Court of Israel has sought to end the torture of detainees in the course of interrogation,[42] the torture and inhuman treatment of detainees continues.[43] Israeli interrogators have used the traditional methods of torture such as sleep deprivation, exposure to persistent noise, beatings, shakings, back bendings and psychological pressure including threats to harm family members, verbal abuse and humiliation. Ex-prisoners recounted to me the methods of torture employed in a coldly factual manner, with an acceptance that this was part of the normal procedure of arrest. That these practices prevail was confirmed to me by the Public Committee against Torture, an Israel NGO that monitors the treatment of prisoners. The methods of interrogation employed against suspects in Israel follow the pattern of those used by the South African security police in the apartheid era.

Since 1967 Israel has imprisoned over eight hundred thousand Palestinians, amounting to more than 20 per cent of the population. There are usually some six thousand political prisoners in Israeli jails, of which several hundred are administrative detainees who have not been convicted of any offence.

Children have suffered under the occupation. Over three thousand have been killed by Israeli security forces since 2000 and some twelve thousand detained. Thousands have been displaced as a result of the forcible transfers of families and house demolitions. Schools have been destroyed and teaching has frequently been interrupted by the military operations of the occupying forces.

Israel's settlement enterprise clearly involves the transfer of Israeli civilians into occupied Palestine in violation of article 49(6) of the Fourth Geneva Convention. This has been confirmed by both the International Court of Justice and the UN Security Council.

There is blatant discrimination against Palestinians in favour of settlers. The worst discrimination occurs in respect of freedom of movement and housing. Other examples of discrimination include the trial of settlers and Palestinians for similar crimes committed in the West Bank. Jewish settlers are tried before civil courts in Israel before proper judges applying the rules of due process of law. Palestinians, on the other hand, are tried by military courts, presided over by military officers, which apply different and more stringent rules relating to procedure, evidence, substantive law and sentencing. No restraints are placed on the marriage of settlers to residents of Israel, but severe restrictions are placed on the marriage of Palestinians from the West Bank and Gaza to Palestinians resident in East Jerusalem and Israel. Similarly no restraints are imposed on the unification of settler families and families in Israel, but serious administrative obstacles are placed on the unification of Palestinian families from the West Bank and Gaza and those from East Jerusalem and Israel. One of the most unfair discriminations occurs in respect of the allocation of water. Some five hundred thousand settlers in the West Bank consume approximately six times the amount of water used by a Palestinian population of 2.7 million, leaving Palestinians without sufficient water to meet their needs.

The evidence is clear. Israel is in serious violation of many of the rules of human rights law and international humanitarian law. But has Israel implemented its occupation of Palestine in such a way that it may be described as apartheid?

27

Apartheid

Apartheid – the systematic and institutionalized oppression of one racial group by another – conjures up images of racism and repression and brings back memories of South Africa's dark history. No state should lightly be accused of practising apartheid. In 2014 US Secretary of State John Kerry was compelled to make an abject apology for suggesting that if a Middle East peace agreement was not achieved, Israel risked becoming an apartheid state, a comparison that the American Israel Public Affairs Committee (AIPAC) condemned as 'offensive and inappropriate'.[44] In 2006 former President Jimmy Carter was likewise admonished for titling a book on the Middle East *Palestine: Peace Not Apartheid.* Others who have made this comparison have been castigated as being misinformed or anti-Semitic. The topic of apartheid and Israel is one that must be approached with caution and circumspection.

In addressing this subject, it is necessary to distinguish between the claim that Israel practises apartheid within Israel itself and the argument that Israel's occupation of the Palestinian Territory has assumed the character of apartheid. Although there is support for the former view, notably from the Russell Tribunal on Palestine in its Cape Town session of 2011,[45] it is difficult to sustain such a claim in the light of the fact that Palestinians in Israel, unlike blacks in apartheid South Africa, are enfranchised[46] and entitled to hold public office. Undeniably Palestinians are discriminated against in Israel and this discrimination is getting worse, but whether this is so grave as to constitute apartheid is questionable. The more pressing question is whether Israel's implementation of the occupation of the Palestinian Territory constitutes a form of apartheid. (Today the term 'Palestinian Territory' is used to describe the 'Palestinian Territories' of West Bank, Gaza and East Jerusalem as it emphasises the unity of the state of Palestine.)

At the outset it must be acknowledged that there are important differences between apartheid in South Africa and Israel's administration of occupied Palestine. The chief difference is that apartheid in South Africa was a policy applied by the government of a state to its own people whereas Israel purports to be acting as an occupying power in an occupied territory that it will return to the people of the territory when a peace treaty is entered into. It insists that it is only a temporary occupying force.[47] The main objection to this argument is that it is impossible to see the occupation of Palestine as a temporary measure. It has been in existence for fifty years and Israel has imprinted itself permanently on the territory by seizing land and facilitating the establishment of colonial settlements throughout the Occupied Palestinian Territory (OPT). There is no sign of the occupation coming to an end and Israel is determined that any peace talks that may be held should not result in the lifting of the occupation. In this sense the situation resembles that of Namibia after the termination of the mandate. Namibia was a territory internationalized by a League of Nations mandate in which South Africa, the occupying force, was judged by the international community to be applying the illegal regime of apartheid. Likewise, Israel may be judged for applying apartheid in Palestine, a territory internationalized by a League of Nations mandate.

There are two ways of approaching the question of apartheid in the OPT. The first is empirical, which entails a judgement based on personal observations of the occupation and life in the OPT. The second is legal, which requires an examination of the occupation in the context of the 1973 International Convention on the Suppression and Punishment of the Crime of Apartheid and the 1998 Rome Statute of the International Court of Justice.[48]

The empirical approach relies on the observation of facts in the OPT, which so closely resemble apartheid in South Africa that it may confidently be said that the two systems are substantially identical – that apartheid in the OPT is akin to that practised in South Africa. This mainly involves an examination of whether the principal features of South African apartheid – discrimination, repression, humiliation and territorial fragmentation – are present in Israel's occupation of the OPT and whether together they provide evidence of systematic racial oppression. This is not a difficult question to answer. There is a dual legal system in the OPT – one for Israeli settlers and the other for Palestinians – which discriminates unfairly against Palestinians in the administration of justice, movement, housing, family unification, the allocation of water and the enjoyment of many basic freedoms. The security system in the OPT contains all the repressive elements that characterized apartheid in South Africa: arbitrary killings, torture, detention without trial, imprisonment of political offenders, and restrictions on freedom of movement, speech and assembly. The fragmentation of the West Bank by the wall, the settlements and the division of the territory into areas A, B and C under the Oslo Accords is reminiscent of the Bantustanization of South Africa.

The humiliation of black people was a cardinal feature of apartheid in South Africa. Subjugation, unequal treatment, white privilege and the assertion of racial superiority together combined to humiliate blacks and to deny their human dignity. Israel's laws and practices in occupied Palestine likewise serve to humiliate Palestinians. The high-handed behaviour of the IDF and settlers, the privileged position of settlers, checkpoints, the seizure of land, house demolitions and, today, virulent racist assertions of Jewish racial superiority have resulted in the humiliation of the Palestinian people.

The highly visible enforcement of the occupation and the protection of the settlements by Israel's occupying forces provide clear evidence that racial discrimination, repression and humiliation are not random, isolated occurrences. They are regular and intended features of a broad system of oppression.

The open display of racism that characterized South Africa is also present in the OPT. In apartheid South Africa, white assaults on blacks that went unpunished were common. In the OPT settlers regularly commit crimes against Palestinians and their property which go unpunished. Racist language is a common phenomenon. The walls of Hebron are replete with racist graffiti. 'Death to Arabs' is a popular slogan on the walls. Sadly, racist language is not confined to settlers. Within Israel itself there has been an increase in hatred for Palestinians and a rise in right-wing political parties that support violence by settlers. Max Blumenthal's *Goliath: Life and Loathing in Greater Israel*[49] describes an Israel as much preoccupied with racial superiority as apartheid South Africa in its heyday, if not more so. For example, in 2014 an Israeli member of Knesset, Ayelet Shaked (who in 2015 became the Israeli minister of justice), called for the genocide of Palestinians on Facebook.[50]

Most South Africans who visit occupied Palestine, particularly black South Africans, compare the occupation with apartheid on the basis of empirical observation. This is, however, too emotive, too impressionistic a manner in which to make an impartial assessment of whether the occupation can be compared to apartheid. Apartheid in the OPT may be akin to apartheid in South Africa, but this is not to say that it is the same. The two countries, their peoples and their historical narratives, are very different. So too are their demography, geography and political structures. Religion was not a divisive factor in South Africa as it is in Palestine. Given these differences it is much fairer and more objective to make an assessment on the basis of an examination of the occupation against the definition of apartheid contained in the International Convention for the Suppression and Punishment of the Crime of Apartheid (the Apartheid Convention) and the Rome Statute of the International Criminal Court.

The Apartheid Convention and the Rome Statute

In 1965 the UN General Assembly gave its approval to the International Convention on the Elimination of All Forms of Racial Discrimination, which prohibits racial discrimination and condemns apartheid. Today 175 states, including Israel, are parties to this Convention and have agreed to prohibit apartheid in their own territories. In 1973 the General Assembly went further when it gave its approval to the International Convention on the Suppression and Punishment of the Crime of Apartheid, which makes apartheid a criminal offence, a species of crime against humanity. A hundred and eight states are party to this convention, not including Israel. In recent years the Apartheid Convention has been endorsed by two important conventions. Additional Protocol I to the Geneva Conventions of 1977 recognizes apartheid as a war crime when practised in the context of an armed conflict,[51] and the Rome Statute of the International Criminal Court of 1998 defines apartheid as a crime against humanity.[52] Altogether, 173 states are party to the Additional Protocol and 124 to the Rome Statute. Israel is not a party to either of these treaties.

Strong opposition to the judging of Israel's occupation in terms of the Apartheid Convention and the Rome Statute comes from Benjamin Pogrund, formerly deputy editor of the *Rand Daily Mail* and a strong opponent of apartheid in South Africa, who today lives in Israel and has become an ardent defender of Israel against the charge of practising apartheid. Pogrund argues that these legal instruments cannot be used to measure Israel's occupation as apartheid because they have not been endorsed by important states such as China, the Russian Federation, the United States and Israel.[53]

This is correct, although Pogrund fails to mention that all European states and thirty-three African states are parties to the Rome Statute. But this misses the point. No one today seriously challenges the definition of apartheid contained in these two instruments, as they accurately reflect the common understanding of apartheid as the systematic oppression of one racial group by another by means of discriminatory and repressive actions. The importance of these conventions is that they indicate that apartheid is a crime, like genocide, crime against humanity or war crime, which applies to any such oppression wherever it occurs in the world. The Apartheid Convention makes this clear in providing that the 'crime of apartheid' shall 'include similar policies and practices of racial segregation and discrimination as practised in southern Africa'. Any doubts on this subject are dispelled by the inclusion of the crime of apartheid in the Rome Statute of the International Criminal Court, which was adopted in 1998, well after the fall of apartheid in South Africa.

That the crime of apartheid is a universal crime is confirmed by the fact that the prosecutor of the International Criminal Court is at present conducting an examination into the question whether Israel's settlement enterprise on Palestinian territory has given rise to the commission of the crime of apartheid.

For the present purposes, the issue is not whether Israelis may be prosecuted under the Rome Statute of the International Criminal Court, but whether Israel's implementation of the occupation of the OPT violates the principles of international law, including the prohibition on apartheid as defined in the Apartheid Convention and the Rome Statute.

The Apartheid Convention defines apartheid as comprising a number of specified 'inhuman acts' committed 'for the purpose of establishing and maintaining domination by one racial group of persons over any other racial group of persons and systematically oppressing them'.[54] The Rome Statute contains a substantially similar definition.[55] This means that three requirements must be satisfied: firstly, the presence of different racial groups; secondly, the commission of certain inhuman acts; and thirdly, the inhuman acts must have been committed for the purpose of establishing domination by one racial group over another and systematically oppressing that group. In essence these requirements reflect the principal features of apartheid as applied in South Africa.

The first requirement of different racial groups requires little comment. International law does not view racial groups in terms of colour. The International Convention on the Elimination of All Forms of Racial Discrimination makes this clear in its definition of racial discrimination, which speaks of any distinction based on 'race, colour, descent or national or ethnic origin'. Human rights monitoring bodies and courts have made it clear that the identification of a racial group is a sociological question and not a biological one.[56] This means that in order to determine the existence of a racial group it is necessary to have regard to the identity of the group on the basis of ancestry, descent, language, religion and national origin, and not on the basis of the skin colour of the group. Clearly, Jews see themselves as distinct from Palestinians on the grounds of descent, religion, history, language and origin. Prime Minister Netanyahu's demand that Israel be recognized as a 'Jewish state' is premised on the existence of Jews as a separate racial group. Palestinians, too, see themselves as a separate group defined by ancestry, history, attachment to the land of historical Palestine, language and origin. Jews and Palestinians are perceived both by themselves and by others as groups distinct from each other and therefore as separate racial groups.

The other two requirements demand more attention and are dealt with separately.

28

Apartheid: Inhuman acts

The Apartheid Convention's list of inhuman acts for the purpose of the convention includes murder, torture, cruel, inhuman or degrading treatment and punishment, arbitrary arrest and imprisonment, denial of freedom of movement and residence, the expropriation of landed property, the division of the population along racial lines by the creation of separate territorial reserves, and the persecution of persons because they oppose apartheid. The Rome Statute's list of inhuman acts is substantially similar but in addition it includes the act of forcible transfer of people.

Many of the inhuman acts committed by the occupying forces and settlers belonging to the Jewish group against members of the Palestinian group have already been described. These include murder in the form of the extra-judicial execution of protesters and militants not participating in hostilities,[57] and the indiscriminate killing of civilians in the bombing of civilian neighbourhoods and in the course of targeted assassinations; the torture and cruel, inhuman and degrading treatment of Palestinian prisoners;[58] the imprisonment of some six thousand Palestinians each year following trial before military courts that fail to comply with international fair-trial standards;[59] and the arbitrary detention of thousands of so-called administrative detainees held for long periods (sometimes over a year) without trial.

Freedom of movement is denied by checkpoints, the wall, settler roads and roadblocks; and freedom of residence is violated by house demolitions.

The expropriation of Palestinian land is crucial to the Zionist enterprise. East Jerusalem has been formally annexed because of its historical importance to Jews. In the West Bank the biblical lands of Judea and Samaria are being stealthily expropriated under the guise of occupation. Outright annexation of the West Bank is impossible because it would provoke an international outcry, although there are suggestions today that Area C or the territory encompassing the settlements should be annexed. Instead, Israel's clear policy is to seize as much Palestinian land as possible without resorting to annexation. The wall has resulted in the de facto annexation of some 10 per cent of Palestinian land. Some 75 per cent of the Jordan valley is under Israeli control: 15 per cent of the land comprises settlements; 40 per cent is designated as closed military zones; and 20 per cent is set aside for 'nature reserves' closed to Palestinians. Overall, more than 40 per cent of the landmass of the West Bank has been appropriated for settlement infrastructure and is entirely closed to Palestinian use.

Although the division of the population along racial lines by the creation of separate reserves is not so obvious as it was in South Africa, with its territorial fragmentation of the country into Bantustans and the division of the cities into separate group areas for different racial groups, there is clear evidence of both territorial fragmentation and residential segregation along racial lines.

The Occupied Palestinian Territory (OPT) has effectively been divided into three sections: Gaza, which has been completely severed from the OPT; East Jerusalem, which has been annexed and is in the process of being 'Judaized'; and the West Bank. The West Bank is further fragmented by the Oslo Accords, which divide it into Areas A, B and C. Area A, consisting of 18 per cent of the West Bank, includes the cities and towns placed under the control of the Palestinian Authority (PA); Area B, constituting 22 per cent of the West Bank, includes the villages and smaller towns and is under the control of both the PA and Israel; and Area C, forming the remainder of the West Bank, covers the rural areas and is entirely controlled by Israel. In addition, checkpoints, the wall and settlements have effectively divided the West Bank into three principal cantons – South around Hebron, Centre around Ramallah, and North around Nablus and Jenin.

Settlements in the West Bank and East Jerusalem resemble the white group areas of apartheid South Africa. They are more affluent and better serviced in terms of water and electricity than Palestinian cities, towns, villages and neighbourhoods. They have better schools, hospitals and recreational facilities. And they are completely isolated from their Palestinian neighbours. The division of the OPT into separate reserves along racial lines, dividing settlers from Palestinians, is more pronounced than in apartheid South Africa, which, despite its ideology of racial separation, never achieved the same degree of segregation.

Persons who oppose the occupation are persecuted relentlessly. Militants are killed, tortured and imprisoned. Non-violent protests, such as those against the wall at the village of Bil'in, are routinely met with excessive force, resulting in mass arrests and sometimes the deaths of protesters. The homes of militants are demolished. Persecution is the price paid for active opposition to apartheid in occupied Palestine.

Israel's determination to suppress peaceful protests is well illustrated by its response to protests along the Gaza border on 14 May 2018 when the IDF killed 61 and wounded over two thousand persons protesting against the Nakba and demanding the right of refugees to return to Israel in what was described as the Great Return March.

As special rapporteur, I was denied access to Israeli prisons, police or armed forces, which would have allowed me to verify or discuss inhuman acts involving the administration of justice or military operations. On the other hand, I was able to observe restrictions on movement and to visit demolished homes, settlements and the wall. These acts, which provide evidence of apartheid, and my experiences in monitoring them, are recounted below.

Freedom of Movement and Checkpoints

Settlers in the West Bank and East Jerusalem move without restriction between settlements in these areas and between Israel and settlements in occupied Palestine. No restraints are placed on their freedom of movement as they drive to work, schools, universities, hospitals and friends. Special separate roads facilitate this freedom. These roads bypass Palestinian areas and allow settlers to move freely without impediment. No notices proclaim these roads for settler use only. Palestinians are simply required to know that these roads are off limits to them. The occupying force is able to enforce this road segregation by reason of the different colour number plates of vehicles. Settler vehicles bear yellow number plates while those of Palestinians are green.

Palestinians, on the other hand, are faced with a wide array of obstacles to free movement. Passage through or past these obstacles is procured by permit. All Palestinians are required to carry identity cards, issued by the Ministry of the Interior of the state of Palestine subject to the oversight of Israel. In addition, Palestinians must obtain permits for every facet of life – work, study, medical treatment, visits – to facilitate movement within occupied Palestine, in much the same way that passes in South Africa facilitated the movement of black people. The regime is characterized by complication and obfuscation. The criteria for obtaining permits are often unpublished, and, when they are, they are issued in Hebrew and not translated into Arabic.[60] Palestinians are expected to find out by trial and error whether they are allowed to pass through a particular checkpoint on a particular day. No respect is shown for the principle of legality requiring laws to be clear, consistent and public. In this respect the system is worse than apartheid's pass laws, which were clearly legislated and published.

Checkpoints constitute the most severe restriction on the movement of Palestinians. Members of the occupying forces who staff checkpoints carefully check the identity of Palestinians wishing to cross and scrutinize their permits. Vehicles and bags are inspected and there are long delays. Every day thousands of Palestinians must pass through these checkpoints in order to travel from home to work, to reach schools and hospitals, and to visit friends and family. Every day Palestinians are compelled to waste hours in this way.

Delays at these points are endemic. During the Second Intifada ambulances were repeatedly held up for hours, resulting in many deaths. Between 2000 and 2006, 68 women gave birth at checkpoints; there were 35 miscarriages; and 5 women died in childbirth. Trips that once took fifteen minutes now take several hours. Qalandia checkpoint, the main crossing from the West Bank to East Jerusalem, is notoriously slow and pedestrians take up to ninety minutes to cross during peak hours.

Movement is also restricted by hundreds of physical obstacles and barriers which include unmanned roadblocks, earth mounds, gates and trenches In many instances these obstacles make it impossible for vehicles to cross highways and oblige Palestinians to leave their vehicles, cross the road on foot, and take a taxi from the other side of the road.

During the Second Intifada a vigorous system of checkpoints and roadblocks was established which had disastrous consequences for the personal lives and economy of Palestinians. In 2007, the final year of my rapporteurship, there were 561 obstacles to freedom of movement, comprising over 80 manned checkpoints and some 476 unmanned locked gates, earth mounds, concrete blocks and ditches. In addition, there were hundreds of temporary checkpoints, known as 'flying checkpoints,' set up by Israeli Defense Forces (IDF) patrols on roads for limited periods, ranging from half an hour to several hours. In 2007 over 400 such checkpoints were recorded. The situation has not changed. In 2015 there were 85 fixed checkpoints in the West Bank and hundreds of 'flying checkpoints'.[61]

Checkpoints were generally manned by young IDF conscripts. Their job was boring and power went to their heads. They frequently did not behave correctly towards us. We were sometimes held up for hours. Soldiers were routinely rude and sought to inspect our vehicle even though they knew full well that UN vehicles were immune from search. On one occasion we were confronted with IDF soldiers feigning sleep on the road in a display of open contempt. When UN vehicles and personnel were treated in such a hostile manner, it was not difficult to imagine the treatment to which Palestinians were subjected.

They were routinely abused and humiliated. This treatment of Palestinians at checkpoints was so bad that a group of Israeli women established Machsom[62] Watch, an organization similar to South Africa's Black Sash, to monitor and ameliorate IDF conduct at checkpoints. It was always good to see these women, old enough to be the mothers or grandmothers of IDF soldiers, as we knew they would shame the IDF into better behaviour. But where Machsom Watch was not present we saw the coarse behaviour of the IDF at checkpoints as we passed through in our privileged UN vehicles. Such conduct must surely have been ordained by those in command.

During the First Intifada, Israelis were free to travel in the West Bank and to witness the excesses of the IDF. Since the Second Intifada they have been prohibited from entering the West Bank, which means that the Israeli public is denied first-hand knowledge of what happens there. Instead they are limited to official information. But, sadly, it seems that Israelis are content not to know what happens in the OPT. Press reports and accounts of the occupation such as those published by the Israeli liberal newspaper *Haaretz* have little impact on the Israeli public. The West Bank remains as unknown to Israelis just as the black townships were to white South Africans. Settlers, despite their residence in the West Bank, are also able to avoid contact with Palestinians. Settler roads and checkpoints have succeeded in isolating them from the Palestinians.

Curfews are not as frequently imposed today as they were during the Second Intifada. However, they are still imposed in villages and towns during military operations or as punishment for offences against the IDF. During the Second Intifada many Palestinian cities were subjected to curfews for long periods. In 2002 all West Bank cities except Jericho were subjected to curfew for several months.[63]

Checkpoints and curfews reminded me strongly of the pass laws of apartheid South Africa. They too served to humiliate, frustrate and intimidate the local population. This explains why my first public statement on the apartheid analogy was in the context of checkpoints and curfews.

House Demolitions

In South Africa the demolition of houses was a feature of apartheid's determination to move blacks from their homes in the cities and the countryside to achieve territorial separation. In the process homes were bulldozed and families were left to fend for themselves, often in some desolated rural area without shelter or access to shops, schools or hospitals.

Israel likewise resorts to house demolition in occupied Palestine but uses this weapon more freely and frequently. House demolitions are justified on a number of grounds: military necessity, collective punishment, administrative sanction, and the construction of the wall. It has been estimated that between 1967 and 2015 over forty-eight thousand Palestinian houses and housing structures were destroyed by Israel.[64] House demolition is on the increase: in 2016 1,089 houses were destroyed, over twice the number for 2015.

'Demolishing a home is always a tragedy,' writes Michael Sfard, Israel's leading human rights lawyer. 'Imagine a bulldozer tearing your house apart. Whatever you managed to save from its iron claws is scattered on the ground where your refuge once stood. Imagine your life after the place where your very core was housed – where you realized yourself and your family, personally and privately – is nothing but rubble. Each home demolition leaves utterly innocent children, the elderly, men and women on the streets, ruined and shamed. The house demolition policy has inflicted dreadful pain on thousands of Palestinians, many of them young, who watched as the home their parents built was destroyed within minutes.'[65]

The most savage destruction of houses has occurred in Gaza in the course of military operations carried out since Israel withdrew its presence in 2005. In Operation Cast Lead of 2008–9 over three thousand houses were destroyed while in Operation Protective Edge some seven thousand houses were razed to the ground. These operations are described in a later chapter on Gaza.

Military operations conducted during the Second Intifada were less devastating but nonetheless severe. In April 2002, in Operation Defensive Shield, the IDF, using armoured Caterpillars, launched a brutal offensive against Palestinian militants in the Jenin refugee camp in the West Bank. As a result fifty-two Palestinians were killed, of which twenty-two were civilians, and twenty-three Israeli soldiers died. Some eight hundred dwellings were destroyed, leaving four thousand homeless. The UN called for an inquiry, and constituted a commission, which included Cyril Ramaphosa, later to become president of South Africa, but Israel refused to allow the commission into the territory, fearing that it might provide evidence of war crimes committed by the IDF. We visited the Jenin refugee camp in August 2002. It was hard to believe that the dusty, levelled plain, punctuated by the crumbling structures that confronted us, had but a few months before been home to a thriving community. The destruction was wanton and there were allegations of looting by the IDF. Nearby, UNRWA had erected tents to accommodate the occupants of the camp. Refugees who had fled their homes in 1948 for fear of the Israelis were again rendered homeless.

Operation Rainbow of May 2004 saw a repetition of Israeli might. This offensive directed at Rafah in the Gaza Strip resulted in the deaths of 43 persons and the destruction of 298 buildings housing over two thousand persons. Again the destruction was wanton. We visited the Brazil Quarter and the Tel es-Sultan neighbourhoods of Rafah soon after Operation Rainbow and met with families who had been rendered homeless. Everywhere we went there was evidence of destruction. Buildings – homes, government buildings and schools – were reduced to rubble, and streets were a mix of mangled pipes and rocks. Tanks, F16 fighter aircraft, Apache helicopter gunships and, above all, the ubiquitous Caterpillar bulldozer had left ruins in their savage wake. The role of the Caterpillar was not to be underestimated. The American student activist Rachel Corrie was killed by a Caterpillar about this time. Much of the damage to property in Palestine was carried out by Caterpillar bulldozers, which had special attachments that allowed them to dig up water and sewerage pipes and electricity wires, and to cause the maximum havoc to roads and property. The Caterpillar bulldozer became the symbol of the occupation, the ugly face of uncaring corporate greed in the Second Intifada.

Until 2005 it was Israel's policy to destroy the homes of those who had committed crimes against Israel. This action was directed at the family of the offender, which meant that it was not necessary for the offender himself to be living in the home at the time of the offence. Between 1967 and 2004 2,464 homes were demolished in this way.[66] Demolitions were carried out in an arbitrary manner without prior warning to house owners. This punitive action clearly constituted a violation of article 33 of the Fourth Geneva Convention prohibiting collective punishment. Innocents are punished for the acts of a family member. Although settlers have often been guilty of committing serious crimes in occupied Palestine, involving the killing of Palestinians, this form of punishment has not been used against them.

In the early years of the Second Intifada the demolition of homes was frequently used as a punishment but in 2005 it was brought to an end when the Israeli army decided that it was counterproductive. In 2014, however, it was revived and the demolition of the homes of militants is once more common practice.

Israel is determined to prevent Palestinians from expanding their presence in East Jerusalem and Area C of the West Bank, the areas over which Israel exercises complete control. In the first instance this is done by refusing permits to Palestinians to build houses. From 2009 to 2013 there were over two thousand applications for permits to build, of which only 34 were granted. In 2014, one permit was issued, but in 2016 no applications were approved.[67] On the other hand, some fifteen hundred building permits are granted each year to settlers to build in occupied Palestine. Frustrated by such refusals and with nowhere to live, Palestinians resort to the construction of houses without permits. Israel's response is to demolish these houses. Israel's explanation that it is simply applying municipal housing laws in the same way as other developed societies is unconvincing. Firstly, it takes no account of the discriminatory manner in which the law is administered in respect of Palestinians. Secondly, it is in violation of international humanitarian law, which prohibits an occupying power from destroying the houses of protected persons (that is, Palestinians) in occupied territory.[68]

So-called administrative demolitions are a frequent occurrence. Thousands of homes have been demolished in East Jerusalem and in Area C of the West Bank. In 2016 alone, 1,100 houses were destroyed.[69] In 2016–17 over a hundred structures – homes, shelters, water networks and schools – funded by the European Union or its members were demolished.

Demolitions are carried out in a spirit of bureaucratic vindictiveness. Two experiences in the Jordan valley spring to mind, one petty and nasty and the other tragic. The first concerned a house owner in a village in Area B who planted geraniums in front of his house. The border of Area C fell just outside his house, with the result that the geraniums were in Area C. The IDF destroyed the geraniums on the ground that they had been planted without permission! The second concerned the Bedouin village or encampment of Hadidiya in Area C near Tubas, which was situated near a settlement. Settlers complained about the proximity of Arabs in much the same way that white South Africans had complained about the presence of neighbouring black communities – called 'black spots'. As a result the encampment was destroyed by the IDF. The community rebuilt Hadidiya and appealed to the Israeli High Court for permission to remain, but the appeal was rejected on the ground that the homes had been erected without permit. While the leader of the community, a wise and well-informed man, traced the history of the community, the building of the nearby settlement and the relations with the settlers over sweetened tea in a shady Bedouin tent surrounded by his family, I recalled the destruction of African communal homes and of District Six in Cape Town in pursuance of the policy of apartheid.

My reports on house demolitions were raised by the NGO Adalah in legal proceedings before the Israeli Supreme Court challenging house demolitions. When the lawyer for the government objected to my reports on the ground that they were clearly biased and therefore inadmissible, the president of the court, Aharon Barak, intervened, saying, 'He's a renowned expert. I know him personally.'[70] The reports were also the subject of a debate in the Knesset. When I was visiting Israel–Palestine in February 2005, I received an invitation from

Michael Eitan of Likud[71] to participate in a debate on 'the position of Israel and international law on the question of house demolitions in the war against terrorism' in the Law, Constitution and Justice Committee of the Knesset. He informed me that the Israeli government had objected to the invitation on the ground that it refused to have anything to do with me, but he had replied that this was the decision of the executive branch of government, which did not bind the legislative branch. David Kretzmer, who had been instrumental in securing the invitation, warned me that I should expect hostility. I opened the debate with a highly critical examination of Israeli practices in respect of house demolitions and the rules of international law. I sat down expecting to be savagely condemned. The first speaker was a member of the Israeli communist party, who was followed by an Arab member of the Knesset. My address had been mild in comparison with their harsh criticisms. Thereafter the debate continued in a forceful but parliamentary manner. I found myself somewhere in the centre of opinion. This experience illustrated one of the many contradictions of Israel and highlighted the freedom of opinion and expression in Israeli society.

Settlements[72]

The Six-Day War and the occupation of Palestine brought with it the construction of Jewish settlements in occupied Palestine. The exact number of settlers in occupied Palestine is uncertain. Most sources give a figure of between six and seven hundred thousand, with nearly four hundred thousand in the West Bank and some three hundred thousand in East Jerusalem. Israel withdrew its settlements from Gaza in 2005. There are about 125 officially authorized settlements and over 100 unauthorized informal outposts, which are often later converted into fully fledged settlements.

Despite protests from the international community, settlements continue to grow. The year 2016 saw one of the greatest increases ever in the settler population. The average birth growth rate in the settlements is 5.3 compared with the average birth growth rate of 1.8 in Israel itself. Settlements vary considerably in size. Beitar Illit (population 45,000), Ariel (population 18,000), Modi'in Illit and Ma'ale Adumim are large cities, with all the facilities and amenities of a city – schools, hospitals, shopping centres and a university in Ariel. Other settlements are very small with populations of several hundred or less. There are settlements scattered around East Jerusalem and in the Old City itself, the Jordan valley and the entire West Bank. And there are newly established settlements termed 'outposts' that are formally illegal under Israeli law but that are allowed to continue their existence until they become fully fledged settlements.[73] Legislation of 2017 is aimed at facilitating this process of 'regularization'. Forty per cent of the settlements are built on land privately owned by Palestinians. Funding comes from the Israeli government itself and Zionist organizations, such as the World Zionist Organization. Settlers may be divided into three categories: ultra-Orthodox, political–religious ideologues and ordinary Israelis in search of comfortable suburban living.

Settlements are clearly unlawful under international law. The Fourth Geneva Convention of 1949[74] prohibits the transfer of the citizens of an occupying power into an occupied territory. The Rome Statute of the International Criminal Court[75] criminalizes such conduct. The International Court of Justice in its 2004 advisory opinion on the wall unanimously found that settlements are unlawful.[76] Both the UN Security Council and the General Assembly have adopted resolutions declaring settlements to be unlawful. As recently as December 2016 the Security Council confirmed this position in Resolution 2334.

Israel has stubbornly refused to accept that settlements are unlawful, despite being advised in September 1967 by its own chief legal adviser, Theodor Meron, that settlements contravened the Fourth Geneva Convention of 1949.[77] It is alone in insisting that settlements are lawful.

The construction of settlements results in the expulsion and displacement of Palestinians from their lands. This constitutes a 'forcible transfer of population' – an inhuman act in terms of the Rome Statute – and the 'expropriation of landed property' – an inhuman act under the Apartheid Convention. This process resembles the taking of land and homes in suburbs occupied by blacks in terms of South Africa's Group Areas Act.

Settlements result in the colonization of an occupied territory. The prohibition on settlements in the Fourth Geneva Convention was aimed at preventing the practice of colonizing occupied territory followed by Nazi Germany in World War II. Consequently, Israel's settlement enterprise must be seen in the context of colonization, which today is contrary to international law.[78] Israeli settlers are foreigners in occupied Palestine and are as much settlers as were British, French, Portuguese and German settlers in Africa during the colonial period. They occupy the land of Palestine, exploit its resources, suppress the local inhabitants, and deny their right to self-determination. The settlement enterprise is simply colonialism under the guise of military occupation. It differs from European colonialism in that it makes no attempt to promote the welfare of the indigenous people in the process of exploitation. Israel and the settlers have not established schools, hospitals or clinics for the Palestinian population. This is left to the UN, foreign governments and the Palestinian Authority despite the fact that Israel is obliged by international humanitarian law to care for the needs of the occupied people. Israel's settlement colonialism is a selfish, brutal exploitation of the territory, totally lacking in idealism or altruism.[79]

I did not visit settlements officially in my capacity as special rapporteur. That I would not be welcome was confirmed by the settlers. Many settlements that I saw from afar were perched on mountain tops, destroying the beauty of the Palestinian hills. We did on occasion drive through some of the major settlements such as Ariel, Ma'ale Adumim and Kiryat Arba. I saw the spacious homes, well-kept gardens, shops and public facilities. Settlements are suburbia at its best.

The consequences of settlements are clear. They displace Palestinians from their homes, seize Palestinian land, obstruct Palestinian farming, seriously interfere with the life of Palestinian villages, disfigure the environment, and are a source of deep humiliation to the Palestinian people, a visible reminder of the occupation. 'Each settlement is the epicenter of a ripple effect of abuses affecting the rights of the surrounding Palestinian communities.'[80] And then there is settler violence. Although most settlers are content to live a peaceful life, there is a minority belonging to the camp of religious and political zealots who are bent on terrorizing Palestinians. They commit random acts of violence against Palestinians and Palestinian property. Olive trees and crops are routinely destroyed. Homes, mosques and churches are set on fire; water wells are poisoned; and roadways are blocked.

Settlers in Hebron are particularly violent. Some eight hundred settlers, protected by over fifteen hundred soldiers, have established settlements, including a Yeshiva, in the centre of the Hebron market from which they terrorize Palestinians and foreign visitors. A body of policemen and women drawn from foreign countries, known as the Temporary International Presence in Hebron (TIPH), patrols Hebron, with the consent of the Israeli government, and seeks to maintain peace in the city. Accompanied by TIPH, we were spat on and abused by settlers with strong American accents; and the TIPH vehicle in which we were travelling was spray-painted. We saw the refuse deposited from settler houses on the streets of Hebron and the anti-Palestinian graffiti on the city walls. I recall one wall slogan with historical connotations: 'Gas the Arabs.' As elsewhere, the IDF made little attempt to control the settlers or to protect Palestinians from settler violence. The arrest and prosecution of settlers for assaulting Palestinians or destroying their property is virtually unknown. The situation is well summed up by *Haaretz* columnist Gideon Levy when he wrote about settlers in Hebron:

> Every day the settlers torment their neighbours here. Every walk to school for a Palestinian child has become a journey of harassment and fear.

> Every shopping outing by a housewife is a journey of humiliation. Settler children kicking old women carrying baskets, settlers sicking their dogs on to the elderly, garbage and feces from the settlers' balconies thrown into the courtyards of Palestinian homes, junk metal blocking the entrances of their houses, rocks thrown at any Palestinian passerby – this is the routine of life in the city. Hundreds of soldiers, border police and cops witness these actions and stand by idly … Israel cannot be considered a state ruled by law, or as democracy, as long as the pogroms continue in Hebron.[81]

The Judaization of East Jerusalem is to be achieved by the expansion of settlements. Small Jewish settlements have sprung up in the Old City itself. I was taken on a tour of the Old City by a Palestinian guide who pointed out buildings with blue-and-white Israeli flags flying from the rooftops. These flags resemble those planted by early European explorers on islands discovered in the Pacific Ocean: they are intended to signify that the building in question is now under Israeli sovereignty. But the real expansion is taking place in greater East Jerusalem where suburbs like Gilo, Ramot and Pisgat Ze'ev, with populations of over forty thousand, have been established. To make matters worse, there are plans to extend the boundaries of Jerusalem to incorporate Ma'ale Adumim, with a population of forty thousand. This will effectively divide the north and the south of the West Bank.

The Wall[82]

The wall Israel is constructing largely on Palestinian territory, ostensibly for security but in reality for the purpose of annexation, has resulted in the expropriation of Palestinian land without compensation and in the displacement of thousands of Palestinians, directly by taking their land and indirectly by making it impossible for them to continue living in the precincts of the wall. It clearly qualifies as an inhuman act for the purpose of defining apartheid. But the history of the construction of this wall is also significant as an illustration of Israel's determination to seize land by false pretences, as an indication of the courage of the International Court of Justice, and as evidence of the spinelessness of the international community in confronting Israel in respect of its illegal act. For this reason this account of the wall is not limited to examining the wall as an 'inhuman act'.

In 2002 Israel began construction of a wall or barrier to separate the West Bank from Israel.[83] When finished, it will run for about seven hundred kilometres. In places, particularly in urban areas, the wall takes the form of an eight-metre-high concrete wall. However, most of the structure is a barrier some sixty to a hundred metres wide, comprising three fences, of which the outer two are protected by coils of barbed wire while the inner fence has electronic equipment that allows intruders to be detected. There are patrol roads on either side of the outer fence and a trace road, which is a strip of sand that allows footprints to be detected. Sometimes the barrier includes trenches. There are fortified guard towers at regular intervals. Some choose to use the term 'barrier' to describe the structure. Within Palestine it is known as 'the wall', or, more frequently, the 'apartheid wall'. In its 2004 advisory opinion on the subject, the International Court of Justice preferred to describe it as a 'wall'. I shall follow this practice.

Had the wall been built on the Israeli side of the Green Line – the Armistice Line of 1949 constituting the accepted border between Israel and Palestine – there would have been no problem. Israel is fully entitled to build a wall on its own territory. But over 80 per cent of the wall is built on Palestinian land, encircling more than sixty major Israeli settlements in the West Bank and 85 per cent of the settler population, and results in the expropriation of some 10 per cent of Palestinian land. It is this fact that gave rise to the charge that the purpose of the wall was less to keep out suicide bombers and more to seize Palestinian land and incorporate settlements into Israel.

In 2002 I was taken to see marks on hills near Qalqilya and Tulkarm which indicated clearly that Israel planned to build the wall inside Palestinian territory. This led me to embark on a campaign to draw public attention to the wall. In 2003 I wrote an op-ed piece for the *International Herald Tribune*,[84] in which I argued that the wall was 'manifestly intended to create facts on the ground' and that it constituted an act of annexation. 'Annexation of this kind', I said, 'goes by another name in international law – conquest.' The Israeli ambassador to the United Nations complained to the secretary-general of the UN about the article, but I responded that comments of this kind fell within my mandate. My report to the UN of September 2003 was equally strong. Israel's choice of the term 'security fence' to describe the wall was a euphemism intended to obfuscate the true nature of the wall. 'The fact must be faced', I wrote, 'that what we are presently witnessing in the West Bank is a visible and clear act of territorial annexation under the guise of security.'[85]

In 2001 and 2002 I presented my report to the Third Committee of the General Assembly in New York and had good reason to assume that I would report again in October 2003. However, I reckoned without the bureaucracy of the Office of the High Commissioner for Human Rights, which sought to prevent me from presenting the report on the ground that it had not been expressly authorized. In exasperation I appealed to the Egyptian ambassador in Geneva to intervene. She did, with the support of other Arab states, and the bureaucratic door was opened. This was the first time I had reason to suspect that there was an obstructive Israeli presence in the Office of the High Commission for Human Rights. It was not to be the last.

In my address to the Third Committee in October 2003 I repeated my view that the wall was not a temporary security measure but a redrawing of the border, an act of de facto annexation. I accused the Quartet, comprising the United States, the Russian Federation, the European Union and the UN, set up in 2002 to advance peace in the Middle East, of appeasement in its failure to condemn the wall. There was overwhelming support for my position, and the Third Committee referred the matter to the General Assembly.

The General Assembly adopted a resolution demanding that Israel 'stop and reverse construction of the wall in the Occupied Palestinian Territory' on the ground that it was a violation of international law.[86] The resolution requested the secretary-general to report on Israel's compliance and in November he reported that Israel had failed to comply. While I was in New York I lobbied for an advisory opinion from the International Court of Justice on the legality of the wall if Israel failed to comply with the resolution of the General Assembly. I was approached by Nasser al-Kidwa, the Palestinian ambassador to the UN, about the form the question to the court should take. Nasser also consulted my friend from Cambridge days, Hussein Hassouna of Egypt, on the subject. Together we advised Nasser to formulate the question to the International Court broadly along the lines of the question posed to the court in the 1971 Namibia opinion, that is, to stress the legal consequences flowing from the construction of the wall. Our advice was followed. On 8 December 2003 the General Assembly adopted a resolution which welcomed my report of 8 September 2003,[87] and asked the court to pronounce on the following question: 'What are the legal consequences arising from the construction of the wall being built by Israel, the occupying power in the Occupied Palestinian Territory?'

My reports featured prominently in the written and oral representations of states to the International Court of Justice in its advisory proceedings. Forty-eight states made written representations to the court and twelve addressed the court, including South Africa. Israel chose to ignore the proceedings after submitting a written statement.

In July 2004 the court gave its opinion.[88] By fourteen votes to one, it held that the wall was illegal, that Israel should stop building the wall, and that it should dismantle the wall and pay compensation to those who had suffered as a result of its construction. The court found that the wall violated principles of international humanitarian law and several human rights conventions. Moreover, it undermined the right of the Palestinian people to self-determination. In its reasoning the court confirmed three issues that are fundamental to the legal dispute between the international community and Israel. Firstly, that the Fourth Geneva Convention of 1949 regulating the military occupation of territory was applicable to Israel's occupation of the Palestinian Territory; secondly, that Israel's settlement enterprise violated article 49(6) of the Fourth Geneva Convention, which prohibits an occupying power from transferring its own citizens into an occupied territory; and, thirdly, that the major human rights conventions were applicable to Israel's administration of Palestine. On these three issues the court was unanimous. The court relied on the account of the impact of the wall on Palestinians living in its shadow contained in my report of 8 September.[89]

The opinion was approved by the General Assembly in a resolution that included member states of the European Union. The United States, however, opposed it from the outset and made sure that it did not feature in the decisions of the Security Council or the Quartet. Predictably, the Israeli government rejected the opinion. This was followed by a decision of the Israeli Supreme Court in *Mara'abe* v. *Prime Minister*,[90] which ruled that the construction of the wall within Palestinian territory was justified as a security measure to protect both Israel itself and the safety of Jewish settlers. The court held that the International Court's opinion was flawed by reason of its failure to have access to the full facts surrounding the wall and accepted without serious examination the assurances of the Israeli military that the wall was constructed for security purposes.[91] My view that the wall also served a political purpose, namely to seize land and to incorporate settlements into Israel, was expressly rejected.[92]

An advisory opinion is by definition advisory. Clearly the opinion itself was not binding on states such as Israel and the United States. On the other hand, both these states were bound by the Fourth Geneva Convention and the International Covenant on Civil and Political Rights, upon which the opinion was based. I took the view[93] that the UN as an institution, including the secretary-general, was bound by the opinion as a result of its approval by the General Assembly. Despite this, the secretary-general, under the influence of his senior advisers and legal counsel,[94] paid little regard to the opinion. In particular, he failed to ensure that the Quartet was guided by the opinion.

The length and course of the wall underwent several adjustments over time, due to court injunctions which accorded minor relief to some Palestinian villages. But the principal unlawful features of the wall were retained. Most of the wall is built in Palestinian territory on the Palestinian side of the Green Line. It seizes over 10 per cent of Palestinian territory, including some of Palestine's most fertile agricultural land and water resources. It incorporates most Israeli settlements and 85 per cent of the settlers in the West Bank into Israel. In some places it extends over twenty kilometres into Palestinian territory in order to incorporate settlements. It includes 42 Palestinian villages with a population of fifty thousand in the 'seam zone' or 'closed zone', that is, the area between the wall built in Palestinian territory and the Green Line or official border.

The restriction on the movement of Palestinians within the seam zone is a replica of South Africa's notorious pass system. Israelis, Jews entitled to Israeli citizenship under the Law of Return,[95] and tourists are free to move within the seam zone without a permit. Palestinians, on the other hand, are required to obtain a permit to access the seam zone. Palestinians who have lived for generations in the territory of the seam zone or whose land is in the seam zone require a permit to enter or to be in the seam zone, while any American tourist may enter and stay in the seam zone without a care. The obvious similarities between this system and South Africa's pass system prompted Israeli human rights lawyers to challenge – unsuccessfully – the legality of the permit system on the ground that the orders applicable to the seam zone constitute 'an intolerable, illegal, immoral legal apartheid'.[96]

This permit system places great hardships on both Palestinians living in the seam zone and those living on the West Bank side of the wall with farmlands in the seam zone. Those living in the seam zone have difficulty in gaining access to family, hospitals, schools, markets and employment within the West Bank. Those living on the West Bank side of the wall require permits to access their own agricultural land on the other side of the wall. Permits are not readily granted and are often issued for only a few months. At least 40 per cent of the applications by farmers for permits are refused; the process of application is humiliating; gates are few and often do not open as scheduled; and those passing through the gates are subject to harassment and abuse. Consequently there is a steady flow of Palestinians displaced from the seam zone and its vicinity to the cities.

We visited villages affected by the wall. One of these, Jayyus, we visited regularly. It had a population of thirty-two hundred, mainly farmers separated by the wall from their farmlands, greenhouses and wells. On each occasion we were hospitably received by the village elders, who pointed to their inaccessible greenhouses and lands across the barrier and in the seam zone while serving Turkish coffee and cakes. They looked to me as the agent of the UN to do something about their plight, but all I could do was report what I had seen, with the knowledge that the UN would do nothing. I asked them whether they had received visits or support from the Palestinian Authority. They had not.

In Jerusalem the wall serves not only to incorporate settlements into Israel but also to Judaize the city. It is built to redefine the outlying Palestinian neighbourhoods of Jerusalem as part of the West Bank, thereby transferring some sixty thousand Palestinians resident in Jerusalem to the West Bank. This has serious consequences for Palestinian Jerusalemites as they lose their right to the social security benefits attached to Jerusalem residency. They are denied access to schools, universities and hospitals in East Jerusalem and must obtain permits to enter Jerusalem. Furthermore, they are unable to access places of worship, notably the al-Aqsa Mosque and the Church of the Holy Sepulchre. Families are physically separated into those with Jerusalem identity documents and those with West Bank documents. We met several families in Abu Dis and al-Eizariya who were separated in this way. The wall in Jerusalem gives the lie to the Israeli argument that it is a security wall, for here it separates Palestinians from Palestinians and demonstrably serves no security purpose.

My claim that the wall constitutes an act of annexation and that it would become the future border between Israel and Palestine was soon confirmed by the statements of Israeli politicians. In 2005 the minister of justice, Tzipi Livni, declared that the wall would serve as 'the future border of the state of Israel',[97] which prompted the Israeli High Court to express concerns that it had been misled by the government on the purpose the wall was intended to serve.[98] That it was Israel's plan to use the wall to redraw the border was also clear from assurances it sought to obtain from the United States that it would be allowed to keep settlements encircled by the wall.[99]

The wall has become a fait accompli. In view of the opposition of the United States to the advisory opinion on the wall, the failure of the Quartet to make any attempt to secure compliance with the opinion, the readiness of European states to fall in line with the United States on this issue, and the reservations of the upper echelons of the Secretariat of the UN about the opinion, the wall has ceased to be a matter of contention between the international community and Israel. In line with this lack of concern for the opinion, the UN has failed to give effect to the finding of the International Court that Israel is obliged to compensate all Palestinians who have suffered any form of material damage as a result of the construction of the wall.[100] Although the General Assembly directed that a register of damages be established in 2004, it was not until 2007 that the secretary-general appointed a board to oversee this process. To date, little if any progress has been made in securing compensation for those who have suffered as a result of the construction of the wall. Claims are being processed, but there is no attempt on the part of the UN to confront Israel on compensation. That the credibility of the International Court of Justice has suffered from the rejection of its opinion is of no concern to the political organs of the UN.

29

Apartheid: Systematic discrimination and oppression

The third requirement for the crime of apartheid is that the inhuman acts are committed 'in the context of an institutionalized regime of systematic oppression and domination by one racial group over any other racial group and committed with the intention of maintaining that regime'.[101] The dominant racial group in occupied Palestine is the Jewish settler group, aided and abetted by Israel's occupying forces. Residence in settlements is restricted to Israeli Jews or to persons of Jewish descent entitled to Israeli citizenship under Israel's Law of Return. Settlers, numbering between six and seven hundred thousand in the West Bank and East Jerusalem, are not part of the security apparatus of occupation, as Israel has long abandoned the pretext that settlers are necessary to secure Israel's occupation. Settlers are colonists who have settled in the OPT for different reasons. They are a mix of Jews in search of a comfortable suburban life within commuting distance of the cities of Israel, religious Jews committed to living in the biblical lands of Judea and Samaria, and Zionist zealots determined to assert Israel's presence in Palestinian lands. As colonists, they resemble the European colonists of a previous era who settled in Africa and Asia and who were protected by the forces of the colonial power. A major difference between colonists of an earlier era and Jewish colonists is that until the 1960s international law placed no prohibition on the institution of colonialism. Indeed, many of its rules were designed to promote and facilitate colonialism. Today, however, international law prohibits colonialism, as manifested by numerous resolutions of the General Assembly,[102] and the decolonization process of the 1960s and 1970s. Colonization in the course of military occupation was prohibited still earlier –

in 1949 – by article 49(6) of the Fourth Geneva Convention and has now been criminalized by the Rome Statute of the International Criminal Court of 1998.[103]

The construction of settlements is not a random exercise designed to cater for the over-population of Israel by allowing Jews to settle near the Israeli border but inside occupied Palestine. Instead it is a project which encourages Jews to settle throughout the West Bank, from the Green Line to the Jordan valley. It aims to fragment the Palestinian territory into a cluster of Palestinian enclaves, like Bantustans, with movement between each enclave carefully controlled. In this way Israel will govern its colony in accordance with the traditional colonial policy of divide and rule.

The primary function of the Israeli civil and military authorities in the OPT is to insulate and privilege Jewish settlers and to ensure that Palestinians intrude as little as possible on the lives of settlers. The inhuman acts described in the previous chapter are not committed in a random manner without purpose. They are part of a systematic and institutionalized oppressive regime that is intended to maintain the domination of the Jewish group – settlers – over the Palestinian group. This regime, like the apartheid regime in South Africa, is founded on a discriminatory ideology that has its roots in the Israeli legal system, which elevates Jews to a higher status than Palestinians.

Israeli law distinguishes between Jewish nationality and Israeli citizenship, with Israel as the state of the Jewish nation and Jewish nationals privileged over non-Jewish Israeli citizens. As the 2009 report of the Human Rights Council fact-finding mission on Operation Cast Lead, chaired by former South African Constitutional Court judge Richard Goldstone, declared: 'The application of Israeli domestic laws has resulted in institutionalized discrimination against Palestinians in the Occupied Palestinian Territory to the benefit of Jewish settlers, both Israeli citizens and others. Exclusive benefits reserved for Jews derive from the two-tiered civil status under Israel's domestic legal system based on "Jewish nationality", which entitles persons of "Jewish race or descendency" to superior rights or privileges.'[104]

This dual legal system is the foundation for the institutionalized system of racial discrimination and domination that prevails in the West Bank. Israel applies Israeli civil law to settlers, affording them full legal protection and rights, whereas Palestinians living in the same area are subject to Israeli military law, which denies such protection and rights. Israel provides settlers with infrastructure, services and subsidies that it denies to Palestinians, thereby creating and sustaining a separate and unequal system of laws and services. In the words of the Association for Civil Rights in Israel: 'In the same territorial area and under the same administration live two populations who are subject to two separate and contrasting legal systems and infrastructure. One population has full civil rights while the other is deprived of those rights.'[105] Inevitably, as shown by the experience of apartheid South Africa, discrimination of this kind results in the domination of the 'superior' group over the 'inferior' group. It serves to humiliate the Palestinian people, deny their human dignity and ensure their oppression.

In occupied Palestine the more powerful racial group in terms of law and military might – the 'superior' group – is the Jewish settler group backed by the occupying forces. It has oppressed and subjugated the Palestinian group by the systematic commission of inhuman acts. This institutionalized racist regime is not a temporary one intended to last only until a peace agreement is reached to end the occupation. It is a permanent state of affairs intended to continue in force indefinitely.

The situation is well summarized by Israeli human rights lawyer Michael Sfard:

> It is hard to look at the way Israel controls the West Bank, with separate legal and administrative systems governing Palestinians and Israelis, and with all local resources used to benefit one group at the expense of the other, without being reminded of a legal term from the not-so-distant past. A person would have to be unconscious not to pick up the whiff of apartheid everywhere there is a settlement. Israel has created not only an occupation that has persisted for generations but also a regime where one group oppresses and discriminates against the other for the sole purpose of preserving its control and supremacy.[106]

There was a benevolent side to apartheid in South Africa that is absent from Israel's occupation of Palestine. The apartheid regime established schools, universities, hospitals and social services for blacks. It promoted industrial development in the Bantustans in order to provide jobs; it built roads and created an infrastructure for development. Israel displays no such concern for the welfare of the Palestinian people; it has not contributed to the infrastructure of the OPT or the establishment of schools, universities or hospitals. Instead it has left the welfare of the Palestinian people to international donors. Apartheid in occupied Palestine is a selfish enterprise designed to serve the indulgence of the settler regime while pursuing the Zionist dream of expanding the territorial boundaries of Israel to the Jordan River.

There is a major difference between apartheid in South Africa and occupied Palestine in respect of the public portrayal of apartheid – a difference that has been exploited by opponents of the apartheid analogy in Palestine. The apartheid regime in South Africa showed no shame for its policy of racial discrimination. Legislation was clear and explicit in its discriminatory intent. Notices in public places openly reserved facilities for different races and made no attempt to provide equal facilities for different races. In Israel, on the other hand, there is no open assertion of racial superiority. Discriminatory and oppressive laws are concealed in unpublished military regulations or de facto military policy without reference to the law. This difference was highlighted by a former Israeli cabinet minister, Shulamit Aloni, who described an example of apartheid in operation in the system of separate roads for Jewish settlers and Palestinians:

> On one occasion I witnessed an encounter between a Palestinian driver and a soldier on a settler road who was taking down the details before confiscating the vehicle and sending its owner away. 'Why?' I asked the soldier. 'It's an order – this is a Jews-only road,' he replied. I inquired as to where the sign was indicating this fact and instructing Palestinian drivers not to use it. His answer was nothing short of amazing. 'It is his responsibility to know it, and besides, what do you want us to do, put up a sign here and let some anti-Semitic reporter or journalist take a photo so that he can show the world that apartheid exists here?'[107]

30

Praise and censure

Both my written and oral reports to the Human Rights Council and the Third Committee of the General Assembly were highly critical of Israel. The reports were well received in certain quarters but were savagely criticized by Israel, pro-Israel NGOs and some states, such as the United States. I responded forcefully to my critics and to those who collaborated with Israel or who remained silent. The mandate on the human rights situation in occupied Palestine was not one for the thin-skinned or faint-hearted.

From Helen Suzman I had learnt two things: be sure of your facts and be bold in your opinions. No critic of human rights violations could be effective if she or he was faulted on fact-finding or was timid in the portrayal of the implications of these findings.

My reports sought to provide the facts of the occupation. Facts were obtained from personal observations, interviews with Palestinians from all walks of life, Palestinian and Israeli NGOs and UN agencies, the media and the reports of the UN, the European Union and international NGOs. In fact-finding I erred on the side of caution in the event of doubt. Consequently my fact-finding was not seriously faulted. Israel and the United States routinely complained that my facts were inaccurate but never took up my challenge to name any inaccuracy. On one occasion the US delegate to the Third Committee, who had declared that my report was riddled with inaccuracies, quietly apologized to me at the adjournment, saying that she had been required to read a speech written by officials of the State Department.

Inevitably my reports were controversial as they dealt with the most politically sensitive issues of the Israel–Palestine conflict: apartheid, terrorism, the wall, checkpoints, house demolitions, settlements, and the response of the

UN and its members to Israel's violation of human rights.

The first reference to apartheid in my reports was in the context of Israel's restrictions on freedom of movement. My 2004 report stated that the permit system governing the movement of Palestinians resembled the notorious pass laws, which determined the right of black South Africans to move and reside in so-called white areas. While the pass laws were administered in a humiliating manner, they were at least administered uniformly whereas the Israeli laws were administered in a humiliating and capricious manner. Restrictions on freedom of movement constituted 'the institutionalized humiliation of the Palestinian people'. Road apartheid, I added, was unknown in South Africa and in this respect Israel 'had gone beyond the restraints imposed on freedom of movement imposed by apartheid'.[108] This passage in the report was picked up by *Haaretz* columnist Aluf Benn, who wrote an account of the report under the title 'UN agent: Apartheid regime in Territories worse than in South Africa'.[109]

My 2007 report declared that Israel's laws and practices in the OPT constituted apartheid, as there was clear evidence of the commission of inhuman acts and it could not seriously be denied that the purpose of these acts was to establish and maintain the domination of Jews over Palestinians and to systematically oppress them. Although Israel denied this intention, 'such an intention or purpose may be inferred from the actions described in this report'.[110]

Reports were not limited to an assessment of the facts. Inevitably they expressed opinions based on the application of the law to these facts. And they included recommendations and calls to Israel, other states, the Palestinians, the EU and the UN to take action to ensure that human rights and humanitarian law were respected. Most controversial were my calls for an arms embargo on Israel and the establishment of a peacekeeping force in the region.

I was critical of the Quartet, the body comprising the UN, the EU, the Russian Federation and the United States, which has been mandated by the Security Council to promote peace between Israel and Palestine. I castigated it for failing to endorse the advisory opinion of the International Court of Justice on the wall. I accused it of imposing economic sanctions on Palestine in order to secure regime change after the 2006 Palestine elections resulted in a government of national unity that included Hamas. I argued that it should be even-handed in its handling of the conflict between Fatah and Hamas and should speak to both parties. I saw the Quartet and its special envoy, Tony Blair, as being biased in favour of Israel, a view widely shared by Palestinians and UN officials working in the OPT. Arguing that the membership of the UN in the Quartet lent legitimacy to it, I urged the secretary-general to withdraw the UN from the Quartet.[111]

I was particularly troubled by the response of Western states to Israel's violations of human rights. The human rights movement, which has dominated international life since 1945 and resulted in the adoption of numerous human rights treaties and the creation of the International Criminal Court, has largely been inspired and promoted by Western European states. Yet they were unwilling to take firm action to constrain Israel. The double standard was obvious. In my report of 2007 I acknowledged that there were regimes other than Israel that suppressed human rights, but I stated that 'there is no other case of a Western-affiliated regime that denies self-determination and human rights to a developing people and has done so for so long. This explains why the OPT has become a test for the West, a test by which its commitment to human rights is to be judged.'

Predictably, the response of Israel and the United States was hostile to the apartheid analogy. Israel protested that it was impossible to compare apartheid in South Africa to the 'state of Israel, a democracy where Jews and Arabs have equal rights', but failed to recognize that my report was confined to Israel's occupation of the OPT and to the privileged position of the settler community there. In the Third Committee of the General Assembly the Israeli delegate described my report as 'patently incendiary' and a 'wildly misleading comparison'. It was 'extremist and inappropriate' and served 'as a window into the psychology and biases of the Report's author'.[112] The United States complained that the comparison with apartheid was 'inappropriate' and 'unhelpful'.[113]

Israel and the United States were highly critical of my even-handed approach to terrorism. My reports strongly condemned real acts of Palestinian terror such as suicide bombings and the indiscriminate bombing of civilians by rockets fired from Gaza. At the same time they condemned Israel's acts of terror in its assaults on Gaza and the killing of civilians in targeted assassinations. I believed that it was incumbent on me to neutralize the language of the conflict by limiting the accusations of terrorism by both sides. I stressed that both parties viewed each other's actions as constituting terrorism and that every effort should be made to end terrorism, whether perpetrated by instruments of the state, organized non-state actors or individuals. I called upon both parties to the conflict to have regard for the principles of international humanitarian law prohibiting, and criminalizing, indiscriminate acts of violence against civilian targets committed by both state and non-state actors. I reminded Israel that one man's terrorist was another man's freedom fighter and that two Israeli prime ministers – Menachem Begin and Yitzhak Shamir – had committed acts of terror against the British while members of the Irgun and Stern gangs.

The United States rebuked me for not attaching sufficient importance to terrorism, describing my reports as 'irresponsible and deeply disturbing'. It rejected my equation of state terror with non-state terror, arguing in the Third

Committee of the General Assembly that there was a clear-cut distinction between military operations by the IDF against terrorists and civilians caught up in the conflict and the deliberate targeting of civilians as practised by Palestinian terrorist organizations.[114] Israel was particularly critical of my refusal to accept that the construction of the wall in Palestinian territory was not a temporary defensive measure which could be justified as legitimate anti-terrorism action. Not surprisingly, it failed to comment on its own history of violent resistance to British rule. Finally, it accused me of encouraging terrorism by refusing to accept that Israel's actions were justified as legitimate anti-terror measures.

These accusations were nasty and I have no doubt that they had the desired effect in some quarters of discrediting my reports. I took some comfort in the knowledge that the United States was wrong in claiming that international law draws a clear distinction between the military operations of the IDF against Palestinians and the violent acts of Palestinian militants against Israelis. Both are legitimate acts if committed against military targets and both are war crimes if indiscriminately directed against civilians. Both are terrorist acts if their purpose is to terrorize civilians. It is not possible to label the acts of only one side as acts of terror.[115]

The Commission on Human Rights and, later, the Human Rights Council provided an opportunity for NGOs to speak in plenary meetings. Pro-Israel NGOs were virulent in their criticism, not hesitating to accuse me of anti-Semitism, an accusation that the Israeli government carefully avoided. NGOs outside the United Nations also had their say. Glen Levy and Abraham Foxman of the Anti-Defamation League wrote to the high commissioner for human rights, Louise Arbour, demanding that I be dismissed for making the 'shameful' comparison of apartheid.[116] Stronger criticism came from the hate mail which followed the publication of each report. I always knew when my report had been published on the UN website as my mailbox was suddenly filled with vitriolic accusations of anti-Semitism, support for terrorism and, as in apartheid South Africa, death threats.

Wider criticism followed. In South Africa the editor of the *South African Jewish Report* described me as a 'courageous outspoken critic of the apartheid regime' who had gone astray. Sadly, many Jewish friends in South Africa agreed. Friendships in the United States suffered more. Many friends, whom I came to know as proponents of racial justice in South Africa, and who admired my opposition to apartheid, resented my criticisms of Israel. In 2008 when the American Society of International Law awarded me honorary membership, a prominent American human rights lawyer with whom I had previously worked, Jerome Shestack, wrote a strong complaint to the society which declared that while I had been 'a courageous voice during South Africa's apartheid', my reports were those of a 'poster boy for Jihadist extremists' and disqualified me from receiving the award.

The response of the UN to my reports was mixed. UN officials in the OPT who provided me with information and agreed with my harsh criticisms of Israel appreciated the fact that I gave expression to many of their own views, which were modified or suppressed by UN bureaucrats in Geneva or New York. I maintained a good relationship with Louise Arbour, the high commissioner for human rights, whom I knew well from a meeting she had attended at Mount Grace and, later, from The Hague, where she had served as prosecutor of the International Criminal Tribunal for the Former Yugoslavia. She encouraged my clear stand on human rights and backed me when I was accused of exceeding my mandate. Less supportive were some of her staff, who did their best to sabotage my work by attempting to interfere with whom I might meet in Palestine,[117] by removing Darka Topali as my assistant before the end of my term, and by being otherwise obstructive.

Both the Human Rights Council and the Third Committee devoted more attention to Israel than to any other country. I benefited from this preoccupation and my reports were warmly acclaimed. My exchanges with the delegates of Israel and the United States in the Third Committee appealed to those who enjoyed seeing these two states confronted with evidence of human rights violations. At times these exchanges became almost theatrical and I was treated like a human rights rock star.

While I welcomed this endorsement of my work I was concerned about the absence of any coherent strategy against Israel. This was manifested by both the tone and substance of resolutions, which largely repeated previous resolutions and took little account of new human rights issues to which I had drawn attention in my reports. The stick was always employed against Israel when the carrot might have been more effective.

My experience with the senior officers of the United Nations who took the real decisions on the Israel–Palestine conflict was less happy. Dismayed by the failure of the Security Council and the secretary-general to take action to enforce the advisory opinion of the International Court of Justice on the wall, I approached Kiernan Prendergast, under-secretary-general for political affairs, who told me quite frankly that 'we do not think the ICJ opinion was a good idea'.[118] Then I learnt that the Office of the UN Legal Adviser had advised the secretary-general that he was not legally required to support the opinion as it was not a binding legal opinion and was not addressed to the UN Secretariat. I strongly disagreed with this view, believing that although the opinion was not binding on states, it bound the UN and the secretary-general.[119] Troubled, I arranged to see Lakhdar Brahimi, perhaps the most experienced and wise person in the upper echelons of the UN hierarchy, then serving as special adviser to the secretary-general. He listened carefully as I complained that UN senior officials seemed to be biased in favour of Israel. Then his face broke into a broad grin. 'Of course, you are right,' he said, 'the United States controls the United Nations and determines how Israel is to be treated. This is a given of the United Nations that one has to live with, however much we may dislike it! But don't let that discourage you from criticizing Israel.'

Another decision of the Secretariat that was of concern to me was its refusal to allow officials of the UN to engage with Hamas. In similar conflict situations, such as South Africa, it had treated parties with different ideologies equally, even if one party espoused violence. However, the UN refused to speak to Hamas and lamely followed the orders of the United States to refuse to have anything to do with it. As an unpaid independent expert I was able to ignore directions from bureaucrats in the Office of the High Commissioner for Human Rights that I should not speak to the leaders of Hamas. Protests followed when I met with Ismail Haniyeh, the leader of Hamas in Gaza in June 2006. My appeal to the UN secretary-general, Ban Ki-moon, to reverse UN policy and instead promote reconciliation between Fatah and Hamas fell on deaf ears.

Public criticism of the Security Council, the Quartet and the Secretariat in my reports was unusual, as most special rapporteurs refrained from criticism of the UN. I was scolded by the under-secretary-general for political affairs, Lynn Pascoe, who told me that as special rapporteur I was a UN insider and should keep my criticisms within the organization.[120]

I met regularly with Secretary-General Kofi Annan when I reported to the Third Committee. Although my reports were critical of both the UN and the secretary-general, he was always friendly and willing to engage in conversation about the Middle East. I was convinced that he would have liked to do more to help the Palestinians but his hands were tied by the need to work with the United States. In June 2006 I wrote to him about my concerns for the situation in the OPT in general and the economic sanctions that had been imposed on Palestine after the 2006 elections, which had resulted in a government of national unity including Hamas. I complained that while Israel was in violation of UN resolutions and had refused to comply with the advisory opinion on the wall and should be subjected to sanctions, it was the Palestinian people who had been subjected to serious economic sanctions for exercising their democratic choice. I added that the UN was losing its credibility in the OPT and that its membership of the Quartet had deprived it of the necessary impartiality to act as a broker of peace in the region. Kofi Annan replied that he shared my concerns relating to human rights and appreciated my 'frank assessment of the current situation … In your role as Special Rapporteur, you are acting as an independent expert, with a mandate to speak out on human rights issues. I fully respect your mandate. As for your concerns on the United Nations' role in the Quartet, you will appreciate that the Quartet's functions are political in nature, and have the backing of the Security Council.'[121]

My experience with Secretary-General Ban Ki-moon was less positive. In September 2007, while I was in Jerusalem, I agreed to give an interview to *Al Jazeera* (Arabic). The interview was conducted in English and later translated into Arabic. In the interview I spoke about the pro-Israel bias of the Quartet and the fact that the United States dictated policy to the Quartet and said that the UN should withdraw from it. I suggested that the secretary-general should place a distance between himself and the United States in order to remove the perception that he was acting on instructions from Washington. I cannot remember exactly what I said but I know that I chose my words carefully to avoid giving affront to the secretary-general while at the same time making it clear that I was concerned about the relationship between him and the United States. Later I received a frantic call from Darka Topali saying that the secretary-general had complained to the high commissioner about my interview and had demanded that I be dismissed from the UN. Apparently the translator had not allowed himself to be influenced by the nuances of my language and had simply translated me as having said that 'the secretary-general and his staff seem to be determined to pursue a pro-Israel line, largely because they are instructed to do so by Washington'. Louise Arbour informed the secretary-general that I could not be dismissed as I was an unpaid expert, not employed by the UN, who had been appointed by the Human Rights Council. She also cautioned that my interview had been translated and that it might not accurately reflect what I had said. Then followed an investigation into what I had exactly said and how it had been translated, from which it appeared that my speech had indeed been translated more boldly than my words permitted. I could not, however, seriously fault the translator because he had captured the essence of what I sought to convey, albeit in more discreet language.

In October 2007 I went to New York to report to the Third Committee and sought an interview with the secretary-general with the purpose of clearing the air. Despite repeated requests, he refused to see me. While in New York I had lunch with Fink Haysom, my friend and former colleague from CALS, who after serving as legal adviser to President Mandela and distinguishing himself in Iraq, Sudan and Burundi in the employment of the UN, had been appointed as director of political affairs in the office of the secretary-general. He told me that he had recently arrived late at a meeting of the inner cabinet of the secretary-general and heard my name mentioned. 'John Dugard is a friend and former colleague from South Africa,' he announced, and asked why I was being discussed. His words were met with stony silence and he realized that the discussion about me had not been favourable. Later he was given the full story. 'Don't attempt to see the secretary-general,' Fink advised. 'He is angry and will not see you under any circumstances.' I took this advice and made no further attempt to meet Ban Ki-moon. I wondered what Kofi Annan would have done in similar circumstances. I have no doubt that he would have met me. This experience ensured that, unlike other special rapporteurs, I would not be asked to serve in any capacity in the UN after my term finished.

My mandate as special rapporteur came to an end in May 2008. A suggestion that the Arab states wished to reappoint me did not materialize. This did not surprise me, as the European states had indicated that I was part of the problem and not of the solution. There were no plaudits from the Human Rights Council or the Office of the High Commissioner for Human Rights. I did, however, receive a generous letter from Ambassador Riyad Mansour of the Palestinian Permanent Observer Mission to the UN in New York, in which he stated that I had been 'an eloquent voice for the just cause of Palestine'.

Israel, the United States and many European states had hoped that they would get a less confrontational special rapporteur to succeed me. They were disappointed. My friend Richard Falk from Princeton University, with whom I had sat as commissioner on the Second Intifada in 2001, was chosen to succeed me. Soon after he had been appointed, Israel declared him to be persona non grata and prohibited him from entering Israel as special rapporteur. Subsequent special rapporteurs have also been refused permission to enter Palestine. This means that they have been compelled to write reports on the basis of visits to neighbouring states (where they have interviewed interlocutors), media reports and official publications. They have not been permitted to hear the sad stories of ordinary Palestinians and to witness the tragedy of a land under occupation and apartheid. I could not have carried out my task without this.

31

Gaza

Imprisoned by Israel and Egypt, battered by successive Israeli military assaults, reduced to poverty and homelessness by economic blockade, denied proper medical attention, deprived of safe drinking water and electricity by the occupying power, and ruled by a repressive Islamist regime, Gaza is today a land of despair. Gaza City is a city of ruins.

It was not always so. When I first visited Gaza City at the start of the Second Intifada in 2001, it was a boom town with a cosmopolitan atmosphere that accommodated the ministries of the Palestinian Authority (PA) and UN agencies. There were building sites everywhere as Palestinians who had returned home from abroad, encouraged by the euphoria of the post-Oslo period, built homes in Gaza. Gaza City was a busy Mediterranean coastal city with hotels and restaurants buzzing with visitors. There were wonderful beachfront terraces where one might gaze at the ocean and enjoy a good meal of meze and seafood. The markets were crowded and the souk sold jewellery set in the yellow gold of the Orient. The traffic was noisy and the streets busy. My most frightening experience in Gaza was not the proximity of Israeli missiles but of being driven in a special Arafat-ordained motorcade by Palestinian security officials through the crowded streets of Gaza City at high speed with the horn replacing the brake. Gaza had an air of excitement, anticipation and prosperity. It was good to visit Gaza City after the reserve of the West Bank. The countryside too was different. The fertile agricultural lands on the coastal plain were so unlike the stony, mountainous hillsides of the West Bank.

There were still Israeli settlements in Gaza, such as Netzarim. And the Israeli security presence surrounding them was intense. The IDF escorted settlers wherever and whenever they went, resulting in tremendous traffic jams, particularly at the junction of Abu Houli, which severed the main highway of Gaza, Salah al-Din Street. Moreover, the IDF took steps to sweep agricultural land and demolish houses in an ever-expanding area surrounding the settlements, ostensibly to improve their security. Sometimes houses were completely sanded over by bulldozers. We visited a house near the settlement of Netzarim which had been sanded up to the top of the first floor, with water and electricity cut off. The settlers in Gaza were a spoilt and privileged community, living in whitewashed bungalows amid spacious, well-watered gardens, protected by the IDF. It was clear that this was a financial and security burden that Israel could not carry indefinitely.

Gaza was the home of Palestinian militants. Hamas, the al-Aqsa brigade of Fatah, Islamic Jihad and the PFLP were all active there. In the early days of the Second Intifada it was the scene of many battles and skirmishes with the Israeli security forces. IDF activity came to focus heavily on Gaza, largely because northern Gaza was used for firing rockets into Israel and because of the tunnels near Rafah leading to Egypt.

In 1948 over seven hundred thousand Palestinians from towns and villages in today's Israel were forced to flee from Israeli forces and seek refuge in the West Bank and Gaza. Consequently every city in Palestine has refugee camps and refugees. Over the years the refugee population has grown as new generations of refugees have been added to the original number. In Gaza their presence is keenly felt, as 1.3 million of the population of 1.8 million are refugees. In a territory only forty-one kilometres long and not more than twelve kilometres wide, there are eight refugee camps, of which the largest are Jabalia, Khan Yunis, Rafah and Beach camp. Gaza is home to the headquarters of the UN Relief and Works Agency for Palestine Refugees in the Near East, better known as UNRWA, which runs schools and clinics, provides food rations for the needy, builds homes for refugees, and generally seeks to protect and assist them. In effect, UNRWA was a government in competition with the PA. When I was special rapporteur, the commissioner-general, Peter Hansen, was more popular than Arafat because UNRWA delivered services rather than merely promising them.

Most refugees believed that one day they would return to the village or town in Israel from which their parents or grandparents had fled in 1948. They naively believed that their villages were still there, that their homes were still intact, that the keys their family had kept would open the doors of their homes to their old way of life. They refused to believe that their homes had been levelled and transformed into Israeli suburbs, shopping malls or parking lots. Initially I refused to accept that children still identified with their family homes in Israel. I mentioned this to a senior UNRWA staff member, himself a Palestinian, while we were visiting a refugee camp. His response was to summon a group of young children below the age of ten playing nearby. One by one he asked them where they came from and one by one they spoke about some town or village in today's Israel. I then turned to him and asked where he came from. He too identified a village in Israel as his home. 'But,' I asked, 'you are an educated man, you have travelled, you understand the situation, I am sure you do not expect to return to your home?' He smiled sadly and said, 'Intellectually I know it is impossible, but emotionally I still believe it. I want to return home.'

In August 2005 Israel withdrew its settlements from Gaza. This was the end of the colonization of Gaza but not of its occupation. Gaza remained an occupied territory over which Israel maintained effective control – the accepted international law test for occupation[122] – by means of control of its landspace, airspace and seaspace. Israel controlled the borders of Gaza and carried out frequent military incursions into the territory to assert its authority. Similarly, Israel asserted its control of the skies above Gaza and the seas off its coast by means of its airforce and navy.

Israel had practised apartheid in Gaza before 2005. The departure of settlers did not change this. The Jewish racial group continued to systematically oppress the Palestinian people of Gaza by committing inhuman acts. The character of these acts changed from systematic violations of human rights by a physically present IDF to military assaults by air, sea and mortar fire from land. The institutionalized regime of systematic oppression took the form of threatened and irregularly executed military assaults and a severe blockade of the territory.

Initially there was joy and euphoria that the settlers had left and Gaza would be free from colonization and apartheid. The Quartet's special envoy, James Wolfensohn, previously head of the World Bank, set out to make life better for the people of Gaza by securing a commitment from Israel that it would allow travel to the West Bank, by raising funds to assist Palestinians to farm the properties vacated by the settlers, and by arranging for the export of Palestinian produce to Israel. At the time I visited, prolific greenhouses previously owned by settlers were now being used by Palestinian farmers to produce flowers and vegetables. They were enthusiastic about the future. It was a time of hope.

It soon became clear that this euphoria was misplaced. Israel reneged on its promise to allow travel to the West Bank, thereby isolating Palestinians in Gaza from their fellow citizens in the West Bank. The export of produce was severely restricted, which meant that greenhouse agricultural produce perished. The import of goods was also restricted. We visited a furniture factory in Gaza City which made furniture for an Israeli buyer who supplied the factory with materials. The import of these materials was prohibited, and the factory was unable to meet its commitments. The Israeli buyer was now suing the factory for failure to deliver on its contract. In this way the co-operation between Israel and Gaza envisaged by James Wolfensohn was brought to an end.

To make matters worse, Israel military incursions became a regular occurrence, with the sonic booms of the Israeli airforce serving as a perpetual reminder of the occupation. The situation was well summed up by *Haaretz* columnist Gideon Levy: 'The IDF departure from Gaza ... did almost nothing to change the living conditions for the residents of the Strip. Gaza is still a prison and its inhabitants are doomed to live in poverty and oppression ... Israel has left the cage, thrown away the keys and left the residents to their bitter fate.'[123]

In January 2006 elections were held in Palestine, which independent observers hailed as free and fair. But Hamas won and this was not what Israel and the West wanted. It soon became clear that the government under Ismail Haniyeh of Hamas could not survive, as Israel, the United States, the EU and Canada withdrew all funding and labelled Hamas a terrorist organization. A government of national unity comprising Hamas, Fatah and independents was established. But it was short-lived. Israel, the United States and the EU made sure that it would not work.

In June 2006 a group of Palestinian militants captured a corporal in the IDF, Gilad Shalit, and demanded that Palestinian women and children in Israeli jails be released in return for his handover. Israel's response to this, and to the continued firing of Qassam rockets from Gaza into Israel, was immediate and savage. The IDF launched two military campaigns, Operation Summer Rains in June 2006, followed by Operation Autumn Clouds in November 2006. Aerial bombing was accompanied by low-flying F16s breaking the sound barrier and causing frightening sonic booms; heavy bombing destroyed Gaza's power plant, leaving half the population with no electricity; water pipelines and sewerage networks were damaged; hundreds of civilians were killed and wounded; homes, schools, hospitals and mosques were destroyed; and agricultural lands were bulldozed.

I visited Gaza regularly from 2001 to 2007. I saw the transformation of Gaza from a bustling, hopeful territory to a besieged land, whose people lived in perpetual fear. I witnessed the devastation caused to the infrastructure of Gaza by Operation Summer Rains and Operation Autumn Clouds. I spoke to bereaved families, saw homes that had been destroyed, visited hospitals where the wounded lay dying, talked to teachers whose schools had been fired on, and spoke to factory owners whose factories had been closed. We visited an UNRWA girls' school shortly after Operation Summer Rains and listened to young girls as they spoke at a counselling session. We heard them speak of their fears and hopes. They spoke of neighbours being killed by IDF soldiers and savaged by sniffer dogs, of homes being destroyed, and of the powerlessness of their parents to help. They repeatedly expressed the wish to live the kind of lives that children led in other parts of the world. But it was not to be. The occupation ensured that children grew up in fear. As they grew older, they would learn to hate those who had stolen their childhood.

Gaza had never been safe. But now it was even less safe. On my last day in Gaza as special rapporteur, in September 2007, Ietje and I were suddenly rerouted by our security officer on our way from Gaza City to the Erez crossing to Israel to avoid an IDF missile attack. Later we learnt that twelve people had been killed on the road we were scheduled to have taken.

In June 2007 the situation worsened when Hamas seized power over Gaza, and Fatah, operating as the Palestinian Authority, became the government of the West Bank. Gaza was designated an 'enemy entity' or 'hostile territory' by Israel and placed under a severe economic blockade. This has resulted in Israel prohibiting the import of basic foodstuffs, fuel, medical supplies, pharmaceutical goods, office equipment and building materials. Poverty followed for 80 per cent of the population. The imprisonment of Gaza was now complete. The joy of living in Gaza was replaced with despair as the people of Gaza resigned themselves to a future without hope. But worse was to come.

Operation Cast Lead 2008–9: First Report

Operation Cast Lead began on 27 December 2008 when Israel launched an aerial, naval and ground bombardment of Gaza from outside the territory, allegedly in response to Palestinian rocket and mortar attacks on southern Israel. The period before that attack had been relatively peaceful as a result of a ceasefire between Hamas and Israel brokered by Egypt in June 2008, which was only broken in November when Israel carried out a military incursion into Gaza. There were, however, suggestions that Israel had been planning the assault ever since Hamas took over control of Gaza in June 2007 and that the purpose of the assault was to effect a regime change. On 3 January Israel expanded the operation to include a ground offensive. Operation Cast Lead ended on 18 January 2009.

Ietje and I heard about Israel's assault on Gaza while we were on holiday in San Francisco in December 2008. We followed this brutal invasion on television and saw images of the Gaza we knew in flames. We listened to radio reports, including from evangelical Christian radio stations that clearly took delight in the bombing of Gaza and the killing of Palestinians. In February I received a call from the League of Arab States asking me to chair a fact-finding committee into Operation Cast Lead.

Although the Arab League had a long history of involvement in the Israel–Palestine conflict, this was the first occasion on which it took the step of establishing a fact-finding committee to examine violations of international humanitarian law and human rights law in the conflict. Indeed, this was the first occasion on which the League had ever established such a committee. In large measure this step was taken on the initiative of the secretary-general of the League, Amr Moussa, and Nabil Elaraby, a friend and former judge on the International Court of Justice. (Later, Nabil himself became secretary-general of the Arab League.)

The committee appointed by the League consisted of me as chair, Paul de Waart (a retired Dutch professor of international law), Fynn Lynghjem (a Norwegian judge, who had worked in Bosnia and Herzegovina and Cambodia), Gonzalo Boye (a national of Chile and Germany practising as an advocate in Spain) and Francisco Côrte-Real (a Portuguese professor of forensic science). On my insistence Raelene Sharp, an Australian lawyer who had been my research assistant at Leiden and who had been part of the investigations into the Hariri killing in Lebanon, was added as rapporteur. The committee was mandated to investigate violations of international humanitarian law and human rights law committed in Operation Cast Lead and to report on responsibility for such violations.

On 22 February we travelled to Gaza via the Rafah border crossing, accompanied by three members of the Arab League and a member of the Egyptian Foreign Ministry, whose task it was, or so we believed, to report to the Egyptian government on our activities.

The committee spent six intense days in Gaza during which time it visited homes, hospitals, schools, mosques, farms, businesses and public buildings that had been attacked, and interviewed victims, refugees, doctors, teachers, journalists, lawyers, university professors and ballistic experts. It also met with members of the Hamas government, the various political factions, civil society, diplomats from foreign governments, the Red Cross and UN agencies, notably UNRWA. Logistical support was provided by the Palestinian Centre for Human Rights under Raji Sourani. The committee made several attempts to secure the co-operation of the Israeli government, but all these approaches were ignored. As a consequence the committee was obliged to rely on Israeli government statements, the Ministry of Foreign Affairs website, NGO reports and the media for information about the conflict from the Israeli perspective. On the basis of this evidence, and reports from NGOs, governments and the media, the committee compiled a report that was submitted to the Arab League on 30 April 2009.[124]

Over 1,400 Palestinians were killed in Operation Cast Lead, including at least 850 civilians (of which 300 were children and 110 women).[125] Over five thousand Palestinians were wounded. Four Israeli civilians were killed by Palestinian rockets; and ten Israeli soldiers were killed (four in friendly fire) and 148 wounded. There was substantial destruction of property in Gaza. Some three thousand homes were destroyed and 11,000 damaged; fifteen hospitals and forty-three primary health-care centres were seriously damaged; thirty mosques and ten schools were destroyed; 80 per cent of the agricultural land and crops were bulldozed; and 215 factories and 700 private businesses were seriously damaged or destroyed. Whereas Palestinian fighters had unsophisticated weapons – Qassam rockets, rocket-propelled grenades (RPGs) and homemade mortars – Israel used the most sophisticated modern weapons to bombard the population of Gaza from air, land and sea. Laser-guided bombs were dropped from F16 warplanes, Hellfire missiles were fired from Apache helicopters, Cobra helicopter gunships and drones, and heavy mortar shells, fleshettes and high explosives were fired by tanks and artillery. In addition, Israel used white phosphorus as an incendiary weapon in densely populated areas. The twenty-two-day offensive with bombing and shelling from the air, land and sea traumatized and terrorized the population, resulting in over two hundred thousand leaving their homes to search for safety. The IDF, which prided itself on being the most moral army in the world,[126] had gone berserk.

The fact-finding committee heard evidence of these events from victims and witnesses. More important, it saw the destruction itself, for our visit occurred so soon after Operation Cast Lead that no attempt had been made to repair the damage. It was all there for us to see and to photograph. I had seen films of World War II and the effects of bombing on London and Berlin. In Gaza 2009 I relived these memories.

Even more distressing than the sight of the destruction caused by Operation Cast Lead were the stories of survivors whose families and friends had been killed by the IDF in their presence. The committee interviewed a number of persons who had seen members of their family killed by the IDF, who had tried to save wounded members, and who had been prevented from using ambulances to evacuate them. Most of these interviews took place *in situ* so the committee was able to fully picture the events that were described.

For me the most painful story was that of Khaled Abed Rabo of East Jabalia, whose three daughters and mother were shot by the IDF.[127] He told the committee:

> On 7 January 2009 I was at home with my wife, mother and three daughters, Souad aged seven, Samar aged four, and Amal aged two. The residents were told to leave the house by an IDF soldier by megaphone. We left the house carrying white flags and saw an Israeli tank 7–10 metres away. There were two IDF soldiers on the tank, we could see them. One was eating chips [crisps], the other was eating chocolate. We were waiting for orders from the soldiers. A third IDF soldier got out of their tank and opened fire at the children. I carried Amal. Her intestines were hanging out of her stomach. I went to carry Samar, she was also shot. I hurried into the house, my wife was crying, and the IDF shot Souad with more than ten bullets. My mother, who is 60 years old, was hit by two bullets and she was also bleeding. We went back to the house and tried to call an ambulance, but nobody came. After a time we decided to leave in small groups. As we left there was firing over our heads and at our feet. I was carrying my dead children and the IDF soldiers came out of their tanks and were laughing at us.

Amal and Souad died from their wounds. Souad suffered a spinal injury and will remain a paraplegic for the rest of her life.

Worse, in terms of the number of persons killed, was the massacre of the extended al-Samouni family of Zaytoun, a rural neighbourhood south of Gaza City.[128] On 4 and 5 January the IDF attacked several of the al-Samouni homes. After tanks and bulldozers had flattened the surrounding agricultural land, houses were shelled from Apache helicopters and grenades tossed into houses sheltering members of the al-Samouni family, comprising mainly women and children. There were no combatants in the houses. Soldiers then entered the homes, deliberately firing at and killing several members of the family. All in all, some twenty-nine persons were killed. Soldiers abused the family, calling them bastards and terrorists and scrawling graffiti on the walls threatening death to all Arabs. Ambulances that attempted to evacuate the wounded were prevented from doing so for several days.

In front of the rubble of the al-Samouni homes, with the bulldozed fields behind us, we heard chilling testimony from family members. Salah al-Samouni testified:

> two shells landed on the house. I thought I was going to die. I went to check on my family. I found my mother, part of her face was gone, my father and my uncle were dead. My daughter was disembowelled. Twenty-two persons were killed by the shells. We told the soldiers we

> were civilians, farmers, telling them they had made a mistake. They said 'go back to death' in classical Arabic.

There were a number of common features of the killings of which we heard evidence. None of the attacks that gave rise to the killings served any military advantage; there were no military targets in the area. None of those killed or wounded were militants and there was no evidence of militant activity in the area. All of those killed were civilians, many were women and children. Many of the killings were callous and committed in cold blood. In most cases the killings were intentional within the meaning of the law: they were acts of murder. Archbishop Desmond Tutu's assessment was accurate:

> Every so often, the world witnesses events of such naked brutality that concerned observers must recoil in outrage and demand an end to the madness. We saw this in my own country after the Sharpeville Massacre, a bloodletting that finally awakened the world to the evils of apartheid … In the waning days of 2008, we saw it once again in the Middle East. Israel had launched a bloody assault on the Gaza Strip … and for three weeks one of the world's most sophisticated armies pummeled a captive Palestinian population … the Gaza conflict exceeded our worst expectations. And offended our deepest understanding of right and wrong.[129]

Our mandate was to report on violations of international humanitarian law, including crimes against humanity and war crimes. Genocide was not mentioned. Yet when I opened discussions about our conclusions at the Al Deira Hotel in Gaza City on the final day of our visit, most members of the fact-finding mission argued in favour of this, the ultimate crime. Emotionally I agreed, but legally I did not. The Genocide Convention of 1948 and a decision of the International Court of Justice made it clear that it was not enough to establish that deliberate unlawful killings of members of one national, ethnic, racial or religious group by another group had occurred. In addition, it was necessary to prove that this had been done with intent to destroy the group in whole or in part.[130] Although Israel's siege and bombardment of Gaza, its brutal and arbitrary killing and wounding of civilians, its wanton destruction of both private and public property, its terrorization of the people of Gaza, and its bombing of hospitals and ambulances pointed in the direction of an intent to destroy the Palestinian people of Gaza in whole or in part, this was not the only inference to be drawn from the facts. I suggested that Israel's intent might rather have been to punish the people of Gaza for having allowed Hamas to seize control of Gaza in 2007, and that we should rather categorize Israel's intent as one of collective punishment. After a long discussion my view prevailed.

So it was that we focused our attention on whether Israel had committed war crimes and crimes against humanity in Operation Cast Lead when we met in Amsterdam to finalize our report at the beginning of April. Applying the principles of customary international law on which there was general consensus among states, we found that Israel had committed war crimes by its indiscriminate and disproportionate attack on civilians, the killing, wounding and terrorization of civilians, the wanton destruction of property not justified by military necessity, and its attack on hospitals and ambulances. We found that in most instances those responsible for such acts had dropped their bombs or fired on civilian objects in densely populated areas where they must have foreseen the consequences of their actions. In many cases there was evidence that they had done so deliberately, but even where this was not the case, they must have foreseen the consequences of their actions and they had acted recklessly. This meant that they had the necessary intent for the commission of war crimes. We also found that Israel had committed crimes against humanity.

Palestinian militants were likewise condemned. We found that they had committed war crimes by firing rockets indiscriminately from Gaza into southern Israel, killing four civilians and wounding 148.

We recommended that our findings be referred to the International Criminal Court (ICC) for the purpose of prosecution. In January 2009 the Palestinian government had recognized the competence of the ICC to prosecute crimes committed in the course of Operation Cast Lead, despite the fact that Palestine was not a signatory to the Rome Statute and its statehood was still uncertain.

The Arab League published our report under the title of *No Safe Place: Report of the Independent Fact Finding Committee on Gaza* with a sad picture of a young girl surrounded by devastation on the cover. The report was placed on the website of the Arab League and it seems that the hard copy was sent to some foreign embassies. Probably it was sent to some international organizations as well. However, the Arab League made little effort to circulate it widely or give it proper coverage. There were no strong statements from the League or any Arab leader calling for justice on the basis of our report. The Israeli government, sensing that the Arab League did not intend to make a big issue out of the report, wisely kept silent. There was no response to the report; no hate mail of the kind I regularly received in response to my reports as special rapporteur. The media in the West failed to give the report attention, treating it as an Arab report and therefore by definition biased – despite the fact that all members of the committee were non-Arabs.

The secretariat of the Arab League, determined to give effect to our report although the League itself was little concerned, arranged a meeting with the prosecutor of the ICC in May 2009 to discuss the recommendation in our report that crimes arising out of Operation Cast Lead be referred to the court. At this meeting, the prosecutor, Luis Moreno Ocampo, indicated an interest in pursuing the matter but made it clear that the main obstacle in the way of prosecution was the question of Palestinian statehood.[131]

Operation Cast Lead: Second Report ('Goldstone Report')

On 3 April 2009 the Human Rights Council established the United Nations Fact-Finding Mission on the Gaza Conflict 'to investigate all violations of international human rights law and international humanitarian law' that had been committed in the course of Operation Cast Lead. The mission comprised Richard Goldstone, Christine Chinkin (professor of international law at the London School of Economics), Hina Jilani (a Pakistani human rights lawyer) and Desmond Travers (a former colonel in Ireland's Defence Forces).

Richard Goldstone was an excellent choice as chair of the mission. As a judge in South Africa, he had succeeded in remaining untainted by the apartheid regime and had been appointed, with the support of both Mandela and De Klerk, to investigate acts of political violence by the mysterious Third Force during South Africa's transition to democracy. Later he became a judge of the Constitutional Court before being appointed as prosecutor of the International Criminal Tribunals for the Former Yugoslavia and Rwanda. A self-identified Zionist, he had close ties with Israel. I had known Richard for over forty years. We had worked together in South Africa and were close friends. This friendship was cemented when he and his wife Noleen introduced me to Ietje.

While I was in Geneva at the International Law Commission in May 2009, I met with all members of the mission to discuss their task informally and to tell them about our experiences in Gaza. I warned Richard that he must expect to be vilified by Israel and the United States. At this time he believed that he, as a Zionist Jew with a record of even-handedness, would be able to persuade the Israeli government to co-operate. I warned him that this was highly unlikely.

As predicted, the Israeli government refused to co-operate with the mission, which, like the Arab League fact-finding committee, was obliged to enter Gaza through Egypt. The mission duly visited Gaza and collected evidence in much the same way that the Arab League committee had done, interviewing many of the same victims and interlocutors. Backed by the Office of the High Commissioner for Human Rights, it made a more thorough investigation than we had been able to do. In September 2009 it presented its report to the Human Rights Council.[132]

The Goldstone Report (as it came to be known) made findings very similar to those of the Arab League committee. It found that Israel had committed war crimes by its indiscriminate attacks on civilians, wanton destruction of property, and attacks on hospitals and ambulances. Furthermore, it emphasized that the IDF had acted deliberately. Its comments on the attacks on civilians were particularly harsh. They were not the result of occasional lapses, said the mission, but 'the result of deliberate guidance issued to soldiers'.[133] The mission found that Israel had intended to punish, humiliate, dehumanize and terrorize the population.[134] It concluded that 'the systematic and deliberate nature of the activities described in this report leave the Mission in no doubt that responsibility lies in the first place with those who designed, planned, ordered and oversaw the operations'.[135] The Goldstone Report also found that Palestinians had committed war crimes by firing rockets indiscriminately into southern Israel.

The recommendations of the Goldstone Report were very similar to those of the Arab League committee, with prosecution before the International Criminal Court a central recommendation.

Unlike that of the Arab League, the Goldstone Report could not be brushed aside. It was immediately seized upon as a credible and authoritative legal assessment of Israel's crimes. There is no doubt that Goldstone's reputation as a lawyer and his credentials as a Jew were largely responsible for this.

The Goldstone Report was warmly received except in Israel and the United States. Some states saw in it a vindication of their views on Israel's occupation of the OPT. Others, particularly European states, found it disturbing and insisted that Israel institute an independent investigation into the conduct of the IDF. The UN General Assembly endorsed the report and called on both Israel and Hamas to carry out investigations into the findings of the Goldstone mission. The opposition of the United States to the report made it clear that no endorsement could be expected from the Security Council.

The response of Israel and the United States was vicious. Israel attacked the impartiality of the mission and accused it of being biased and inaccurate. Prime Minister Netanyahu said that there were three threats facing Israel – the nuclear threat, the missile threat and the Goldstone threat. The US House of Representatives passed a resolution condemning the Goldstone Report by a vote of 344 to 36, describing it as 'irredeemably biased and unworthy of further consideration or legitimacy'. The Obama administration condemned the report as 'unbalanced, one-sided and basically unacceptable'.

Much of the criticism of the report was directed very personally at the chief messenger, Richard Goldstone. He was vilified as a self-hating Jew and the perpetrator of a blood libel. President Shimon Peres called him 'a small man, devoid of any sense of justice'. Harvard law professor Alan Dershowitz said that Goldstone was 'an evil man, a despicable human being and a traitor to the Jewish people'. The Israeli media condemned him as an apartheid judge who had 'sentenced dozens of blacks mercilessly to their death'.[136]

In South Africa, too, Goldstone was harshly condemned by sections of the Jewish community. South Africa's chief rabbi, Warren Goldstein, accused him of 'delegitimizing Israel' and prohibited him from attending his grandson's bar mitzvah in Johannesburg, a decision that was applauded by the South African Zionist Federation. (This decision was later revoked.) Friends and former colleagues rallied to support Goldstone. Archbishop Desmond Tutu said he greatly admired Richard's integrity and courage.[137] Two Jewish Constitutional Court judges, Arthur Chaskalson and Albie Sachs, came to his defence.[138] I too defended him and declared that it should be a matter of pride to Jews that a Jewish lawyer was prepared to conduct an inquiry into Operation Cast Lead.[139]

Later, the Human Rights Council appointed a follow-up committee to investigate whether credible investigations into the crimes alleged in the Goldstone Report had been carried out. This committee, chaired by Mary McGowan Davis, a former New York federal judge, reported in March 2011[140] that Israel had not conducted a credible, transparent or impartial investigation or any serious prosecutions.[141] It found no decision had been taken as to whether to prosecute anyone for the killing of the al-Samouni family.[142] Israel was unwilling to investigate the policies and decisions of the military and there was no indication that it had opened investigations into the actions of those who had planned, ordered and overseen Operation Cast Lead.[143]

On Friday, 1 April 2011, an op-ed piece appeared in the *Washington Post* by Richard Goldstone titled 'Reconsidering the Goldstone Report on Israel and War Crimes', which in effect killed the report.[144] The article makes strange reading. Richard stated that the Goldstone Report would have been a different document 'had I known then what I know now'. To support his change of heart, he invoked the McGowan Davis report, which he claimed showed that Israel had conducted proper investigations into allegations of operational misconduct 'to a significant degree'. This, despite the fact that the McGowan Davis report was critical of Israel's investigations and found that they were lacking in transparency, credibility and impartiality, and had not resulted in any meaningful prosecutions. Goldstone declared that Israel was investigating the al-Samouni killings and that he was confident that this investigation would be properly handled, despite the McGowan Davis committee's critical assessment of this investigation. He invoked the McGowan Davis report to show that civilians in Gaza were 'not intentionally targeted as a matter of policy' although this report had found that Israel was unwilling to investigate the actions of those who had planned, ordered or overseen Operation Cast Lead. In short, there were no facts in the McGowan Davis report that could have changed Goldstone's mind.

The article did not claim to repudiate the Goldstone Report in full. Although it failed to indicate precisely the findings in respect of which Goldstone had changed his mind, it seems that it was the findings of the intentionality of the killings of civilians that troubled him. It is true that the Goldstone mission had been severe in its finding that Israel's actions had been deliberate and systematic. But even if Israel had not 'intentionally targeted civilians as a matter of policy' (in the words of the op-ed), in law the IDF had the necessary intention to commit war crimes. This is because the intention required for the commission of war crimes is not deliberate or premeditated intention but whether the person engaging in the action in question foresaw the consequences of his action and was reckless as to whether they would occur. Israel's indiscriminate and disproportionate attacks on civilians were carried out with full knowledge that the consequence of the actions would be the killing and wounding of civilians.

Much of the article was devoted to a castigation of Hamas – for purposely attacking civilian targets and for failing to investigate the crimes attributed to it by the Goldstone Report. Goldstone reminded readers that 'his' report was the first to have investigated the 'illegal acts of terrorism' committed by Hamas. In addition, he accused the Human Rights Council of bias against Israel.

I read and reread Richard's op-ed, trying to make sense of it. I recognized none of the clarity and certainty in it that had characterized Richard's judicial decisions or his writings. To aggravate matters, it was a retraction in part – if not in full – of a report written by four commissioners. And the other three commissioners soon made it clear that they had not been consulted on the op-ed. The first they knew of it was after it had been published.

I wrote an article on Richard's op-ed piece on the *New Statesman* blog on 6 April.[145] In it I pointed out that the McGowan Davis report did not provide support for Richard's change of mind and stressed that the op-ed was not a retraction of the report, as this could only be done with the consent of the three other commissioners and the approval of the Human Rights Council. However, I acknowledged that the piece had undermined the effect of the report.[146]

Why Richard wrote the op-ed remains a mystery. We can only speculate as to what caused him to take such an unprecedented step. However, as one who himself was subjected to vilification from the pro-Israeli lobby, I suspect that intense pressure was brought on him to recant.

Both Israel and the United States were delighted with Richard's op-ed, which, as was to be expected, was interpreted as a total retraction of the report. Prime Minister Netanyahu declared that it showed that 'everything we said proved to be true'.

Richard's fellow commissioners publicly declared that they stood by the report and that there was no need to reconsider it. The Human Rights Council stated that it would not revoke the report on the basis of a newspaper article by one of the members of the mission which was unsupported by the other members. The Goldstone Report therefore remained valid.

But, in effect, the Goldstone Report was dead and, with it, all other reports on Operation Cast Lead, including that of the Arab League committee. Neither Israel nor Hamas made any serious attempt to investigate the crimes identified in the reports. In 2012 Israel announced that there would be no prosecution arising from the killing of the al-Samouni family on the ground that their killing was not done knowingly or negligently 'in a manner that would indicate criminal responsibility'.[147]

The final nail in the coffin of the reports on Operation Cast Lead was hammered in by the International Criminal Court. On 3 April 2012, Prosecutor Luis Moreno Ocampo ruled, after three years of consideration, that Palestine did not qualify as a state, as required by the ICC Statute; and consequently the court could not consider Palestine's request that the court investigate international crimes committed in Operation Cast Lead.[148] Palestine's statehood was later confirmed by the UN General Assembly on 29 November 2012,[149] but the new prosecutor, Fatou Bensouda, insisted that this was still insufficient for the ICC to exercise jurisdiction over the crimes committed in Operation Cast Lead. Clearly, the ICC was determined not to offend two states that were not even parties to the Rome Statute – the United States and Israel.

I still have images of the destruction caused by Operation Cast Lead.

I see flattened, broken buildings and bulldozed farms. I hear the stories of Israel's assault and I see fear in the eyes of children and grown men and women as they recount the brutal events of that time. No one has been held accountable.

Operation Protective Edge

Conflict has continued to plague Gaza. In 2009, in the wake of Operation Cast Lead, Israel imposed a naval blockade off the coast of Gaza. In May 2010 a flotilla of eight vessels set sail for Gaza with humanitarian aid and construction materials in an attempt to break the blockade. The largest vessel was the *Mavi Marmara*, a ship owned by a Turkish NGO,[150] but registered in the Comoros Islands, with 590 passengers on board. The flotilla was intercepted by the IDF on the high seas and the *Mavi Marmara* was boarded by IDF commandos. In the melee that ensued, nine passengers, eight Turkish nationals and one American national, were killed and fifty-five wounded. Nine IDF soldiers were wounded. UN commissions of inquiry predictably failed to achieve accountability, but Comoros Islands, a state party to the Rome Statute of the ICC, initiated a prosecution against the Israeli commandos responsible for killing passengers on board the *Mavi Marmara*. In what has been interpreted as deference to the will of the United States and Israel, neither of which is a party to the Rome Statute, the prosecutor has refused to pursue a prosecution.

In November 2012 Israel assassinated a prominent Hamas militant, Ahmed al-Jabari, which resulted in rocket fire from Gaza into southern Israel. Israel retaliated by launching Operation Pillar of Defence. This attack on Gaza lasted for eight days, during which 174 Palestinians were killed, of which 107 were civilians, and 840 Palestinians were wounded. Four Israeli soldiers and two civilians were killed by Palestinian rocket fire.

Operation Pillar of Defence was followed by Operation Protective Edge, to date the most extensive and severe attack on Gaza. This operation was carried out from 8 July to 26 August 2014 in response to rocket fire from Gaza and the kidnapping and killing of three Israeli teenagers by supporters of Hamas in the West Bank.[151] The assault, vividly portrayed on Al Jazeera, CNN and BBC World screens, brought back memories of the brutality, callousness and indifference of Operation Cast Lead. Once again, there were claims that the IDF was the most moral army in the world, which was impossible to reconcile with the pictures of schools and hospitals being bombed and of civilians being targeted. There were images of whole neighbourhoods transformed into wastelands, of women and children desperately seeking shelter in destroyed structures that could no longer be described as buildings, of the bloody wounded being carried to safety, and of the dead in the streets and rubble that once was Gaza City. Statistics confirmed that this was a more devastating operation than those that had preceded it. Some 2,200 Palestinians were killed and over ten thousand wounded in the aerial strikes and ground offensive. Of those killed, 1,492 were civilians, of whom over five hundred were children and three hundred women. Some seven thousand homes were razed to the ground and eighty-nine thousand were seriously damaged. Almost a third of the population of Gaza was displaced. Throughout the offensive, Palestinians continued to fire rockets from Gaza and to tunnel into Israel itself. During the conflict sixty-six Israeli soldiers were killed and six civilians were killed in Israel from rocket and mortar fire from Gaza. As in previous attacks on Gaza, the world watched spellbound and did nothing.

As before, the UN Human Rights Council established a commission of inquiry to examine and report on the operation. The commission was not, however, able to enter Gaza to carry out its mission, as both Israel and Egypt denied it access. Not surprisingly, the commission found that both Israel and Palestinian factions had committed acts constituting war crimes. The report[152] lacked the forcefulness of the Goldstone Report on Operation Cast Lead and failed to receive the same degree of attention. No doubt another reason for this failure was that the credibility of UN fact-finding missions had been seriously undermined by Richard Goldstone's retraction of the Operation Cast Lead report. This retraction conveyed the message that reports of such missions, unlike judicial decisions, were not final statements on the facts and the law, and might be freely amended or withdrawn at the whim of the fact-finders. As such, they were not to be taken seriously.

Operation Protective Edge was an obvious matter for the International Criminal Court (ICC). Its statehood having been confirmed by the General Assembly in November 2012, the government of Palestine acceded to the Statute of the ICC on 31 December 2014. On 1 April 2015 Palestine became the 123rd member of the ICC. At the request of Palestine, the prosecutor has embarked on a preliminary examination into the situation with a view to deciding whether to investigate and prosecute the commission of war crimes and crimes against humanity arising out of the Gaza conflict and the construction of settlements in the West Bank and East Jerusalem. Both the Palestinian Authority and NGOs have made comprehensive submissions to the prosecutor. The Palestine–Israel conflict has now moved to the ICC. Will it take steps to ensure that international humanitarian law is at last enforced in the conflict? Or will the prosecutor defer to political pressure from Israel, the United States and some European states to refrain from prosecuting Israeli military and political leaders?

The failure of international institutions to secure accountability on the part of Israel led civil society to establish a 'people's tribunal' to investigate Israel's crimes. Modelled on the Russell Tribunal established by Bertrand Russell and Jean-Paul Sartre to examine war crimes committed by the United States in Vietnam, the Russell Tribunal on Palestine was established after Operation Cast Lead with the goal of drawing attention to the failure of states, corporations and international organizations to confront Israel on its violations of international law. The tribunal held six sessions between 2010 and 2014, culminating in the session on Operation Protective Edge in 2014.

Although it was not a court of law, the Russell Tribunal broadly followed legal procedures. Evidence was presented to the jury by witnesses comprising scholars, lawyers, journalists, members of civil society and victims. Assisted by legal experts, the jury then delivered a verdict which was widely disseminated in the media.

The Russell Tribunal's jury was a 'people's jury' composed of a mix of persons from many different countries who had distinguished themselves in politics, music, literature, scholarship, films, TV, human rights activism and the law. The driving force behind the Russell Tribunal was Pierre Galand, a former Belgian senator with a long history of involvement in the promotion of human rights through civil society. Jurors in its six sessions included Stéphane Hessel, member of the French Resistance deported to Buchenwald, who later assisted in the drafting of the Universal Declaration of Human Rights; Alice Walker, author of the Pulitzer-Prize winning novel *The Color Purple*; Mairead Corrigan Maguire, Nobel Peace Laureate from Northern Ireland; Michael Mansfield QC, English barrister and president of the Haldane Society of socialist lawyers; Miguel Ángel Estrella, Argentine pianist; Angela Davis, American professor and political activist; Ronnie Kasrils, anti-apartheid veteran and former South African cabinet minister; Cynthia McKinney, former US congresswoman; Roger Waters, founding member of the band Pink Floyd; Richard Falk, Princeton professor and former special rapporteur on human rights in Palestine; and Ken Loach, English film and TV director. I was a member of this jury in four sessions, including its final session on Operation Protective Edge.

The final session of the Russell Tribunal, which considered Operation Protective Edge, heard evidence from journalists and doctors who had been present in Gaza at the time, military experts and members of civil society. They testified about the onslaught and about the hate speech directed at Palestinians by public figures in Israel. The tribunal had no difficulty in finding that this testimony and the public record provided evidence that war crimes and crimes against humanity had been committed by Israel. The jury stopped short of finding that the evidence supported a charge of genocide but it expressed concern about statements that could be construed as incitement to genocide. In the light of Israel's actions and its failure to prevent or punish statements of this kind, the tribunal declared that it was 'compelled to place the international community on notice as to the risk of the crime of genocide being perpetrated'.

The Great Return March

Conditions in Gaza have engendered a mood of despair among its population. Imprisoned in an overpopulated enclave with an infrastructure destroyed by Israel's blockade, repeated Israeli invasions, high unemployment, limited electricity, uncontrolled sewerage, inadequate health care and pervasive sanctions, the people have been reduced to hopelessness. To vent their frustrations, on 30 March 2018, Gazans embarked on a protest over several weeks to commemorate the 70th anniversary of the Nakba, demand the right of return to their ancestral homes in Israel, and condemn the move of the US embassy to Jerusalem. In what became known as the Great Return March, thousands of protesters assembled on Gaza's border with Israel.

While most protesters remained far from the border, the more daring approached the fence, burning tyres and attempting to break through. Protesters were mainly unarmed; few used slingshots or threw Molotov cocktails. They posed no threat to the soldiers of the IDF some one hundred metres away. Predictably no IDF soldiers were killed or wounded in this confrontation. Over several weeks 120 Palestinians were killed by live fire or tear gas and thirteen thousand seriously wounded, mainly by gunshots in the legs. On 14 May, the last day of the protest, sixty-one were killed and 2,700 wounded.

Israel's use of excessive force was widely condemned, and South Africa recalled its ambassador from Israel in protest. As expected, the United States vetoed a resolution condemning Israel in the Security Council. The Human Rights Council resolved to establish a fact-finding mission but it is unlikely, in the light of the history of the Goldstone mission, that it will have any real effect. More significantly, the government of Palestine responded by referring accusations of international criminal conduct on the part of Israel to the International Criminal Court in The Hague.

32

Is there hope?

It was a strange quirk of fate that led me to devote most of my adult life to living with and confronting apartheid. South Africa, the land of my birth, was understandable. So perhaps was its neighbour, Namibia. But I had no connection with Israel or Palestine until the chance withdrawal of speakers from a conference determined that I should become a participant in the life and politics of that region. I have no regrets. Denis Kuny, friend and human rights lawyer from Johannesburg, once said that we had been privileged to work as lawyers against apartheid. He was right. Being able to use one's legal skills to oppose a wicked system was both a challenge and a privilege.

In two of the societies in which I have worked, apartheid has been brought to an end. I would like to live to celebrate the end of apartheid in Palestine. I express no clear preference for either a two-state or a single-state solution.

A single democratic state within the borders of the mandate for Palestine, extending from the Mediterranean Sea to the Jordan River, is an attractive and idealistic option, provided the state is fully democratic with universal suffrage and not an apartheid state in which the Jewish minority (as it already is or soon will be) rules over the Palestinian majority. On the other hand, a 'two-state solution' of the state of Israel and a fully recognized and independent state of Palestine coexisting together within pre-1967 borders[153] is perhaps a more realistic – and pessimistic – option premised on the real likelihood that past history will make it impossible for the two communities to coexist in a single state.

I am frustrated by the absence of any serious efforts to find a solution to the conflict. Israel and Palestine are clearly unable to negotiate a settlement on their own. The inequality of the parties and the intransigence of their leaders make it imperative that the international community, operating through either the UN or the European Union, takes a firm position on both the terms of the settlement and the procedures for achieving it. The United States is disqualified from playing the role of honest broker, as it has demonstrated that it is incapable of impartiality in this process.[154] This has been apparent for some time but, strangely, the Palestinians persisted in viewing the United States as a mediator. The advent of Donald Trump as US president has changed everything. His decisions to recognize Jerusalem as the capital of Israel, to move the US embassy from Tel Aviv to Jerusalem, and to substantially reduce US funding of UNRWA have made it clear where his loyalties lie. In the case of South Africa and Namibia, the UN and Western states were prepared to exercise a leadership role without the full support of the United States. Whether they will be willing to fill the vacuum left by the United States in respect of Palestine is still to be seen.

It does not follow from the fact that South Africa was subjected to sanctions by the UN and isolated by the community of nations for applying apartheid in South Africa and Namibia that Israel will likewise suffer sanctions in the foreseeable future for applying apartheid in occupied Palestine. Israel's policies and practices in occupied Palestine resemble those of apartheid South Africa. Whether they result in even more human suffering and humiliation is open to debate. Certainly they violate more rules of international law than did apartheid in South Africa. But this does not mean that Israel will soon suffer the same fate as South Africa.

Why this difference in the response of the international community to a serial violator of international law? What explains the silence and indifference of states, particularly of the West, that claim to be concerned about human rights and the rule of law? What allows states to treat Israel as an exception, to permit Israel to violate international law with impunity, but to insist that other states respect international law? What makes Western states unconcerned about the credibility of international law in their support for Israeli exceptionalism?

The principal explanations for this exceptionalism are to be found in the uncritical, unquestioning and unswerving support given to Israel by the United States, in the strength of Israeli lobbies in the United States and elsewhere, in the memories of the Holocaust, in the guilt that this still engenders in the psyche of European political leaders, and in the fear that criticism of Israel will be labelled as anti-Semitism.

The support of the United States for Israel is pervasive. In addition to giving moral, political, economic and financial support, the United States provides Israel with military aid to enable it to remain the dominant power in the Middle East. Since 2007 Israel has received an average of $3 billion military aid each year, a figure set to increase to $3.8 billion in 2019.The United States has consistently protected Israel in the UN. It has successfully used its veto as a permanent member of the Security Council to block resolutions condemning Israel. On over forty occasions it has cast its veto to block resolutions on all sorts of issues, including the condemnation of settlements, the construction of the wall, and the halting of attacks on Gaza and, most recently, the United States has decided to recognize Jerusalem as the capital of Israel. As the dominant member of the Quartet, it makes sure that this body is biased in favour of Israel. This is the factor that distinguishes the case of apartheid South Africa from that of Israel. Although South Africa, a strong ally of the West in World War II, could initially rely on the West for protection against a hostile world, it could not rely on it for unconditional support. The West, determined to secure the moral high ground in the promotion of human rights, made its support conditional on the abandonment of apartheid. South Africa had no Great Power fairy godmother on which it could rely for unquestioning political, military or economic support.

Not only the US president and the executive branch of government give support to Israel, the legislative branch – the Congress – is completely, and pathetically, subservient to Israel. It has repeatedly invited Prime Minister Netanyahu to address it and to give him standing ovations. It never fails to give approval to Israel's actions. In 2014, for instance, both the House of Representatives[155] and the Senate[156] unanimously adopted resolutions giving support to Israel's invasion of Gaza.

Powerful pro-Israeli lobbies are largely responsible for the subservience of both the White House and the Congress to the interests of Israel.[157] Pro-Israel lobbies are to be found in Europe, Latin America, Canada, South Africa and Australia, but these lack the influence of lobbies in the United States. This is because the American political system allows well-funded and well-organized special interest groups to wield significant power and influence on political figures, including the president.[158] (President Trump has described himself as the most pro-Israel president ever.) No American politician can be seen to be weak in his or her defence of Israel. Those that have tried to present a more balanced and independent view have frequently not been re-elected to office owing to the intervention of pro-Israel lobbies.

Both Jewish and Christian special interest groups constitute the Israel lobby in the United States. The most powerful Jewish lobby is the American Israel Public Affairs Committee (AIPAC), but there are a host of think tanks and NGOs, such as the Anti-Defamation League, which together make up this lobby.[159] Christian Zionist and many fundamentalist evangelical Christians[160] support the state of Israel because they believe that Jews must return to the Holy Land to await the Second Coming of Christ, when they will either accept Christ or be damned. Despite the inherently anti-Semitic nature of the beliefs which lead them to endorse the state of Israel, their support has been welcomed by Israel. As Israel does not believe in the Second Coming, it can afford to reap the benefits of this relationship without incurring any obligations. As the Jewish lobby is particularly powerful in the Democratic Party and the evangelical Christians in the Republican Party, Israel is able to rely on bipartisan support in the Congress and the White House.

European states allow themselves to be guided by Washington in their relations with Israel and the search for peace in the region. They raise no serious objections to Israel's destruction of EU-funded projects in occupied Palestine. This is largely the result of Europe's acceptance of the United States as the leader of the West. But there are other factors which lead Europe to support Israel. Lobbies play an important role, but to this must be added two other factors: firstly, Holocaust guilt; and, secondly, the fear of being labelled as anti-Semitic.

Holocaust guilt operates in the psyche and subconscious of many Europeans who remember the failures of their forefathers to protect Jews from the Nazis. That this influences German foreign policy is undeniable but it also impacts upon the decision-making of leaders in other European countries, such as France and the Netherlands. This portrayal of Jews as victims – and hence of Israel as a victim state – has been manipulated by Israel. So much so that an American Jewish scholar, Norman Finkelstein, has described it as 'the Holocaust industry'.[161] To make matters worse, it is suggested that the Palestinians are in some strange way responsible for the Holocaust. As the English historian Arnold Toynbee said in 1961: 'It was not the Palestinian Arabs who committed genocide against the European Jews. It was the Germans. The Germans murdered the Jews: the Palestinian Arabs have been made to pay for what the Germans did.'[162]

Related to Holocaust guilt is anti-Semitism, which has also been exploited by Israel to suppress disagreement with its policies and practices. Anti-Semitism has been extended beyond its meaning of prejudice, hatred or discrimination against Jews as a racial, national or religious group to encompass criticism of the policies and practices of the state of Israel. To criticize the Israeli government or to demand of Israel a higher standard of behaviour in respect of human rights than from other human rights transgressors is labelled as anti-Semitism. It thus becomes easy to dismiss critics of Israel's occupation of the Palestinian Territory as anti-Semites. I was frequently labelled as anti-Semitic for my criticisms of the occupation – as was my successor, Richard Falk, himself a Jew. The publication of my reports on the UN website was always heralded by a spate of emails accusing me of anti-Semitism. Recently one of my reports was singled out as evidence of anti-Semitism in the *Jerusalem Post* because I had described Palestinian opposition to the occupation as similar to that of the French Resistance to Nazi occupation.[163]

The accusation of anti-Semitism is painful, however unfair it may be. Undoubtedly it deters many public figures and the media from open criticism of Israel. A chance remark construed as anti-Semitism can destroy a career. Even in private conversations most people are guarded when they talk about Israel. No one wishes to be labelled an anti-Semite.

Pro-Israel lobbies, Holocaust guilt and fear of being accused of anti-Semitism are a powerful cocktail. This concatenation ensures that the media in most Western countries, particularly the United States, seldom dare to challenge the Israeli narrative and present a balanced perspective – let alone a pro-Palestinian position.

The advocacy of an end to apartheid in occupied Palestine is not an easy or popular pursuit in this environment. Many see it as anti-Semitism. Others view it as support for terrorism or Islamic fundamentalism. Most, particularly non-Jews, take no position at all, either because they sympathize with Israel or because they do not wish to express an opinion that might be construed as anti-Semitism, with all the consequences that follow from such a labelling. Most people prefer to remain silent or to politely change the subject when the question of Israel's actions in Palestine is raised. In Western society the subject of Palestine has become a taboo. Ietje and I make no attempt to conceal our concern for human rights in Palestine, even if it carries with it certain costs. Ietje has been excluded from a lunch group for criticizing settlements in the OPT, and I have good reason to believe that I have been overlooked for certain positions because of my advocacy of the Palestinian cause.

I often contrast this exclusion with the reception I received outside South Africa, and particularly in the United States, during the apartheid era. I was welcomed as a human rights activist engaged in the struggle for a laudable cause. I was in demand as a lecturer at universities, acclaimed by staff and students. I was asked to comment on developments in South Africa to the press and on mainstream television programmes.

Israel's present immunity from international sanctions or pressure does not mean that it enjoys the respect of the peoples of the world. As long as the occupation continues – and, with it, apartheid – Israel will remain a pariah state subject to the quiet disdain of many and the vocal disapproval of civil society. This disdain will grow as the characterization of Israel's occupation as apartheid becomes more accepted. Opposition to this reality remains strong among public office-bearers in the United States and in the foreign ministries of European countries, but there are signs of change. In Israel itself the apartheid analogy is today invoked by lawyers, journalists, politicians and academics. Civil society organisations, including Jewish groups, in the United States have become more strident in their criticisms of Israel. Undoubtedly the Trump administration's harnessing of evangelicals, often virulently anti-Semitic, in its support for Israel has alienated younger American Jews. Voices within the Democratic Party are also questioning the morality of support for Israel.

South Africans, such as Archbishop Tutu, have not hesitated to describe the occupation as similar to or worse than apartheid. A study conducted by the South African Human Sciences Research Council concluded that Israeli domination of the Palestinians in the OPT was oppressive and discriminatory and could be described as a form of apartheid.[164] The South African government has declared that the practices of Israel in the OPT are reminiscent of apartheid,[165] and in May 2018 it was one of only three states to recall its ambassador after Israel's killing of protesters in the Great Return March.

The Middle East is the most volatile region of the world, one in which allegiances change overnight and in which conflict is an ever-present possibility. In the past Israel has successfully withstood these dangers, but the future cannot be predicted. On the international political level, too, there are forces at work which threaten Israel's impunity and expose it to possible concerted international action. The first is the Boycott, Divestment and Sanctions campaign – BDS – which seeks to apply sanctions against Israel and to isolate it. The second is international legal action before the International Criminal Court or other legal institutions which delegitimises Israel's occupation of the OPT and sways international opinion against Israel.

In 2005 BDS was launched by 171 Palestinian NGOs on the first anniversary of the advisory opinion of the International Court of Justice on the Israeli-built wall. This campaign, which is modelled on the South African Anti-Apartheid Movement (AAM), seeks to use economic, cultural, sport and political pressure against Israel to compel it to comply with international law and to end the occupation, grant equality to Palestinians in Israel, and recognize the right of return of refugees. In recent times it has met with considerable success in the United States, some European and Latin American states, Canada, Australia, New Zealand and South Africa. State pension funds have blacklisted Israeli companies and banks; banks have severed ties with Israeli banks; churches have announced their divestment from companies doing business with Israel in the OPT; corporations have cancelled agreements with Israel on projects affecting the OPT; scholars (notably Stephen Hawking) have refused to participate in conferences in Israel; entertainers have refused or cancelled visits; sports fixtures have been cancelled; university teacher and student associations have decided not to co-operate with Israeli universities; and Israeli companies selling products from settlements and foreign companies doing business with Israel in the OPT, such as Caterpillar, Motorola, Hewlett-Packard and G4S, have been subjected to consumer boycotts, shareholder disapproval and protest action. The experience of South Africa's Anti-Apartheid Movement shows that a campaign of the kind employed by BDS takes time to have serious effect, but in the long run its consequences are severe. In the case of South Africa the AAM succeeded in isolating South Africa and in damaging the country's economy. BDS has already made headway and is likely to grow. In response, several countries have attempted to criminalize the advocacy of BDS, but these measures are more likely to publicize BDS and what it stands for than to suppress it. Protest action of this kind will not go away until the reason for the protest disappears.

International legal action should not be underestimated. In recent times the government of Palestine has started to invoke remedies under international law to compel Israel to comply with its obligations. It is considering a further advisory opinion from the International Court of Justice in order to obtain legal endorsement of the illegality of Israel's occupation. In 2018 it filed a complaint against Israel in terms of the International Convention on the Elimination of all Forms of Racial Discrimination (CERD) in which it claimed that Israel was guilty of practising racial discrimination and apartheid in occupied Palestine. This is the first time in the fifty-year history of CERD that such a complaint has been filed by one state against another. This complaint will be considered in the first instance by the Committee on the Elimination of Racial Discrimination, the committee charged with the monitoring of CERD. If it is unable to resolve the dispute to the satisfaction of parties, the matter will be referred to an ad hoc Conciliation Commission to consider the facts and to make recommendations for the resolution of the dispute. Undoubtedly, a finding that Israel practises apartheid in the OPT will have serious political repercussions.

A more serious threat is posed to Israel by the International Criminal Court (ICC). Palestine became a party to the Rome Statute of the ICC in 2015. This allows the ICC to exercise jurisdiction over international crimes committed within its territory, even by the nationals of a state that is not a party to the Rome Statute. At present the prosecutor of the ICC is conducting a preliminary examination into the question whether Israeli officials and military leaders may be investigated and prosecuted for war crimes and crimes against humanity arising out of the construction of settlements and the application of apartheid in the West Bank and the attack on Gaza in 2014. A boost was given to this process on 22 May 2018 when the government of Palestine decided to expedite investigation of Israel's crimes by itself referring Israel's criminal conduct to the

Office of the Prosecutor, despite threats from the United States that it would impose sanctions on Palestine if it resorted to such measures. While it is unlikely that senior Israeli political and military figures will face prosecution before the ICC, there is no doubt that if the prosecutor decides to open an investigation and prosecution into Israel's actions this will seriously damage Israel's reputation and legitimacy. It will also bring pressure on other states to take concerted action to enforce international law, among other things by arresting and transferring to the ICC any Israeli official indicted for such crimes. An advisory opinion of the International Court of Justice, such as that rendered in 2004, may be disregarded, but the stigma attached to criminality may prove difficult for states to ignore.

Demands for the enforcement of fundamental rules of international law inherent in a criminal investigation by the ICC, a finding that Israel practises apartheid under CERD, and support for BDS cannot be ignored indefinitely by the Western nations that have traditionally led the way in promoting respect for the rule of law in international relations. In the long term, governments of the West and international institutions will be compelled to respond to these violations by taking action against Israel. International public opinion will demand it. The government of Israel is aware of this. Hence its determination to suppress BDS and civil society activism and to oppose and evade the reach of the ICC. The case of Israel is similar to that of Namibia. Israel has violated well-established rules of international law relating to the ban on settlements, the annexation of territory, apartheid, self-determination, humanitarian law and human rights law. Many of these violations have already been confirmed by the International Court of Justice and the Security Council. In the long run the UN, with the support of European states, will not be able to resist action based on international law.

Israel endangers its future by focusing on how to oppose and suppress its critics rather than addressing the ending of the occupation and establishing normal relations with its neighbour. Failure to do this will have political, economic and security consequences for the state of Israel. It will also have severe consequences for the people of Israel. Like white South Africans under apartheid, they will become a pariah people, tolerated but not respected, increasingly isolated from the world, and damned with the stigma of apartheid. Inevitably this isolation will intensify. Apartheid delegitimized white-ruled South Africa. It has already delegitimized the occupation of Palestine. If continued, the stigma of apartheid will be used to delegitimize Israel itself. Already many have widened the concept of apartheid to include discriminatory policies and practices in Israel itself.

South Africa has a special interest in a just solution to the Israel–Palestine conflict. Historically it has a close relationship with Israel. General Smuts endorsed the Balfour Declaration and ensured that the South African government supported both the partition of Palestine in 1947 and the recognition of the state of Israel in 1948. The apartheid regime maintained close ties with Israel at a time when other allies scorned it.[166] These ties were cemented by the presence of a substantial Jewish community, numbering some one hundred and twenty thousand in the 1970s, which undoubtedly constituted the most liberal section of the white community during the apartheid era. The end of apartheid brought about a reversal of policy on the part of the South African government. South Africa now recognizes Palestine as an independent state, maintains diplomatic relations with Palestine, and consistently votes in favour of UN resolutions condemning Israel for its treatment of the Palestinians. Policy is guided by the declaration of Nelson Mandela shortly after he was released from prison that 'We know too well that our freedom is incomplete without the freedom of the Palestinians'. Although policies have changed over the years, South Africa has always had, and still has, a special relationship with Israel. Today this special relationship extends to Palestine. It is therefore incumbent on South Africa with its experience of apartheid to use its good offices and influence to promote and facilitate a just solution to the conflict.

That a solution to the conflict in the Middle East will be found is clear. History teaches us that conflicts of this kind cannot continue for ever. Whether such a solution will be fair to both Jews and Palestinians is unpredictable. But it is the very unpredictability of history that makes me optimistic. For most of my life I believed that apartheid in South Africa would end in bloodshed, that civil war would engulf us all, and that we would take years to recover. But then a miracle occurred. Overnight both parties came to their senses under wise leadership, the bloodbath was avoided, and a constitutional democracy was established. The land between the Mediterranean Sea and the Jordan River is the land of miracles.

Notes

CHAPTERS 1 and 2

1 Article 7(2)(h) of the Rome Statute of the International Criminal Court.

2 See B. Pogrund, *Drawing Fire: Investigating the Accusations of Apartheid in Israel*, London: Rowman and Littlefield, 2014.

3 N. Mandela, *Long Walk to Freedom*, Boston: Little, Brown, 1994, pp. 31–32. See further on Healdtown: T. Webster, *Healdtown: Under Eagle's Wings: The Legacy of an African Mission School*, Cape Town: Methodist Publishing House, 2013; Jack Dugard, *Fragments of My Fleece*, Pietermaritzburg: Kendall & Strachan, 1985, pp. 20–39.

4 See further on the Defiance Campaign and the constitutional crisis, John Dugard, *Human Rights and the South African Legal Order*, Princeton: Princeton University Press, 1978, pp. 28–34, 212–213.

5 See A. Sparks's autobiography, *The Sword and the Pen: Six Decades on the Political Frontier*, Cape Town: Jonathan Ball, 2016, particularly pp. 48–54.

6 See D. Welsh, *The Rise and Fall of Apartheid*, Cape Town: Jonathan Ball, 2009, pp. 113–116.

7 See Dugard, *Human Rights*, pp. 28–34.

8 Act 47 of 1953.

9 Dugard, *Fragments of My Fleece*, p. 88.

10 John, a good friend and gifted scholar, who had just commenced his studies at Oxford, died shortly after we separated when he and a friend were lost while climbing in the Alps.

11 Act 45 of 1959.

12 On Eleanor and Ronnie, see R. Kasrils, *The Unlikely Secret Agent*, Johannesburg: Jacana Media, 2010.

13 Section 21 of the General Law Amendment Act 76 of 1962.

14 Section 17 of the General Law Amendment Act 37 of 1963.

15 1963 (1) *South African Law Reports* 692 (AD).

16 See *State* v. *Arenstein*, 1963 (3) *South African Law Reports* 243 (N).

17 For an account of Hepple's involvement in the Rivonia arrests, see B. Hepple, *Young Man with a Red Tie: A Memoir of Mandela and the Failed Revolution 1960–1963*, Johannesburg: Jacana Media, 2013.

PART 1: SOUTH WEST AFRICA/NAMIBIA

1 See, generally, J. Dugard (ed.), *The South West Africa/Namibia Dispute: Documents and Scholarly Writings on the Controversy between South Africa and the United Nations*, Berkeley: University of California Press, 1973.
2 Article 77 of the UN Charter.
3 1950 *ICJ Reports* 128.
4 *Voting Procedure on Questions Relating to Reports and Petitions Concerning the Territory of South West Africa*, 1955 *ICJ Reports* 67; *Admissibility of Hearings of Petitioners by the Committee on South West Africa*, 1956 *ICJ Reports* 23.
5 See C. and M. Legum, *South Africa: Crisis for the West*, London: Pall Mall, 1964; R. Segal (ed.), *Sanctions against South Africa*, Harmondsworth: Penguin Books, 1964.
6 'Objections to the Revision of the 1962 Judgment of the International Court of Justice in the South West Africa Case', (1965) 82 *South African Law Journal* 178.
7 Later it emerged that the president of the court, Sir Percy Spender, had falsely informed Judge Zafrulla Khan of Pakistan that the majority of the judges believed he should recuse himself because he had in 1962 been asked by the applicant states to sit as their judge ad hoc, an invitation that he had declined. In fact, only two judges supported such a recusal.
8 Resolution 2372(XXII).
9 See J. Dugard, 'The Revocation of the Mandate for South West Africa', (1968) 62 *American Journal of International Law* 78.
10 *R* v. *Christian*, 1924 *South African Law Reports, Appellate Division* 101.
11 See Carlson's account of the trial in J. Carlson, *No Neutral Ground*, New York: Thomas Y. Crowell, 1973, pp. 150–216.
12 For Bizos's account of the trial, see G. Bizos, *Odyssey to Freedom*, Johannesburg: Random House, 2007, pp. 322–331.
13 D. Herbstein, *White Lies: Canon Collins and the Secret War against Apartheid*, Oxford: James Currey Publishers, 2002, pp. 146–150.
14 *State* v. *Tuhadeleni and Others*, 1967 (4) *South African Law Reports* 511 (T).
15 Resolution 245 (1968). See also Resolution 246 (1968).
16 See *Written Pleadings*, United States, p. 860.
17 1971 *ICJ Reports* 215.
18 1971 *ICJ Reports* 16.
19 See, for, example, J. Dugard, 'The Opinion on South West Africa (Namibia): The Teleologists Triumph', (1971) 88 *South African Law Journal* 35.
20 See 'The South West Africa/Namibia Dispute', address at the AGM of the South African Institute of Race Relations, Durban, 18 March 1976.
21 1983 (1) *South African Law Reports* 833 (SWA).
22 See Charles Yeats's account of his ordeal as a conscientious objector in C. Yeats, *Prisoner of Conscience: One Man's Remarkable Journey from Repression to Freedom*, Johannesburg: Random House, 2005.
23 See the account of the trial of Ivan Toms in R. Abel, *Politics by Other Means: Law in the Struggle against Apartheid*, New York: Routledge, 1995, pp. 78–92.

PART 2: SOUTH AFRICA

1 See J. Dugard, *Human Rights and the South African Legal Order*, Princeton: Princeton University Press, 1978; J. Dugard, N. Haysom and G. Marcus, *The Last Years of Apartheid: Civil Liberties in South Africa*, New York: Ford Foundation, South Africa Update Series, 1992; D. Welsh, *The Rise and Fall of Apartheid*, Cape Town: Jonathan Ball, 2009.
2 Act 55 of 1949.
3 Immorality Amendment Act, 21 of 1950, section 1.
4 Act 30 of 1950.

5 Act 49 of 1953.
6 Act 41 of 1950. This was later consolidated by Act 36 of 1966.
7 See *Minister of the Interior* v. *Lockhat,* 1961 (2) *South African Law Reports* 587 (AD).
8 Act 47 of 1953.
9 See *Brown* v. *The Board of Education of Topeka*, 347 U.S. 483 (1954) at 494.
10 Act 45 of 1959.
11 See Industrial Conciliation Act 28 of 1956.
12 See Dugard, *Human Rights and the South African Legal Order*, pp. 28–34.
13 *Harris* v. *Minister of the Interior (Vote Case)*, 1952 (2) *South African Law Reports* 428 (AD); *Minister of the Interior* v. *Harris (High Court of Parliament Case)*, 1952 (4) *South African Law Reports* 769 (AD).
14 *Collins* v. *Minister of the Interior (Senate Case)*, 1957 (1) *South African Law Reports* 552 (AD).
15 Act 67 of 1952. See too the Bantu (Urban Areas) Consolidation Act, as amended in 1952.
16 Act 44 of 1950.
17 Act 8 of 1953.
18 Act 34 of 1960.
19 General Law Amendment Act, 76 of 1962, section 21.
20 General Law Amendment Act, 37 of 1963, section 17.
21 Criminal Procedure Amendment Act, 96 of 1965, section 7, inserting section 215 *bis* into the Criminal Procedure Act of 1955.
22 For further on this trial, B. Hepple, *Young Man with a Red Tie: A Memoir of Mandela and the Failed Revolution*, Johannesburg: Jacana Media, 2013.
23 See the Promotion of Bantu Self-Government Act, 46 of 1959.
24 A.S. Mathews and R.C. Albino, 'The Permanence of the Temporary: An Examination of the 90- and 180-day Detention Laws', (1966) 83 *South African Law Journal* 16. See on the impact and consequences of this article, J. Dugard, 'Tony Mathews and Criticism of the Judiciary', in M. Carnelley and S. Hoctor (eds.), *Law, Order and Liberty: Essays in Honour of Tony Mathews*, Durban: University of KwaZulu-Natal Press, 2011, p. 3.
25 The *Rand Dail Mail* carried a full report of the speech on 25 July 1967. Later I published a slightly different version in *Law, Justice and Society*, Report of the Legal Commission of the Study Project on Christianity in Apartheid Society (SPROCAS), Johannesburg, 1972.
26 B. van Niekerk, 'Hanged by the Neck until You Are Dead', (1969) 86 *South African Law Journal* 470 and (1970) 87 *South African Law Journal* 60.
27 *State* v. *Van Niekerk*, 1970 (3) *South African Law Reports* 655 (T).
28 347 US 483 (1954).
29 This lecture was published as 'The Judicial Process, Positivism and Civil Liberty', (1972) 88 *South African Law Journal* 181.
30 *Rand Daily Mail*, 25 March 1971.
31 *Sunday Tim*es, 28 March 1971.
32 *Daily Dispatch*, 20 November 1981.
33 *City Press*, 15 May 1983.
34 *State* v. *Van Niekerk*, 1972 (3) *South African Law Reports* 711 (AD). See further, J. Dugard, 'Judges, Academics and Unjust Laws: The Van Niekerk Contempt Case', (1972) 89 *South African Law Journal* 271.
35 Government Notice No. 1062 of 9 June 1978.
36 *Die Beeld*, 7 September 1978.
37 In terms of the Criminal Law Amendment Act, 8 of 1953, enacted to put an end to the 1952 Defiance Campaign.
38 Act 51 of 1968.

39 See further, H. Suzman, *In No Uncertain Terms*, Cape Town: Jonathan Ball, 1993; J. Strangwayes-Booth, *A Cricket in the Thorn Tree*, Bloomington, Indiana: Indiana University Press, 1976; P. Lewsen (ed.), *Helen Suzman's Solo Years*, Cape Town: Jonathan Ball, 1976; R. Lee (ed.), *Values Alive: A Tribute to Helen Suzman*, Cape Town: Jonathan Ball, 1990 (particularly my contribution 'Laws That Are a Travesty of Justice', pp. 101–114); R. Renwick, *Helen Suzman: Bright Star in a Dark Chamber*, Cape Town: Jonathan Ball, 2014.

40 See J. Allen, *Rabble-Rouser for Peace: The Authorized Biography of Desmond Tutu*, London: Rider Books, 2006; A. Sparks and M. Tutu, *Tutu: The Authorized Portrait*, Johannesburg: Pan Macmillan, 2011.

41 *Tutu* v. *Minister of Internal Affairs*, 1982(4) *South African Law Reports* 571(T).

42 See below in the section on the South African Institute of Race Relations.

43 See *S* v. *Naude*, 1975 (1) *South African Law Reports* 681 (A); *S* v. *Naude*, 1977 (1) *South African Law Reports* 46 (T); Dugard, *Human Rights and the South African Legal Order*, pp. 225, 357–358.

44 *S* v. *Wood*, 1976 (1) *South African Law Reports* 707 (AD).

45 See on Wits University before 1959, B. Murray, *Wits University: The 'Open' Years. A History of the University of the Witwatersrand 1939–1959*, Johannesburg: Witwatersrand University Press, 1997.

46 See *The Star*, 4 June 1969.

47 Act 31 of 1974.

48 J. Dugard, *Failure of a Fiction*, Johannesburg: South African Institute of Race Relations, 1979, p. 15.

49 J. Dugard, *A National Strategy for 1980*, Johannesburg: South African Institute of Race Relations, 1980.

50 See further on this case, R. Abel, *Politics by Other Means: Law in the Struggle Against Apartheid, 1980–1994*, New York: Routledge, 1995, pp. 219–243.

51 For an account of the history of the BLA, see D. Moseneke, *My Own Liberator*, Johannesburg: Picador Africa, 2016, pp. 206–220.

52 See H. Kenney, *Verwoerd: Architect of Apartheid*, Cape Town: Jonathan Ball, 2016, pp. 195ff.

53 See Status of Transkei Act, 100 of 1976.

54 Resolution 31/6A (1976).

55 Resolution 407 (1977).

56 *House of Assembly Debates*, 72, col. 579 (7 February 1978).

57 J. Dugard, 'South Africa's "Independent" Homelands: An Exercise in Denationalization', (1980) 10 *Denver Journal of International Law and Policy* 11.

58 Other participants included Kader Asmal, Judge Keba Mbaye, Peter Kooijmans, professor of international law at the University of Leiden, and Niall McDermott, secretary-general of the International Commission of Jurists.

59 1989 (4) *South African Law Reports* 519 (B).

60 For a full account of the 'Moutse affair', see Abel, *Politics by Other Means*, pp. 435–473.

61 *Mathebe* v. *Government of the RSA*, 1988(3) *South African Law Reports* 667 (A).

62 *State President* v. *Lefuo*, 1990(2) *South African Law Reports* 679 (AD).

63 See J. Dugard, 'Failure of the TBVC States', (1992) 8 *South African Journal of Human Rights* (editorial comment). For the opposing view, see M. Wiechers, 'Reincorporation of the TBVC Countries', (1990-91) *South African Yearbook of International Law* 119.

64 Section 239 of the Republic of South Africa Constitution Act, 200 of 1993.

65 Restoration and Extension of South African Citizenship Act, 196 of 1993.

66 Some hotels were designated as 'international', which allowed them to admit black guests.

67 Act 41 of 1950.

68 1961 (2) *South African Law Reports* 587 (AD).
69 Ibid. at p. 602.
70 *S* v. *Adams*, *S* v. *Werner*, 1981(1) *South African Law Reports* 187 (AD).
71 *S* v. *Cassim*, unreported, and *S* v. *Govender*, 1986(3) *South African Law Reports* 969 (T).
72 Republic of South Africa Constitution Act, 110 of 1983.
73 Abolition of Racially Based Land Measures Act, 108 of 1991.
74 Bantu (Abolition of Passes and Co-ordination of Documents) Act, 67 of 1952; and Bantu (Urban Areas Consolidation) Act, 25 of 1945, as substantially amended in 1952.
75 Abolition of Influx Control Act, 68 of 1986.
76 Act 83 of 1967.
77 Section 2.
78 *S* v. *ffrench-Beytagh*, 1972 (3) *South African Law Reports* 430 (AD).
79 Section 6 of Act 83 of 1967.
80 See G. Bizos, *Odyssey to Freedom*, Johannesburg: Random House, 2007, pp. 425–428.
81 Ibid., pp. 434–437.
82 *S* v. *Wood*, 1976 (1) *South African Law Reports* 707 (AD).
83 See B. Pogrund, *How Can Man Die Better? The Life of Robert Sobukwe*, Cape Town: Jonathan Ball, 1997.
84 *Sobukwe and Another* v. *Minister of Justice*, 1972 (1) *South African Law Reports* 693 (AD).
85 Act 74 of 1982.
86 See G. Marcus, 'Civil Liberties under Emergency Rule', in J. Dugard, N. Haysom and G. Marcus (eds.), *The Last Years of Apartheid: Civil Liberties in South Africa*, New York: Ford Foundation, 1992, pp. 39–48.
87 On the nature of the political trial and its history in South Africa, see Dugard, *Human Rights and the South African Legal Order*, chapter 7.
88 See D. Herbstein, *White Lies: Canon Collins and the Secret War against Apartheid*, Oxford: James Currey, 2004.
89 For an account of many of these trials, see Bizos, *Odyssey to Freedom*.
90 This law was later included in section 29 of the Internal Security Act, 74 of 1982.
91 Dugard, *Human Rights*, p. 120.
92 *The Star*, 11 May 1970; *Wits Student*, 15 May 1970.
93 *Rand Daily Mail*, editorial, 20 May 1970.
94 *S* v. *Ndou and Others*, 1971 (1) *South African Law Reports* 668 (AD).
95 *S* v. *Van Niekerk*, 1972 (3) *South African Law Reports* 711 (AD). See, too, Dugard, 'Judges, Academics and Unjust Laws: The Van Niekerk Contempt Case'.
96 *Sunday Times*, 11 June 1972.
97 *Rand Daily Mail*, 2 November 1972.
98 *Sunday Times*, 5 November 1972.
99 See statement by Mr F. Herman MP in *Rand Daily Mail*, 19 September 1970.
100 See further on the role of blacks in the police force, J. Dlamini, *Askari: A Story of Collaboration and Betrayal in the Anti-Apartheid Struggle*, Johannesburg: Jacana Media, 2014.
101 See G. Moss, *The New Radicals: A Generational Memoir of the 1970s*, Johannesburg: Jacana Media, 2014.
102 Ibid., pp. 230–234, 247–248.
103 H. Arendt, *Eichmann in Jerusalem: A Report on the Banality of Evil*, London: Penguin Books, 2006.
104 *Die Vaderland*, 15 July 1972.
105 *Die Vaderland*, 18 July 1972.
106 *Rapport*, 23 July 1972.
107 See K. van Rooyen, *A South African Censor's Tale*, Pretoria: Protea Books House, 2011, p. 137.

108 See *Rand Daily Mail*, 30 November 1984; *The Star*, 30 November 1984.
109 This letter, sent from Gaborone on 12 October 1977, read: 'Dear John, Thank you for the nice things you had to say about me in your references. Also for the trouble you took in contacting Phyllis and John. It is all much appreciated. I'll be writing to Phyllis personally to thank her. Jen joins me in sending love. Our baby is coming in March. My love to Jane. Yours, Marius.'
110 Letter marked 'Secret' for Captain Williamson from A.J. Kruger, Divisional Head 052. Reference 052/208/1980, 8 September 1980. See *Mail & Guardian*, 29 July to 4 August 1994.
111 Van Niekerk, 'Hanged by the Neck', p. 60.
112 Ibid.
113 *S* v. *Van Niekerk*, 1970 (3) *South African Law Reports* 655 (T).
114 See further on this case, Hugh Lewin, *Stones against the Mirror*, Cape Town: Umuzi, 2011.
115 Discussed by Christina Murray, 'The Status of the ANC and SWAPO and International Humanitarian Law', (1983) 100 *South African Law Journal* 402. See, too, *S* v. *Sagarius*, 1983 (1) *South African Law Reports* 836 (SWA); and *S* v. *Mncube*, 1991 (3) *South African Law Reports* 132 (A).
116 *House of Assembly Debates*, 25, cols. 257ff (14 March 1969).
117 This case was known as 'the Sharpeville Six'.
118 1995 (3) *South African Law Reports* 391 (CC).
119 *House of Assembly Debates*, 62, col. 6306 (7 May 1976).
120 Section 1 of Act 44 of 1950.
121 Riotous Assemblies Act, 17 of 1956, section 17.
122 Publications and Entertainment Act, 26 of 1963.
123 Act 42 of 1974.
124 Section 47(2) of Act 42 of 1974.
125 See *Race Relations News*, March 1978.
126 See Kobus van Rooyen's account of his experiences in *A South African Censor's Tale*.
127 Published by Taurus Press, Johannesburg, 1980.
128 Van Rooyen, *A South African Censor's Tale,* pp. 117–118.
129 Ibid., p. 126.
130 There is a preface to Van Rooyen's book by the writer André Brink, who himself was dealt with harshly by the censors, which acknowledges the positive role played by Van Rooyen.
131 Literally this might be translated as 'language box'. But the word *doos* has acquired the secondary meaning of vagina or cunt.
132 Act 8 of 1959.
133 *S* v. *South African Associated Newspapers, Ltd*, 1970 (1) *South African Law Reports* 469 (W).
134 Republic of South Africa Constitution Act, 110 of 1983, section 34.
135 Mathews and Albino, 'The Permanence of the Temporary', p. 16.
136 Van Niekerk, 'Hanged by the Neck'.
137 *S* v. *van Niekerk*, 1970 (3) *South African Law Reports* 655 (T).
138 J. Dugard, 'The Judicial Process, Positivism and Civil Liberty', (1971) 88 *South African Law Journal* 181.
139 *S* v. *van Niekerk*, 1972(3) *South African Law Reports* 711(AD).
140 See A. Sachs, *Justice in South Africa*, Berkeley: University of California Press, 1973; Dugard, *Human Rights and the South African Legal Order*, Part 4; E. Cameron, 'Legal Chauvinism, Executive-Mindedness and Justice: L.C. Steyn's Impact on South African Law', (1982) 99 *South African Law Journal* 38; Hugh Corder, *Judges at Work: The Role and Attitudes of the South African Appellate Judiciary, 1910–1950*, Cape Town: Juta, 1984; C. Forsyth, *In Danger of Their Talents: A Study of the Appellate*

Division of the Supreme Court of South Africa 1950-1980, Cape Town: Juta, 1985. For later studies, see D. Dyzenhaus, *Hard Cases in Wicked Legal Systems: Pathologies of Legality*, Oxford: Oxford University Press, 2010; D. Dyzenhaus, *Judging the Judges, Judging Ourselves: Truth, Reconciliation and the Apartheid Legal Order*, Oxford: Hart Publishing, 1998; S. Ellmann, *In a Time of Trouble: Law and Liberty in South Africa's State of Emergency*, Oxford: Clarendon Press, 1992.

141 See the Report of this Commission in RP 78/1983, Government Printer, Pretoria.

142 Personal letter of 8 August 1988.

143 R. Wacks, 'Judges and Injustice', (1984) 101 *South African Law Journal* 266.

144 J. Dugard, 'Should Judges Resign? A Reply to Professor Wacks', (1984) 101 *South African Law Journal* 286.

145 *Sunday Tribune*, 3 April 1983.

146 Today Mount Grace is a very different luxury hotel.

147 *R* v. *Pitje*, 1960 (4) *South African Law Reports* 709 (AD).

148 See further on this National Convention, L.M. Thompson, *The Unification of South Africa 1902–1910*, Oxford: Clarendon Press, 1960.

149 See Dugard, 'The Judiciary and Constitutional Change', in D.J. van Vuuren and D.J. Kriek (eds.), *Political Alternatives for Southern Africa*, Johannesburg: Macmillan, 1983, pp. 332–333.

150 See the book by a former student of mine in the National Intelligence Service, M. Spaarwater, *A Spook's Progress: From Making War to Peace*, Cape Town: Zebra Press, 2012.

151 Articles 55 and 56 of the UN Charter.

152 Resolution 418 (1977).

153 Resolution 569 (1985).

154 Resolutions 1761(XVII), 39/72 of 13 December 1984.

155 Such as FAO, UNESCO, ILO, WHO, ITU, WIPO and ICAO.

156 Universal Postal Union (UPU).

157 *Debates of Parliament (Hansard)*, col. 2 (2 February 1990), pp. 15–16.

158 See A. Sampson, *Mandela: The Authorized Biography*, Johannesburg: Jonathan Ball, 1999, p. 581; Welsh, *The Rise and Fall of Apartheid*, pp. 251–259.

159 See further, N. Mandela, *Long Walk to Freedom*, Boston: Little, Brown and Company, 1994; Sampson, *Mandela*.

160 Letter of 4 March 1985, in possession of author.

161 For a full account of the activities of the IBIIR, see P. Harris, *In a Different Time: The Inside Story of the Delmas Four*, Cape Town: Umuzi, 2008. See too Dlamini, *Askari*.

162 For a study of De Kock and whether he genuinely felt remorse for his crimes, see P. Gobodo-Madikizela, *A Human Being Died That Night: A South African Woman Confronts the Legacy of Apartheid*, Johannesburg: Mariner Books, 2004.

163 *Sunday Star*, 27 September 1992.

164 See R. Keightley, 'Political Offences and Indemnity in South Africa', (1993) 9 *South African Journal of Human Rights* 347.

165 Act 34 of 1995.

166 See J. Dugard, 'Dealing with Crimes of a Past Regime: Is Amnesty Still an Option?' (1999) 12 *Leiden Journal of International Law* 1001; A. Boraine, *A Country Unmasked: Inside South Africa's Truth and Reconciliation Commission*, Oxford: Oxford University Press, 2000.

167 Debate on 20 January 1991.

168 P. Waldmeir, *The Anatomy of a Miracle: The End of Apartheid and the Birth of the New South Africa*, London: Penguin, 1997, p. 241; Welsh, *Rise and Fall*, p. 482.

169 Constitution of the Republic of South Africa Act, 200 of 1993.

170 Mandela, *Long Walk to Freedom*, p. 539.

171 Constitutional Assembly, Constitutional Committee Subcommittee, *Draft Bill of*

Rights, volume I, Explanatory Memoranda, 9 October 1995, p. 154.

172 See S. Liebenberg, *Socio-Economic Rights: Adjudication under a Transformative Constitution*, Cape Town: Juta, 2010.

173 Act 108 of 1996.

174 For a positive assessment of the work of the Constitutional Court, see E. Cameron, *Justice: A Personal Account*, Cape Town: Tafelberg, 2014.

175 T. Leon, *On the Contrary: Leading the Opposition in a Democratic South Africa*, Cape Town: Jonathan Ball Publishers, 2008, p. 266.

176 In 1991 Wits University was led to believe that the apartheid government was about to take money from the university's pension fund to provide 'golden handshakes' for its officials who were likely to soon find themselves without jobs in the new South Africa. Staff were accordingly advised to withdraw their pension savings and to invest elsewhere. I had unfortunately taken this advice.

177 *Sunday Times*, 30 August 1998.

178 Article 92.

179 Article 6, Statute of International Court of Justice.

180 Letter dated November 2002.

181 *Case Concerning Armed Activities on the Territory of the Congo (DRC* v. *Rwanda), Jurisdiction and Admissibility*, 2006 *International Court of Justice Reports* 6.

182 *Case Concerning Sovereignty over Pedra Branca/Pulau Batu Puteh, Middle Rocks and South Ledge (Malaysia/Singapore)*, 2008 *International Court of Justice Reports* 12.

183 *Certain Activities Carried Out by Nicaragua in the Border Area (Costa Rica* v. *Nicaragua); Construction of a Road in Costa Rica along the San Juan River (Nicaragua* v. *Costa Rica)*, 2015 *International Court of Justice Reports* 665.

PART 3: PALESTINE

1 For comprehensive histories of Palestine, see A. Shlaim, *The Iron Wall: Israel and the Arab World*, London: Penguin, 2000; I. Pappe, *A History of Modern Palestine*, Cambridge: Cambridge University Press, 2000.

2 See V. Kattan, *From Coexistence to Conquest: International Law Origins of the Arab–Israeli Conflict, 1891–1949*, London: Pluto Press, 2005, pp. 39–42, 98–116; J. Barr, *A Line in the Sand: The Anglo-French Struggle for the Middle East, 1914–1948*, New York: W.W. Norton & Company, 2012.

3 See J. Schneer, *The Balfour Declaration: The Origins of the Arab-Israeli Conflict*, New York: Random House, 2010.

4 See T. Segev, *One Palestine, Complete: Jews and Arabs under the British Mandate*, New York: Henry Holt, 1999.

5 See B. Hoffman, *Anonymous Soldiers: The Struggle for Israel, 1917–1947*, New York: Knopf, 2015.

6 Ibid., pp. 166–167.

7 For accounts of Harry Truman's role in the recognition of Israel, see A. Radosh and R. Radosh, *A Safe Haven: Harry S. Truman and the Founding of Israel*, New York: HarperCollins, 2009; J.B. Judis, *Genesis: Truman, American Jews, and the Origins of the Arab/Israeli Conflict*, New York: Farrar, Straus and Giroux, 2014.

8 See J. Crawford, *The Creation of States in International Law*, 2nd edn, Oxford: Oxford University Press, 2006, p. 434.

9 I. Pappe, *The Ethnic Cleansing of Palestine*, Oxford: Oneworld, 2007.

10 See P. O'Malley, *The Two-State Delusion: Israel and Palestine – A Tale of Two Narratives*, New York: Viking, 2015, chapter 6.

11 See, for example, M. Oren, *Six Days of War*, Oxford: Oxford University Press, 2002, in support of Israel's position; and J. Quigley, *The Six-Day War and Israeli Self-Defense: Questioning the Legal Basis for Preventive War*, Cambridge: Cambridge

University Press, 2013, against the Israeli position.

12 See, on these talks, L. Wright, *Thirteen Days in September: Carter, Begin and Sadat at Camp David*, New York: Alfred A. Knopf, 2014.

13 Article 1.

14 Much has been written about the Oslo Accords. Perhaps the most official account is that of Mahmoud Abbas (Abu Mazen), *Through Secret Channels*, Reading: Garnet Publishing, 1995.

15 S. Ben-Ami, *Scars of War, Wounds of Peace: The Israeli–Arab Tragedy*, London: Weidenfeld and Nicholson, 2005, p. 212.

16 C. Swisher, *The Truth about Camp David*, New York: Nation Books, 2004. See, further, D. Ross, *The Missing Peace: The Inside Story of the Fight for the Middle East*, New York: Farrar, Straus and Giroux, 2004.

17 See G. Sher, *The Israeli–Palestinian Peace Negotiations, 1999–2001: Within Reach*, Abingdon: Routledge, 2004. See, further on this period, A.D. Miller, *The Much Too Promised Land: America's Elusive Search for Arab–Israeli Peace*, New York: Bantam Books, 2009.

18 The report of my research was published in 'Israel and the International Community: The Legal Debate', (1984) 10 *South African Yearbook of International Law* 35.

19 See D. Kretzmer, *The Occupation of Justice: The Supreme Court of Israel and the Occupied Territories*, Albany: State University of New York Press, 2002.

20 For an account of this family history, see R. Shehadeh, *Strangers in the House*, London: Profile Books, 2002.

21 See A. Shlaim, *The Iron Wall: Israel and the Arab World*, London: Penguin Books, 2000, pp. 450–460.

22 The proceedings of the conference were later published in E. Playfair (ed.), *International Law and the Administration of Occupied Territories: Two Decades of Israeli Occupation of the West Bank and Gaza Strip*, Oxford: Clarendon Press, 1992.

23 *Public Committee against Torture* v. *State of Israel*, HCJ 5100/94, 53 (4) PD 815.

24 Ibid., paras. 39, 40.

25 *Public Committee against Torture* v. *State of Israel*, HCJ 769/02, Judgment of 13 December 2006.

26 For a helpful account of the Second Intifada, see A. Bregman, *Cursed Victory: A History of Israel and the Occupied Territories*, London: Penguin Books, 2014, chapters 12–14.

27 Resolution S-5/1.

28 See Declaration on Fact-Finding by the United Nations in the Field of the Maintenance of International Peace and Security, General Assembly Resolution 46/59 of 9 December 1991.

29 Israel calls its armed forces the Israeli Defense Forces (IDF). Palestinians object to this term for the reason that much of their work cannot be described as defensive and the term does not include the Israeli police. Instead they use the term Israeli Occupation Forces (IOF). I have chosen to use the term Israel Defense Forces and the acronym IDF to describe Israel's security forces, as this is the most commonly used term.

30 *Report of the Human Rights Inquiry Commission Established Pursuant to Commission Resolution 5/1 of 19 October 2000, E/CN.42001/121*, 16 March 2001.

31 Ibid., para. 51.

32 Ibid., para. 108.

33 U. Davis, *Israel: An Apartheid State*, London: Zed Books, 1987.

34 René Felber of Switzerland (1993–5); Hannu Halinen of Finland (1996–8); and Giorgio Giacomelli of Italy (1999–2001).

35 I hold no firm view on whether Arafat died of natural causes or was assassinated. Ahron Bregman examines the evidence on this subject and concludes 'while we do not have the smoking gun to show that Israel killed Arafat, the weight of evidence is such

that one should not exclude this possibility' (*Cursed Victory*, p. 298).

36 R. Bergman, *Rise and Kill First: The Secret History of Israel's Targeted Assassinations*, New York: Random House, 2018. See also R. Bergman, 'How Arafat Eluded Israel's Assassination Machine', *New York Times Magazine*, 23 January 2018.

37 For an excellent account of the part played by Israeli lawyers in opposing the occupation, see M. Sfard, *The Wall and the Gate: Israel, Palestine and the Legal Battle for Human Rights* (translated by Maya Johnston), New York: Metropolitan Books, Henry Holt & Co., 2018.

38 *Legal Consequences of the Construction of a Wall in the Occupied Palestinian Territory*, 2004 *ICJ Reports*, 136 at paras. 102–13.

39 Ibid., paras. 90–101.

40 See Bergman, *Rise and Kill First*.

41 Sfard, *The Wall and the Gate*, p. 412.

42 *Public Committee against Torture* v. *State of Israel*, HCJ 5100/94, 53 (4) PD 815.

43 See Sfard, *The Wall and the Gate*, chapter 4.

44 *International New York Times*, 30 April 2014, p. 8.

45 See Russell Tribunal on Palestine, Cape Town, *Findings of the South Africa Session* (November 2011), paras. 5.44 and 5.45. See, too, U. Davis, *Israel: An Apartheid State* (1987); S. Nathan, *The Other Side of Israel: My Journey across the Jewish–Arab Divide*, Detroit: Nan A. Talese, 2005; U. Davis, *Apartheid Israel*, London: Zed Books, 2003. In March 2017 Richard Falk and Virginia Tilley wrote a report on *Israeli Practices towards the Palestinian People and the Question of Apartheid* for the UN Economic and Social Commission for Western Asia (ESCWA) which argued that Israel practised apartheid in Israel itself. This report was removed from the ESCWA website on the instructions of the UN secretary-general.

46 In the 2015 Israeli election the Palestinian political parties in Israel combined to form a Joint List which secured sufficient support to make it the third-largest political party in the Knesset.

47 See Y. Zilbershats, 'Apartheid, International Law and the Occupied Palestinian Territories: A Reply to John Dugard and John Reynolds', (2013) 24 *European Journal of International Law* 914.

48 See, further, J. Dugard and J. Reynolds, 'Apartheid, International Law and the Occupied Palestinian Territory', (2013) 24 *European Journal of International Law* 867; V. Tilley (ed.), *Beyond Occupation: Apartheid, Colonialism and International Law in the Occupied Palestinian Territories*, London: Pluto Press, 2012.

49 M. Blumenthal, *Goliath: Life and Loathing in Greater Israel*, London: Nation Books, 2013.

50 Shaked is a senior member of the Habeyit Hayehudi (Jewish Home) party. See Abu Abunimah, 'Israel Lawmaker's Call for Genocide of Palestinians', *Electronic Intifada*, 10 July 2014.

51 Article 85(4).

52 Article 7(1)(jj).

53 B. Pogrund, *Drawing Fire: Investigating the Accusations of Apartheid in Israel*, London: Rowman and Littlefield, 2014, p. 198.

54 Article 2.

55 Article 7 (1)(j) and (2)(h).

56 See Dugard and Reynolds, 'Apartheid, International Law and the Occupied Palestinian Territory', pp. 885–889.

57 The Israeli Supreme Court has ordered that restraints be placed on this practice but the IDF has failed to comply with the conditions imposed by the Supreme Court. See *The Public Committee against Torture in Israel* v. *Government of Israel et al.*, HJJ 769/02, 13 December 2006.

58 See B'Tselem and HaMoked, *Absolute Prohibition: The Torture and Ill-Treatment of*

Palestinian Detainees (2007), www.btselem.org/publications.

59 See A. Baker and A. Matar (eds.), *Threat: Palestinian Political Prisoners in Israel*, London: Pluto Press, 2011.

60 Gisha, *Procedures and Policies* (2015), www.gisha.org/legal/procedures-and-protocols.

61 Report of the Office of the High Commissioner for Human Rights, A/HRC/31/44 of 20 January 2016, pp. 5–7.

62 *Machsom* is Hebrew for 'checkpoint'.

63 For a moving account of life under curfew in Ramallah, see Raja Shehadeh, *When the Bulbul Stopped Singing: A Diary of Ramallah under Siege*, London: Profile Books, 2003.

64 Israeli Committee Against House Demolitions, http://icahd.org/get-the-facts.

65 Sfard, *The Wall and the Gate*, pp. 395–396.

66 B'Tselem, *Through No Fault of their Own: Punitive House Demolitions During the al-Aqsa Intifada*, Jerusalem: B' Tselem, November 2004.

67 Y. Berger, 'EU Slams Israel's Destruction of Palestinian Houses in West Bank's Area C', *Haaretz*, 28 July, 2016

68 See Article 23(g) of the Hague Regulations respecting the Laws and Customs of War on Land annexed to The Hague Convention of 1907 and Article 53 of the Fourth Geneva Convention of 1949.

69 Office of the Co-ordination of Humanitarian Affairs, *Humanitarian Bulletin: Occupied Palestinian Territory* (January 2017).

70 Dan Izenberg in *Jerusalem Post*, 16 November 2004.

71 Michael Eitan was a long-serving member of the Knesset who held cabinet office and in 2009 was elected speaker of the Knesset.

72 For an excellent account of the history of settlements and Israeli litigation on settlements, see Sfard, *The Wall and the Gate*, chapter 3.

73 See further on outposts, ibid., chapter 6.

74 Article 49(6).

75 Article 8(2)(viii).

76 2004 *ICJ Reports* 136 at para. 120. Dissenting Judge Buergenthal agreed with this finding.

77 Theodor Meron later became a distinguished professor of law at New York University, before being appointed as a judge (and later president) of the International Criminal Tribunal for the Former Yugoslavia. In 2017 he wrote a powerful article reaffirming his view that settlements are unlawful: 'The West Bank and International Humanitarian Law on the Eve of the Fiftieth Anniversary of the Six-Day War', (2017) 111 *American Journal of International Law* 357.

78 See General Assembly Resolution 1514(XV), the Declaration on the Granting of Independence to Colonial Countries and Peoples.

79 See, too, Bregman, *Cursed Victory*, p. 308.

80 Sfard, *The Wall and the Gate*, p. 122 n. 321.

81 G. Levy, 'The Real Uprooting is Taking Place in Hebron', *Haaretz*, 11 September 2005.

82 See Sfard, *The Wall and the Gate*, chapter 5.

83 See R. Dolphin, *The West Bank Wall: Unmaking Palestine*, London: Pluto Press, 2006.

84 *International Herald Tribune*, 2/3 August 2003.

85 E/CN.4/2004/6 of 8 September 2003, para. 6.

86 A/Res/ES-10/13 of 21 October 2003.

87 E/CN.4/2004/6 of 8 September 2003.

88 2004 *ICJ Reports* 136. See further on this decision, J. Dugard, 'Legal Consequences of the Construction of a Wall in the Occupied Palestinian Territory', in E. Bjorge and C. Miles (eds.), *Landmark Cases in Public International Law*, Oxford: Hart Publishing, 2017, p. 539.

89 Para. 133.

90 (2006) 45 *International Legal Materials* 2002. See, further, Sfard, *The Wall and the Gate*, pp. 299–312.
91 Paras. 62, 65, 70–74.
92 Paras. 43, 44, 61, 63.
93 See J. Dugard, 'Advisory Opinions and the Secretary-General with Special Reference to the 2004 Advisory Opinion on the Wall', in L. Boisson de Chazournes and M. Kohen (eds.), *International Law and the Quest for Its Implementation: Liber Amicorum Vera Gowlland-Debbas*, Leiden: Brill, 2010, p. 403.
94 Ibid., p. 409.
95 This allows Jews from any part of the world to claim Israeli citizenship.
96 Sfard, *The Wall and the Gate*, p. 331.
97 Y. Yoaz, 'Justice Minister: West Bank Fence Is Israel's Future Border', *Haaretz*, 1 December 2005.
98 *Head of the Azzun Municipal Council, Abed Alatif Hassin and Others* v. *State of Israel and the Military Commander of the West Bank*, H.C.J. 2733/05.
99 Bregman, *Cursed Victory*, p. 295.
100 2004 *ICJ Reports* 136 at paras. 152–153.
101 Article 7(2)(h).
102 See in particular the Resolution 1514 (XV) on the Granting of Independence to Colonial Countries and Peoples of 1960.
103 Article 8(2)(b)(viiii).
104 *Report of the UN Fact-Finding Mission on the Gaza Conflict*, UN Doc.A/AHRC/12/48, 15 September 2009, para. 206. In an op-ed in the *New York Times* of 1 November 2011, written in response to the session on Israeli apartheid of the Russell Tribunal on Palestine, Richard Goldstone denounced any suggestion that apartheid applied in the OPT as 'slanderous' and 'pernicious'. He made no mention of the statement in the report cited above. I drew attention to this contradiction in Richard's views in a letter to the *New York Times* of 3 November 2011 titled 'Israel and the Lightning-rod Word'.
105 *The State of Human Rights in Israel and the Occupied Territories, 2008 Report* (2008), p. 17.
106 Sfard, *The Wall and the Gate*, pp. 126–127.
107 S. Aloni, 'Indeed There Is Apartheid in Israel', *Middle East News Service*, 10 January 2007 (translation of Hebrew original published in *Yediot Aharonot*, 31 December 2006).
108 Report of 12 August 2004, A/59/256.
109 *Haaretz*, August 2004.
110 A/HRC/4/17 of 29 January 2007, paras. 50–1.
111 See Report A/62/275 of 17 August 2007.
112 See the statement by Mr Tuvia Israeli of the Permanent Mission of Israel to the UN in the Third Committee on 28 October 2004.
113 See the statement by Ambassador Grover Joseph Rees in the Third Committee on 24 October 2007.
114 See the comments of Ambassador Grover Joseph Rees in Third Committee on 24 October 2007.
115 See A. Cassese and P. Gaeta (eds.), *Cassese's International Criminal Law*, 3rd edn, Oxford, Oxford University Press, 2013, pp. 146–148.
116 Letter of 1 March 2007.
117 My arrangement to meet Ismail Haniyeh of Hamas in Gaza was opposed by a bureaucrat in the Office of the High Commissioner for Human Rights on the ground that the UN had a policy of not speaking to Hamas. I insisted that as an independent expert I was not bound by UN policy on this subject.
118 Meeting of 29 October 2004.
119 See the opinion of Mr Ralph Zacklin printed in Dugard, 'Advisory Opinions and the

Secretary-General with Special Reference to the 2004 Advisory Opinion on the Wall', p. 409.

120 Meeting of 23 October 2007.

121 Letter of 13 July 2006.

122 See *United States of America* v. *Wilhelm List et al. (the Hostages case)*, United Nations War Crimes Commission, *Law Reports of Trials of War Criminals*, vol. 8, 1949; *Democratic Republic of Congo* v. *Uganda*, 2005 *ICJ Reports*, paras. 173–174.

123 *Haaretz*, 7 July 2006.

124 *No Safe Place: Report of the Independent Fact-Finding Committee on Gaza*, Cairo: League of Arab States, 30 April 2009. The executive summary is contained in C. Meloni and G. Tognoni (eds.), *Is There a Court for Gaza? A Test Bench for International Justice*, The Hague: Asser Press, 2012, p. 586.

125 These are very conservative figures. Palestinian sources estimated a higher number of civilian deaths.

126 According to Defence Minister Ehud Barak and the IDF Chief of Staff Gabi Ashkenazi.

127 His evidence is to be found in Annexure 4 to the Committee's report. A similar statement by Abed Rabo appears in the Human Rights Council Report: A/HRC/12/48 of 15 September 2009, paras. 768–777.

128 This massacre was also the subject of investigation by the Human Rights Council fact-finding mission. See ibid., paras. 704–723, Arab League report, Annexure 4.

129 D. Tutu, 'Foreword: A Call to the Community Conscience', in A. Horowitz, L. Ratner and P. Weiss, *The Goldstone Report: The Legacy of the Landmark Investigation of the Gaza Conflict*, New York: Nation Books, 2011, p. vii.

130 *Genocide Case (Bosnia* v. *Serbia)*, 2007 *ICJ Reports* 1 at p. 70, para. 187.

131 At the suggestion of Ocampo I wrote an op-ed in favour of Palestinian statehood: 'Take the Case', *International Herald Tribune*, 23 July 2009.

132 A/HRC/12/48 of 15 September 2009. For a comprehensive examination of this report, see N. Finkelstein, *Gaza: An Inquest into Its Martyrdom*, Berkeley: University of California Press, 2018.

133 A/HRC/12/48 of 15 September 2009, para. 1686.

134 Ibid., paras. 1689–1690.

135 Ibid., para. 1692.

136 Most of these criticisms are to be found in L.C. Pogrebin, 'The Unholy Assault on Richard Goldstone', in Horowitz, Ratner and Weiss, *The Goldstone Report*, pp. 409–416.

137 Ibid., p. viii.

138 Ibid., pp. 411–412.

139 *Mail & Guardian*, 19–25 February 2010.

140 *Report of the Committee of Independent Experts in International Humanitarian Law and Human Rights Law Established Pursuant to Council Resolution 13/9* (A/HRC/16/24 of 18 March 2011).

141 Ibid., paras. 40-45.

142 Ibid., para. 27.

143 Ibid., paras. 47, 79.

144 For a critical account of this op-ed, see Finkelstein, *Gaza*: *An Inquest into Its Martyrdom*, pp. 117–132.

145 See http://www.newstatesman.com/blogs/the-staggers/2011/04/goldstone-report-israel-rights.

146 For a thorough examination and criticism of Goldstone's retraction, see N. Finkelstein, *Gaza: An Inquest into Its Martyrdom*, pp. 117–132.

147 Report of 1 May 2012, http:/www.haaretz.com/news/diplomacy-defense/idf-closes-probe-into-israeli-air-strikes-thatkilled-21-members-of–gaza-family-1,427583.

148 ICC, Office of the Prosecutor, *Update on Situation in Palestine*, 3 April 2012. See, further, J. Dugard, 'Palestine and the International Criminal Court: Institutional Failure or Bias?', (2013) 11 *Journal of International Criminal Justice* 563.
149 Resolution 67/19.
150 The Foundation for Human Rights and Freedoms and Humanitarian Relief (IHH).
151 See Finkelstein, *Gaza: An Inquest into Its Martyrdom*, pp. 211–356; M. Blumenthal, *The 51 Day War: Ruin and Resistance in Gaza (2015)*, London: Verso, 2015; O'Malley, *The Two-State Delusion*, pp. 154–163.
152 *Report of the Detailed Findings of the Independent Commission of Inquiry Established Pursuant to Human Rights Council Resolution S-21/1*, A/HRC/29/CRP4 of 22 June 2015. For a comprehensive examination of Operation Protective Edge, see Finkelstein, *Gaza: An Inquest into Its Martyrdom*.
153 For a critical examination of this solution, see O'Malley, *The Two-State Delusion*.
154 The United States has consistently appointed as negotiators men who on their own admission acted as 'Israel's lawyers'. See Miller, *The Much Too Promised Land*, pp. 75–80. America's principal negotiators, Dennis Ross, Aaron David Miller, Elliott Abrams and Martin Indyk, are all Jewish.
155 Resolution 657 of 11 July 2014.
156 Resolution 498 of 17 July 2014.
157 See generally on these lobbies, J. Mearsheimer and S. Walt, *The Israel Lobby and US Foreign Policy*, New York: Farrar, Straus and Giroux, 2007; P. Beinart, *The Crisis of Zionism*, New York: Times Books, 2012.
158 Under pressure from Jewish lobbies, President Truman gave support to both the 1947 Partition Proposal and the recognition of the state of Israel. See Radosh and Radosh, *A Safe Haven*; Judis, *Genesis*.
159 See Mearsheimer and Walt, *The Israel Lobby*, pp. 115–132.
160 Ibid., pp. 132–139; Miller, *The Much Too Promised Land*, pp. 239, 108–118.
161 N.G. Finkelstein, *The Holocaust Industry: Reflections on the Exploitation of Jewish Suffering*, 2nd edn, London: Verso, 2003.
162 A. Toynbee, 'Two Aspects of the Palestine Question' (Lecture delivered at the Cairo Governorate, 17 December 1961), in A. Toynbee, *Importance of the Arab World*, London: National Publications House Press, 1962, p. 57.
163 E. Mandel, 'Is the United Nations Anti-Semitic?', *Jerusalem Post*, 8 July 2014.
164 See Tilley, *Beyond Occupation*.
165 See J. Dugard and J. Reynolds, 'Apartheid, International Law and the Occupied Palestinian Territory', pp. 868–869.
166 See S. Polakow-Suransky, *The Unspoken Alliance: Israel's Secret Relationship with Apartheid South Africa*, New York: Pantheon Books, 2010.

Index

C